Teaching American English Pronunciation

Also published in
Oxford Handbooks for Language Teachers

Teaching English Overseas: An Introduction
Sandra Lee McKay

How Languages are Learned (second edition)
Patsy M. Lightbown and Nina Spada

Teaching Business English
Mark Ellis and Christine Johnson

Explaining English Grammar
George Yule

Communication in the Language Classroom
Tony Lynch

Teaching American English Pronunciation

Peter Avery and Susan Ehrlich

Oxford University Press

Oxford University Press,
Great Clarendon Street, Oxford OX2 6DP

Oxford New York
Auckland Bangkok Buenos Aires Cape Town Chennai
Dar es Salaam Delhi Hong Kong Istanbul Karachi Kolkata
Kuala Lumpur Madrid Melbourne Mexico City Mumbai Nairobi
São Paulo Shanghai Singapore Taipei Tokyo Toronto

with an associated company in Berlin

Oxford and *Oxford English*
are trade marks of Oxford University Press

ISBN 0 19 432 815 5

© Peter Avery and Susan Ehrlich 1992

First published 1992
Ninth impression 2002

Set in Adobe Garamond
by Tradespools Ltd, Frome, Somerset, UK

Printed in China

To the memory of Carlos Yorio

CONTENTS

PART ONE: The sound system of English

PREFACE

This book is intended as both a textbook and a reference manual for teachers of English as a Second Language. While there are many other introductory phonetics textbooks on the market, none has been written specifically for the ESL teacher. This book attempts to fill this gap by providing an accessible introduction to the fields of phonetics and phonology as they relate to second language learning.

Part One is an introduction to the English sound system, with many of the descriptions and concepts exemplified through typical errors made by ESL students. Part Two describes pronunciation problems common to most ESL students in addition to the specific pronunciation problems of fourteen different language groups. Part Three, a set of articles written by practitioners in the field, considers practical issues in the teaching of pronunciation.

This book is based, to a large extent, on a book previously published by the Ministry of Citizenship, Government of Ontario. We acknowledge the Queen's Printer for Ontario for permission to reprint portions of our previous book. In preparing this book for Oxford University Press, we have substantially revised Chapters 1 to 4 and Chapters 7 and 8 for a wider international audience. Chapters 11, 12, and 16 in Part Three have been substantially revised and rewritten for the present volume. The other chapters in Part Three have undergone minor revisions.

Numerous individuals have contributed to the preparation of this book and our previous Ministry of Citizenship publication. First, we acknowledge our many ESL students whose enthusiasm for pronunciation made us understand the importance of a book such as this. We thank Jack Chambers and Keren Rice for material and moral support over the last decade. Ed Burstynsky, Rob Fink, Jila Ghomeshi, Bill Idsardi, Michael Kay, Ruth King, Fouad Krichel, Maureen McNerney, Younghee Na, Jura Seskus, Ian Smith, and Mark Webber provided us with insights and information regarding pronunciation problems of specific language groups. John Archibald and Ilsa Mendelson Burns assisted in the original research for Chapter 8 and Doug Jull and John Archibald did much of the research for the Annotated Bibliography. We would also like to acknowledge the detailed and helpful comments of two anonymous reviewers for Oxford University Press. Their comments have allowed us to make many needed improvements to the volume.

We are most grateful to Esther Podoliak of the Ministry of Citizenship, Government of Ontario, who was involved in every stage of the original project. Esther's insistence on clarity and accessibility played a large role in making this book as readable as it is. We would also like to thank Sandy Feldman who did the original artwork. Finally, we acknowledge our enormous debt to Carlos Yorio, whose commitment to the application of linguistics to second language teaching made us both better linguists and better second language practitioners. Without Carlos, we probably would never have embarked upon this project. Peter Avery would like to express special thanks to Mary Ann Neary for her continuing support and patience.

INTRODUCTION
Preliminary considerations in the teaching of pronunciation

Peter Avery and Susan Ehrlich

Let us begin by considering two opposing views on the teaching of pronunciation in the ESL classroom. One view holds that the purpose of teaching pronunciation is to eradicate all traces of a 'foreign' accent through pronunciation drills. The other view holds that the teaching of pronunciation is futile after a certain age due to a decreasing ability among learners to develop native-like pronunciation in a second language. In this section, we will point out that neither of these views is completely accurate by considering biological, socio-cultural, personality, and linguistic factors which are known to affect the acquisition of the sound system of a second language. This will lead to the understanding that while practice in pronunciation may not make perfect, ignoring pronunciation totally can be a great disservice to ESL students.

Biological factors

A common observation made by people involved in the field of second language learning is that adult second language learners almost always have a 'foreign' accent while child second language learners almost always attain native-like pronunciation. One hypothesis that has been proposed to explain this difference between adults and children is the 'critical period hypothesis'. This hypothesis holds that languages are learned differently by children and adults, and that this is a direct result of the maturation of the brain.

As all experienced ESL teachers know, adult learners do have difficulty in acquiring native-like pronunciation in a second language. Thus, there may be some truth to the critical period hypothesis. However, it is also true that some adult learners do achieve native-like pronunciation and, among other adult learners, the degree of pronunciation accuracy varies considerably from individual to individual. The critical period hypothesis, therefore, does not absolve ESL teachers of the responsibility of teaching pronunciation. The very fact that variability exists among adult learners means that ESL classroom time can profitably be devoted to improving students' pronunciation.

Socio-cultural factors

The great variability in pronunciation accuracy of adult learners has led other researchers to conclude that it is socio-cultural factors that largely determine this success or lack of success in achieving native-like pronunciation. More specifically, it has been claimed that the more strongly second language learners identify with members of the second language culture, the more likely they are to 'sound' like members of that culture. Conversely, if it is important for learners to preserve their own cultural identity, they may hold on to their foreign accent as a marker of this identity.

We can see examples of this phenomenon in our own experience with native speakers of English who speak a different dialect (British English, Jamaican English, Australian English, etc.). Such speakers rarely lose their 'accent' primarily because their accent serves as a strong marker of their social identity. This is especially true when the accent is viewed positively by members of the society in which they live. However, even when the particular accent is viewed negatively by members of the culture at large, the accent may be retained because the speaker may feel at a social distance from members of that culture.

For ESL teachers, it is important to be aware of the way in which these socio-cultural factors may influence their students. Students may wish to improve their pronunciation in order to make themselves more comprehensible but, at the same time, they may not be interested in sounding like native-speakers of English. Such considerations become important in setting realistic goals in the pronunciation class.

Personality factors

Other factors affecting the acquisition of the sound system of a second language are related to the personality of the learner. Learners who are out-going, confident, and willing to take risks probably have more opportunities to practise their pronunciation of the second language simply because they are more often involved in interactions with native speakers. Conversely, learners who are introverted, inhibited, and unwilling to take risks lack opportunities for practice.

ESL teachers should be aware that such personality factors can affect progress in a second language and should strive to create a non-threatening atmosphere in their classrooms so that student participation is encouraged. Furthermore, students should not be forced to participate if they are not ready, as the pressure to perform can be paralyzing for some students.

The role of the native language

The nature of a foreign accent is determined to a large extent by a learner's native language. Thus, speakers of English are able to recognize Spanish accents, Russian accents, Chinese accents, etc. This is an indication that the sound patterns of the native language are being transferred into the second language. Every language has a different inventory of sounds, different rules for combining these sounds into words, and different stress and intonation patterns. The pronunciation errors that second language learners make are not just random attempts to produce unfamiliar sounds. Rather, they reflect the sound inventory, rules of combination, and the stress and intonation patterns of the native language.

The sound system of the native language can be seen to influence our students' pronunciation of English in at least three ways. First, difficulties may arise when a learner encounters sounds in English that are not part of the sound inventory of the learner's native language. As we will show in the following sections, the pronunciation of sounds depends on the proper use of the musculature in the mouth. Thus, adult learners may be unable to produce new sounds because they have never exercised their mouth in the particular way required to pronounce certain English sounds. Secondly, difficulties may arise because the rules for combining sounds into words are different in the learner's native language. This type of difficulty can occur even when a particular sound is part of the inventory of both English and the native language. Thirdly, the patterns of stress and intonation, which determine the overall rhythm and melody of a language, can be transferred from the native language into the second language.

The native language not only affects the ability to produce English sounds but also the ability to hear English sounds. Experienced teachers certainly know the frustration involved in having students continually repeat a mispronounced word in the same way. Students may seem impervious to correction but, in fact, the problem often arises because the word is heard through the sound system of the native language. Thus, sounds which occur in the native language will be heard rather than the actual sounds of English which are being produced by the teacher. This highlights a very important point concerning the influence of the native language. It is as if learners hear the second language through a 'filter', the filter being the sound system of the native language.

One question that a teacher might ask concerns the degree of difficulty that different native languages pose for learning the pronunciation of English. For example, because the sound systems of English and Cantonese differ more than the sound systems of English and Polish, is it more difficult for a Cantonese speaker to acquire English pronunciation than for a Polish speaker? If so, does this mean that it is more important to teach pronunciation to Cantonese speakers than to Polish speakers? The answer to both of these questions is 'perhaps'. Cantonese speakers' pronunciation problems may cause their speech to be more incomprehensible than the speech of Polish learners. This, of course, would suggest that it is more important to teach pronunciation to Cantonese speakers. However, it is not necessarily the case that their English will be more incomprehensible than Polish speakers' English. Socio-cultural and personality factors such as those discussed above will also determine the degree of a learner's pronunciation problems. In other words, the native language of a learner is not the only factor affecting pronunciation ability in a second language. It is one of several factors, suggesting that teachers cannot decide, without first listening to their students, which learners will necessarily need more pronunciation practice.

Setting realistic goals

Given that biological, socio-cultural, and personality factors may prevent a student from ever attaining native-like pronunciation in a second language, it is important that teachers set realistic goals. Attempting to completely eradicate a foreign accent is an unrealistic goal. However, this is not to say that pronunciation should be ignored in the ESL classroom. We know that it is possible for adult learners to improve their pronunciation. And sometimes these improvements can be quite dramatic.

What the teacher must focus on in the pronunciation class are critical errors, features of a student's speech most responsible for incomprehensibility. This requires work in two areas. First, students must be made aware of aspects of their pronunciation that result in other people being unable to understand them. Students will not necessarily have this awareness before entering the classroom due to the 'filter' of their native language. In other words, they may not hear the points at which their pronunciation does not correspond to that of a native-English speaker. Secondly, students must be given the opportunity to practice aspects of the English sound system which are crucial for their own improvement. It is important that this be done in meaningful contexts as students often produce sounds correctly in isolation but are unable to carry this over into their everyday speech.

In the sections that follow, we present a description of the major features of English pronunciation. A knowledge of the English sound system will aid you in identifying and isolating the most important pronunciation problems of your students. In addition, this information will make the pronunciation class both interesting and enjoyable for you and your students.

PART ONE

The sound system of English

1 SPELLING AND PRONUNCIATION

Peter Avery and Susan Ehrlich

The English spelling system

Before discussing the sound system of English in any detail, it is necessary to make a distinction between the sounds of English and the spelling of English. The English spelling system often fails to represent the sounds of English in a straightforward manner. In other words, there is often no one-to-one correspondence between the sounds that we hear and the letters we see on a page. An examination of the English spelling system reveals many examples of this discrepancy between spelling and sounds, for example:

Different letters may represent the same sound Pronounce the words below:

     to   two   too   through   threw   clue   shoe   Sioux

All of these words contain the same vowel sound but it is represented by eight different spellings.

The same letter represents different sounds Pronounce the words below and notice that the letter *a* is pronounced as five different vowel sounds.

     cake   mat   call   any   sofa

Now pronounce the next set of words and notice that the letter *s* is pronounced as three different sounds.

     see   pleasure   resign

In the first word, 'see', the letter *s* is pronounced in its usual way. In the word 'pleasure', it is pronounced like the final sound in the word 'beige', and in the word 'resign', it is pronounced like the first sound in the word 'zoo'.

Combinations of letters may represent one sound It is possible for a combination of letters to represent only one sound. If you pronounce the words below, you will notice that the *gh*, the *ph*, and the *ea* each represent only one sound even though the spelling represents this single sound as two letters.

     rough   physics   head

Letters may represent no sounds It is also possible for no sound to be represented by a particular letter. Pronounce the words below and notice that the letters in italics are not pronounced at all.

bom*b*   cak*e*   *p*neumonia   *k*nee   thou*gh*   de*b*t   recei*p*t

Again, the lack of correpondence between sounds and spelling can be observed in these words containing 'silent' letters.

After this brief examination of the English spelling system, we can begin to understand what led George Bernard Shaw to suggest that the English spelling system could be used to spell the word 'fish' as *ghoti*—the *gh* as it sounds in a word like 'rough', the *o* as it sounds in a word like 'women', and the *ti* as it sounds in a word like 'nation'. Shaw's suggested spelling, at first glance, might seem quite ridiculous; however, it illustrates clearly the way in which a particular sound in English can be spelled in quite different ways.

Sound-spelling correspondences

The lack of sound-spelling correspondence illustrated in the previous examples should not be taken to mean that there are no sound-spelling regularities in English. In fact, many of the consonant letters display a consistent relationship to the sounds they represent. For example, letters such as *b*, *m*, and *n* only have one pronunciation, unless they are silent.

b	*m*	*n*
boat	moat	no
rubber	hammer	winner
robe	home	wine

Other consonant letters are also consistent in their pronunciation but may appear in combination with another letter giving them a different pronunciation. For example, a letter such as *p* is normally pronounced in one way when it is alone but when it is combined with *h*, it is pronounced in a different way, that is, like the letter *f*.

p alone	*p + h = f*
pat	philosophy
top	physics
copper	photograph

The pronunciation of still other consonant letters can be predicted on the basis of their combination with vowel letters. For example, the letter *c* is pronounced like the letter *s* as in 'sent' when followed by the vowel letters *i*, *e*, or *y*, and like the letter *k* as in 'kite' when followed by the vowel letters *a*, *o*, or *u*, or when it occurs at the end of a word. Thus:

c before *i*, *e*, and *y* = *s*
e.g. city, cigar, certain, census, cent, cyst

c before *a*, *o*, and *u* and at the end of a word = *k*
e.g. cat, call, cone, come, custom, cup, plastic

This predictable difference in the pronunciation of the letter *c* can also be observed in pairs of words that are related in meaning:

electric   electricity

Notice that the English spelling system preserves the same spelling in these related words even though the pronunciation of the letter *c* changes.

The range of pronunciation of consonant letters is somewhat more predictable than the pronunciation of vowel letters. This is because there are many more vowel sounds in English than vowel letters in the Roman alphabet and because historical changes in the pronunciation of English have affected vowel sounds much more than consonant sounds. It is often the case that English spelling represents pronunciations that are now obsolete.

Traditionally, English vowel letters have been divided into two categories based on their pronunciation as either long or short vowels. When the vowel letters *a*, *e*, *i*, *o*, and *u* occur in words ending in a silent *e* letter, they are pronounced with their 'long' sound which is the sound heard when these letters are pronounced in isolation (e.g. when reciting the alphabet). When the same vowel letters occur in words without a silent *e*, they are pronounced with their 'short' sounds:

Long vowels	Short vowels
mate	mat
Pete	pet
hide	hid
note	not
cute	cut

This is, then, one generalization that can be made regarding the sound-spelling correspondence of English vowels. This regularity can also be observed in pairs of words that are related in meaning:

sane	sanity
serene	serenity
divine	divinity

Here we see that the unsuffixed form with the silent *e* has the 'long' sound, while the suffixed form without the silent *e* has the 'short' sound. Many people have observed that the English spelling system is advantageous in that spelling is consistent (even though the pronunciation may differ) among words related in meaning.

While there are many more vowel letter-sound correspondences that could be listed here, their large number (Prator and Robinett (1985) list 57 different vowel-letter combinations with predictable pronunciations) and many exceptions make their usefulness to ESL students somewhat questionable. However, once students have mastered enough spelling, they usually become quite proficient at guessing the pronunciation of an unknown word based solely on the spelling.

Spelling in other languages

Many languages, including English, use the Roman alphabet. Differences between the sound-spelling correspondences of such languages and of English can often be the source of mispronunciations. For example, the spelling systems of languages such as Spanish, Polish, and Hungarian are more straightforward than the English spelling system in representing sounds. That is, there is usually a one-to-one correspondence between sounds and spelling. Speakers of such languages may pronounce every letter of an English word, assuming incorrectly that the English spelling system is like the spelling system of their native language. In addition, these speakers may assign the sound values of their spelling system to the letters of English. This often results in what we term a *spelling pronunciation*. Pronouncing words on the basis of one's native language spelling system does not necessarily constitute a pronunciation problem. It may merely reflect a lack of knowledge regarding the often complex sound-spelling correspondences of English. If you have a large number of literate students from a language background using the Roman alphabet, it may be wise to familiarize yourself with the sound-spelling correspondences in that language. Then you can point out to students the places in which the sound-spelling correspondences of English and their native language differ.

The phonetic alphabet

Given the complexity of sound-spelling correspondences in English, it would be difficult to use the Roman alphabet to symbolize English sounds. Consider trying to represent the first sound of 'cat' using the English spelling system. If we were to use the letter *c* to represent this sound, then how would we represent the first sound in a word such as 'certain'? Furthermore, would we also use the letter *c* to represent the first sound in a word like 'kite', given that the first sound of 'kite' is the same sound that begins 'cat'? You can see the problems that would arise in using the English spelling system for such a purpose.

In order to avoid the problems that a spelling system like English poses for the representation of sounds, it is helpful to use a phonetic alphabet when discussing sounds in languages. In the phonetic alphabet, each symbol represents only one sound and each sound is represented by only one symbol. Therefore, the vowel sounds in the words 'to', 'two', 'too', 'through', 'threw', 'clue', 'shoe', and 'suit' would be represented by one phonetic symbol because each of these words has the same vowel sound. On the other hand, the letter *s* in the words 'see', 'pleasure', and 'resign' would be represented by three distinct phonetic symbols, as this letter represents three different sounds. Throughout this book, we will use symbols from the phonetic alphabet to represent English sounds. When you encounter these symbols, remember that they are intended to represent sounds. That is, they are not letters, but symbols for sounds.

Table 1.1: Phonetic symbols used in this book

vowels and diphthongs				consonants			
ɪ	as in	'sit'	[sɪt]	p	as in	'pen'	[pɛn]
ɛ	as in	'pen'	[pɛn]	b	as in	'bad'	[bæd]
æ	as in	'hat'	[hæt]	t	as in	'tea'	[tiy]
a	as in	'pot'	[pat]	d	as in	'dog'	[dag]
ɔ	as in	'bought'	[bɔt] (some dialects)	k	as in	'cat'	[kæt]
ʊ	as in	'put'	[pʊt]	g	as in	'got'	[gat]
ʌ	as in	'but'	[bʌt]	f	as in	'fair'	[fer]
ə	as in	'about'	[əbawt]	v	as in	'voice'	[voys]
iy	as in	'see'	[siy]	θ	as in	'thin'	[θɪn]
ey	as in	'say'	[sey]	ð	as in	'then'	[ðɛn]
uw	as in	'too'	[tuw]	s	as in	'sew'	[sow]
ow	as in	'go'	[gow]	z	as in	'zoo'	[zuw]
ay	as in	'buy'	[bay]	ʃ	as in	'she'	[ʃiy]
aw	as in	'now'	[naw]	ʒ	as in	'vision'	[vɪʒən]
oy	as in	'coin'	[koyn]	tʃ	as in	'chin'	[tʃɪn]
ir	as in	'fear'	[fir]	dʒ	as in	'jump'	[dʒʌmp]
er	as in	'bear'	[ber]	m	as in	'may'	[mey]
ur	as in	'boor'	[bur]	n	as in	'no'	[now]
or	as in	'bore'	[bor]	ŋ	as in	'sing'	[sɪŋ]
ər	as in	'her'	[hər]	l	as in	'let'	[lɛt]
				r	as in	'red'	[rɛd]
				y	as in	'yes'	[yɛs]
				w	as in	'will'	[wɪl]
				h	as in	'he'	[hiy]

Exercises

1 Read the following poem and list the different pronunciations represented by the following letter combinations:

   ough   ea   oth

Can you think of any more pronunciations for these letter combinations?

Hints on pronunciation for foreigners

I take it you already know
Of tough and bough and cough and dough?
Others may stumble but not you,
On hiccough, thorough, laugh and through.
Well done! And now you wish, perhaps,
To learn of less familiar traps?

Beware of heard, a dreadful word
That looks like beard and sounds like bird,
And dead: it's said like bed, not bead—
For goodness' sake don't call it 'deed'!
Watch out for meat and great and threat
(They rhyme with suite and straight and debt).

A moth is not a moth in mother
Nor both in bother, broth in brother,
And here is not a match for there
Nor dear and fear for bear and pear,
And then there's dose and rose and lose—
Just look them up—and goose and choose,
And cork and work and card and ward,
And font and front and word and sword,
And do and go and thwart and cart—
Come, come, I've hardly made a start!
A dreadful language? Man alive!
I'd mastered it when I was five!

From a letter published in the London *Sunday Times*
(3 January, 1965)

2 Consider the way the letter *g* is pronounced at the beginning of the following words:

gorge	gig	gem	guest
gut	got	gag	George
genius	gypsy	gust	guilt
gel	garage	giggle	gymnast
German	genetic	general	guess

a. Can you determine any regularity in the way *g* is pronounced, based on the following vowel letter?

b. Now consider the following words. Do they affect the generalization you have formulated above? Explain.

geyser   geld   get   gist   giraffe   gin

3 Look up the sound-spelling correspondences for a language (other than English) that uses the Roman alphabet or a modified version of it (for example, Italian, Spanish, Polish, Vietnamese). Based on your findings, what difficulties might a learner with that native language encounter in learning the English sound-spelling correspondences? (Usually sound-spelling correspondences can be found at the beginning of a primer on the language.)

2 INDIVIDUAL SOUNDS OF ENGLISH

Peter Avery and Susan Ehrlich

To be effective as a teacher of pronunciation, it is essential to have an understanding of how the speech sounds of English are produced. Such knowledge will enable you to understand why your students have a 'foreign accent', since a foreign accent results partially from an inability to produce the speech sounds of English. In addition, it will enable you to take the necessary steps for correction of your students' pronunciation problems. When your student pronounces the world 'think' as 'fink' or 'sink' or 'tink', that student is obviously having difficulty making the English sound that begins the word 'think'. Understanding how this sound is made will allow you to help your student to produce it correctly. The study of how sounds are produced and how the position of the mouth can be changed to produce different sounds is called *phonetics*. In the sections that follow, some basic concepts from phonetics will be presented.

How speech sounds are made

Speech sounds are made by air moving outward from the lungs through the mouth or nose. Different speech sounds result when the airstream is altered in some way by the positioning of various parts of the mouth. Some sounds are made as a result of the lips altering the airstream while other sounds are made as a result of the tongue altering the airstream.

In Figure 2.1, we label the parts of the mouth that are involved in the production of speech sounds. The movable parts of the mouth—the bottom lip, the bottom teeth, the tongue, and the jaw—are referred to as *articulators*. In the production of speech sounds, the articulators approach the upper unmovable parts of the mouth, causing the airstream to be altered in different ways. The unmovable parts of the mouth involved in the articulation of speech sounds are referred to as *places of articulation*.

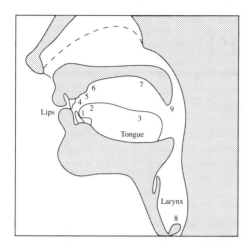

Figure 2.1: Articulators and places of articulation

Articulators
1 Tip of tongue
2 Blade of tongue
3 Back of tongue

Places of Articulation
4 Teeth
5 Tooth (alveolar) ridge
6 Hard palate
7 Soft palate (velum)
8 Glottis
9 Uvula

Consonants and vowels

A basic distinction, in terms of how sounds are formed, is made between consonants and vowels. *Consonants* involve a narrowing in the mouth which in turn causes some obstruction of the airstream. With *vowels*, air passes rather freely through the mouth because there is very little narrowing. In order to become aware of this difference between consonants and vowels, pronounce the word 'palm'. You can feel your mouth widening when you pronounce the vowel sound and narrowing when you pronounce the initial and final consonants.

The description of English consonants

In our discussion of consonants, we will refer to three basic characteristics:

1 Place of articulation—where in the mouth the airstream is obstructed.
2 Manner of articulation—the way in which the airstream is obstructed.
3 Voicing—whether there is vibration of the vocal cords.

Place of articulation

In English, there are six places in the mouth where the airstream is obstructed in the formation of consonants. The various places of articulation are labelled in the diagram of the mouth in Figure 2.1.

We will discuss each consonant in terms of the articulators involved and the place in the mouth where the articulators cause an obstruction of the airstream.

Sounds made with the lips

Both lips (bilabial)   Pronounce the words 'pat', 'bat', and 'mat', paying attention to the way the first consonant of each word is made. The first sound in each of these words is made with the two lips coming together and touching momentarily. The obstruction of the airstream thus occurs at the lips. The phonetic symbols for these three sounds are the same as the English letters. We use the symbols /p/, /b/, and /m/ to represent the first sounds of 'pat', 'bat', and 'mat'.

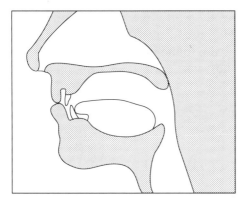

Figure 2.2: The position of the lips in the production of /p/, /b/, *and* /m/

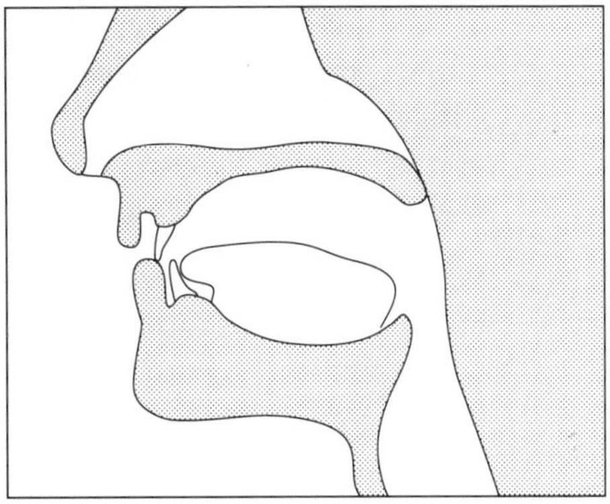

Figure 2.3: The position of the teeth and lips in the production of /f/ *and* /v/

Photocopiable © Oxford University Press

The sounds /p/, /b/, and /m/ are referred to as *bilabial* sounds because the two (bi-) lips (labial) are involved in their production.

Lower lip and upper teeth (labiodental)   Now produce the words 'fat' and 'vat', again paying attention to the way the first sounds of these words are formed. The initial sounds of 'fat' and 'vat' are made with the top teeth touching the bottom lip. Therefore, in the case of these two sounds, the obstruction of the airstream occurs not because the two lips come together but because the bottom lip and the top teeth come together. Again, the phonetic symbols for these two sounds are the same as the English letters. We use the symbols /f/ and /v/ to represent the initial sounds of 'fat' and 'vat'.

The sounds /f/ and /v/ are referred to as *labiodental* sounds because the lips (labio) and the teeth (dental) are involved in their production.

Sounds made with the tip of the tongue

Tip of the tongue and the teeth (interdental)   Pronounce the words 'thigh' and 'thy', paying attention to the way the first consonant sounds of these words are formed. With these two sounds the obstruction of the airstream occurs because the tip of the tongue is between the teeth or just behind the teeth. The phonetic symbols for these sounds are not the same as the English letters. The *th* sound in the word 'thigh' is represented by the symbol /θ/ and the *th* sound in the word 'thy' is represented by the symbol /ð/.

The sounds /θ/ and /ð/ are referred to as *interdental* sounds because the tongue is placed between (inter) the teeth (dental).

The two *th* sounds are notoriously difficult for second language learners because they are not common sounds in many of the world's languages. While not many words in English contain the /ð/ sound as in 'thy', the words that do contain this sound are among the most frequently used words in the English language. For example, the words 'the', 'this', 'that', 'these', 'those', 'then', 'than', 'there', 'though', 'they', 'them', and 'their' all begin with the /ð/ sound. The /ð/ sound is also found in such common words as 'mother', 'father', and 'brother'. Thus, you can see how important this sound is in English.

With the knowledge that you have regarding place of articulation, it becomes easier to correct a student who says 'I fink so' when attempting to say 'I think so'. To produce 'think' rather than 'fink', it is necessary to place the tip of the tongue between the teeth instead of placing the top teeth on the bottom lip. Thus, we can see that the substitution of /f/ for /θ/ is a pronunciation error that results from incorrect place of articulation.

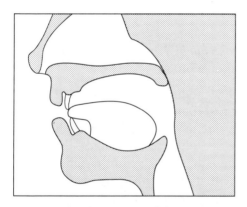

Figure 2.4: The position of the tongue in the production of /θ/ and /ð/

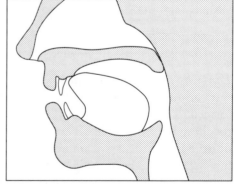

Figure 2.5: The position of the tongue in the production of /t/, /d/, /n/, and /l/

Photocopiable © Oxford University Press

Tip of the tongue and the tooth ridge (alveolar)   Other English sounds made with the tip of the tongue include the initial sounds of 'tip', 'dip', 'nip', and 'lip'. When you pronounce the initial consonants of these words, you should feel the tip of your tongue touching the roof of your mouth just behind your upper teeth. We refer to this place of articulation as the *tooth ridge* or the *alveolar ridge*. (See Figure 2.1 above.) Again, the phonetic symbols for these sounds are the same as the English letters. We use /t/, /d/, /n/, and /l/ to represent the initial sounds of 'tip', 'dip', 'nip', and 'lip'.

Other tooth ridge sounds in English include the initial sounds of the words 'sip' and 'zip'. Again, the phonetic symbols for these sounds are the same as the English letters. We use /s/ and /z/, respectively.

The sounds /s/ and /z/ are not made in precisely the same way as /t/, /d/, /n/, and /l/ as the tip of the tongue does not actually touch the tooth ridge. They are, nevertheless, tooth ridge sounds as the tip of the tongue does approach the tooth ridge. To confirm that this is the case, pronounce the /θ/ as in 'think' followed immediately by the /s/ as in 'sink'. You should feel your tongue moving from a position between the upper teeth to a position behind the upper teeth approaching the tooth ridge.

The initial sound of 'rip' is also a tooth ridge sound and is represented by the phonetic symbol /r/. It is a little more problematic in terms of its description and will be discussed in more detail later in this chapter (see page 37).

The sounds /t/, /d/, /n/, /l/, /s/, /z/, and /r/ are referred to as *alveolar* sounds because the tongue either touches or approaches the alveolar ridge (tooth ridge) in their production.

In languages such as French, Italian, and Spanish, these sounds are not made in the same way as in English. In these languages, the tip of the tongue does not touch the tooth ridge but rather touches behind the teeth. While this may sound like a very trivial difference, it is such differences between sounds in languages that partially cause what we know as a 'foreign accent'.

Sounds made with the blade of the tongue

Blade of the tongue and the hard palate (alveo-palatal)   Pronounce the words 'wish' and 'beige', concentrating on the position of the tongue in the production of the final sounds. These sounds are made with the blade of the tongue approaching the *hard palate* just behind the tooth ridge. (See Figure 2.1 above.) The phonetic symbols for these sounds are not the same as the English letters. We use the symbol /ʃ/ to represent the final sound of 'wish' and the symbol /ʒ/ to represent the fnal sound of 'beige'. Note that the /ʒ/ sound very rarely begins a word in English. Only words of foreign origin such as 'genre' or 'Jacques' begin with this sound.

You may be able to feel the position of the tongue for /ʃ/ and /ʒ/ more easily if you make a /s/ as in 'sip' followed immediately by a /ʃ/ as in ship. When you move to the /ʃ/ sound, you will feel the blade of the tongue rising to approach the hard palate. Now, make the /ʃ/ sound and hold your tongue in that position while breathing in through the mouth. The incoming air should cool the blade of your tongue and the roof of your mouth just behind the tooth ridge.

One other important aspect of the pronunciation of / ʃ / and / ʒ / involves the lips. Notice that the lips are rounded when you pronounce these sounds.

The / ʃ / sounds often presents difficulty for learners of English. When pronouncing words such as 'sheep' and 'sheet', Greek speakers, for example, may substitute a / s / sound for the correct / ʃ / sound at the beginning of these words. Thus, instead of pronouncing the intended words 'sheep' and 'sheet', they will say what sounds like 'seep' and 'seat'. These, of course, are critical errors as they could interfere with comprehensibility. In order to produce the correct sounds, the student must use the blade of the tongue rather than the tip and be sure that it is approaching the hard palate just behind the tooth ridge.

There are two other sounds that are made with the blade of the tongue at the hard palate. These are the initial consonants in the words 'chug' and 'jug'. We use the complex symbol / tʃ / for the initial sound in the word 'chug' and / dʒ / for the initial sound in the word 'jug'.

The sounds / ʃ /, / ʒ /, / tʃ /, and / dʒ / are referred to as *alveopalatal* sounds because the tongue is just behind the alveolar ridge at the hard palate in the production of these sounds.

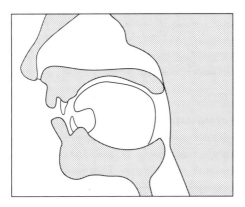

Figure 2.6: The position of the tongue in the production of / ʃ /, / ʒ /, / tʃ /, and / dʒ /

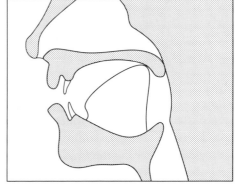

Figure 2.7: The position of the tongue in the production of / k /, / g /, and / ŋ /

Sounds made with the back of the tongue

Back of the tongue and soft palate (velar)   Pronounce the words 'coat' and 'goat', exaggerating the formation of the initial sounds. In producing the initial sounds, the back part of your tongue touches the back part of your mouth momentarily, causing an obstruction of the airstream. Contrast the position of your tongue in the formation of the first and last sounds in a word such as 'tack'. You should feel the tip of your tongue rising to the tooth ridge as you pronounce the /t/, and the back part of your tongue rising as you pronounce the final sound of the word. The back part of the tongue rises to touch the *soft palate* or *velum*. You will probably find it difficult to feel the back part of the tongue touching the soft palate. In general, it is harder for speakers to become aware of obstruction in the back of the mouth. Thus, as a teacher you may have difficulty making your students aware of the precise positioning of the tongue with sounds made at the back of the mouth. Again, the phonetic symbols for these sounds are the same as the English letters. We use /k/ and /g/ to represent the initial sounds of 'coat' and 'goat'.

The final sound in a word such as 'sing' has the same place of articulation as /k/ and /g/. We use the phonetic symbol /ŋ/ to represent this sound. Pronounce the word 'sing' and prolong the final consonant. The back part of your tongue touches the soft palate as it does with the initial sounds of 'coat' and 'goat'. Many English speakers feel that a word such as 'sing' ends in a /g/ sound, but for most English speakers it actually does not. This perception is influenced by the spelling of a word like 'sing'. Compare the words 'singer' and 'finger'. For most speakers, there is only one consonant sound, /ŋ/, in the middle of 'singer' but two, /ŋg/, in the middle of 'finger'.

In informal styles of English, some speakers pronounce words such as 'hunting' and 'fishing' as 'huntin'' and 'fishin''. We generally say that these speakers are dropping their *g*'s. In fact, there are no /g/'s in the pronunciation of these words. Rather, these speakers have substituted /n/ for /ŋ/ at the end of these words. This is a change in the place of articulation not the deletion of a sound.

The sounds /k/, /g/ and /ŋ/ are referred to as *velar* sounds because they are made with the back of the tongue rising to touch the soft palate or velum.

A pronunciation error often made by Spanish-speaking students involves substituting /n/ for the /ŋ/ sound at the end of an English word. Notice the potential for confusion if a student produced 'I want to sin' instead of 'I want to sing'. In correcting this error, it is necessary to have the student raise the back part of the tongue so that it touches the soft palate rather than allowing the tip of the tongue to touch the tooth ridge. Often by producing the sounds /k/ or /g/ (which have the same place of articulation as /ŋ/), the student can become aware of this tongue position.

Places of articulation   A chart that classifies the consonants of English according to their place of articulation is provided in Table 2.1 below:

Table 2.1: Classification of consonants according to place of articulation

bilabial	labiodental	interdental	alveolar	alveopalatal	velar
p			t		k
b			d		g
	f	θ	s	ʃ	
	v	ð	z	ʒ	
				tʃ	
				dʒ	
m			n		ŋ
			l		
			r		

Manner of articulation

Manner of articulation refers to the way in which the obstruction of the air-stream, which characterizes all consonants, is achieved. At the different places of articulation in the mouth, there are several basic ways that the air-stream can be obstructed.

Complete obstruction of the airstream—stops

The air that passes from the lungs into the mouth can be completely stopped because the lips or the tongue actually touch some part of the upper mouth. Consonants that involve this complete blockage of the airstream are called *stops*. The initial sounds of 'pill' and 'bill', 'till' and 'dill', and 'kill' and 'gill', are all stop consonants. Notice that the place in the mouth where the air-stream is blocked differs with these three pairs of sounds. With /p/ and /b/, the air is blocked because the two lips come together. With /t/ and /d/, the air is blocked because the tip of the tongue touches the tooth ridge. With /k/ and /g/, the air is blocked because the back of the tongue touches the soft palate.

Table 2.2: The stop consonants of English

lips (bilabial)	/p/ and /b/
tooth ridge (alveolar)	/t/ and /d/
soft palate (velar)	/k/ and /g/

bilabial	labiodental	interdental	alveolar	alveopalatal	velar
p			t		k
b			d		g

Partial obstruction of the airstream—fricatives

Some consonants in English do not involve a complete stoppage of the airstream but rather a partial obstruction. This partial obstruction results from the lips or the tongue coming close to some part of the upper mouth. These consonants are called *fricatives* because the close approximation of the articulators causes turbulence or friction in the airflow. The initial sounds of 'fat' and 'vat', 'thigh' and 'thy', 'sip' and 'zip' and the final sounds of 'wish' and 'beige' are all fricatives.

Compare the initial consonants of the words 'tip' and 'sip'. Both of these sounds are made at the same place of articulation—the tooth ridge. They differ, however, in their manner of articulation. The /t/ is made with complete blockage of the airstream while the /s/ is made with only partial blockage of the airstream. Air continues to pass through the mouth in the pronunciation of /s/ (a fricative) which means that the sound can be prolonged in a way that the /t/ cannot be. Try prolonging the /t/ and notice the impossibility of prolonging a stop consonant.

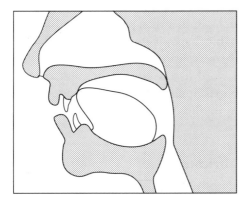
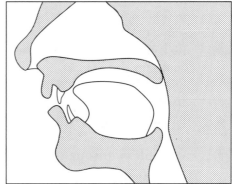

Figure 2.8: Complete blockage of the airstream as in the stops /t/ and /d/

Figure 2.9: Partial blockage of the airstream as in the fricatives /s/ and /z/

Photocopiable © Oxford University Press

ESL students will sometimes substitute stops for fricatives. The student who pronounces 'I think so' as 'I tink so' is making an error in terms of manner of articulation. The initial sound of 'think', /θ/, is a fricative sound but the /t/ sound is a stop. Therefore, in order to correct this pronunciation problem, the student must place the tip of the tongue between the teeth and allow air to move out of the mouth during the pronunciation of the sound.

ESL students may also substitute fricatives for stops. Spanish-speaking students will often produce fricatives at the end of a word rather than the appropriate stops, saying, for example, 'lathe' instead of 'laid'. A /ð/ (the initial sound of 'the') is substituted for a /d/ in this word. In order to produce the correct sound, the Spanish speaker must make sure that there is contact between the tip of the tongue and the tooth ridge so that a /d/ rather than a /ð/ is pronounced.

Table 2.3: The fricative consonants of English
lower lip/upper teeth (labiodental)   /f/ and /v/
teeth (interdental)   /θ/ and /ð/
tooth ridge (alveolar)   /s/ and /z/
hard palate (alveopalatal)   /ʃ/ and /ʒ/

bilabial	labiodental	interdental	alveolar	alveopalatal	velar
	f	θ	s	ʃ	
	v	ð	z	ʒ	

The eight fricatives of English are not the only fricatives that we find among the languages of the world. For example, many languages have velar fricatives or bilabial fricatives. We sometimes use a velar fricative in English in the pronunciation of the name 'Bach'. Rather than pronouncing the final sound of this word as a /k/, we do not block the air completely but bring the back of the tongue close to the soft palate, causing partial obstruction of the airstream. In Spanish, the /b/ of a word like 'Cuba' is pronounced as a bilabial fricative. That is, rather than stopping the airstream as English speakers do, Spanish speakers bring the lips close together, causing only partial obstruction of the airstream.

Complex consonant sounds—affricates

There are two complex consonant sounds in English, /tʃ/ as in 'chug' and /dʒ/ as in 'jug'. We introduced both of these sounds previously as hard palate sounds. Each is a combination of a stop followed immediately by a fricative and they are referred to as *affricates*. The initial consonant of 'chug' begins as the stop consonant /t/, and is released as the fricative /ʒ/. Similarly, the initial consonant of 'jug' begins as the stop consonant /d/, and is released as the fricative /ʒ/. Pronounce these two sounds ans see if you can feel the tip of the tongue making contact with the top of the mouth and then separating slightly so that a fricative is made immediately after the stop.

A common pronunciation problem of Vietnamese speakers is the substitution of the fricative /ʃ/ for the complex affricate sound /tʃ/. For example, Vietnamese speakers will typically produce 'too mush' when attempting to say 'too much', failing to block the airstream before the fricative is produced. To correct this, students should place the tip of their tongue at the tooth ridge as if they were about to pronounce a /t/ and then release the sound as a /ʃ/.

Table 2.4: The complex consonants of English—affricates
hard palate (alveopalatal)   /tʃ/ and /dʒ/

bilabial	labiodental	interdental	alveolar	alveopalatal	velar
				tʃ	
				dʒ	

The two complex consonants of English are not the only possible complex consonant sounds found in the languages of the world. Many languages have complex consonants such as /ts/ (/t/ + /s/) or /dz/ (/d/ + /z/). Korean learners of English will substitute a /dz/ sound for the initial /z/ sound in 'zoo', producing a word like 'dzoo'. Whilst this does not result in a different English word, it can lead to incomprehensibility.

Sounds made with the air escaping through the nose—nasals

All of the consonant sounds that we have discussed up to this point are made with air passing through the mouth. *Nasal* sounds, on the other hand, are made with air passing through the nose. Air is blocked in the mouth in the same way as it is for stop consonants. However, the soft palate is lowered, allowing air to escape through the nose.

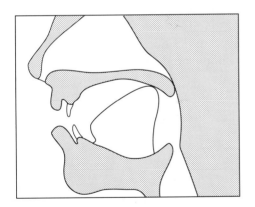

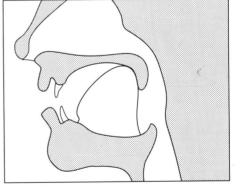

Figure 2.10: The position of the velum in the production of /k/ or /g/

Figure 2.11: The position of the velum in the production of the nasal consonant /ŋ/

There are three nasal consonants in English: /m/, /n/, and /ŋ/ as in 'ram', 'ran', and 'rang'. These three sounds differ in terms of place of articulation. The /m/ is produced when the two lips touch, the /n/ is produced when the tip of the tongue touches the tooth ridge and the /ŋ/ is produced when the back of the tongue touches the soft palate. In each case, this contact prevents air from escaping out of the mouth.

You may have noticed that when you have a cold, your nasal consonants become distorted. This is because your nose is plugged. As nasal consonants are, by definition, sounds produced by air escaping out of the nose, any blockage of the nose passage will have an effect on the pronunciation of these sounds. What often happens is that your nasals end up sounding like non-nasal sounds. For example, 'my mommy' may sound like 'by bobby'. As /b/ and /m/ sounds are made with the two lips coming together, the /b/ results when the nasality is removed from the /m/. (Try holding your nose and saying 'my mommy'. How does it sound?)

Table 2.5: The nasal consonants of English
lips (bilabial)   /m/
tooth ridge (alveolar)   /n/
soft palate (velar)   /ŋ/

bilabial	labiodental	interdental	alveolar	alveopalatal	velar
m			n		ŋ

Photocopiable © Oxford University Press

Liquids

The initial sounds of 'rip' and 'lip' are called *liquids* because, in the pronunciation of these sounds, the air passes through the mouth in a somewhat fluid manner. Compare the quality of the airstream in the pronunciation of the /z/ sound (a fricative) and the /l/ sound (a liquid). Make both of these sounds alternately, prolonging the pronunciation of each. You should notice a clearer, less turbulent airflow in the production of the /l/.

The lateral /l/   The consonant /l/ is made with the tip of the tongue touching the tooth ridge and air passing through the mouth over the sides of

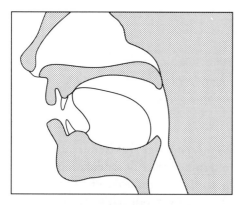

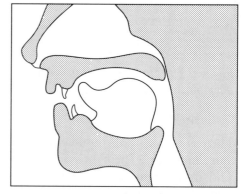

Figure 2.12: The position of the tongue in the production of the lateral /l/

Figure 2.13: The position of the tongue in the production of the retroflex /ɾ/

Photocopiable © Oxford University Press

the tongue. For some speakers of English, the /l/ may be made with air passing out of the mouth over one side of the tongue only. Because the air passes out the side of the mouth, the /l/ sound is referred to as a *lateral* consonant.

The retroflex /r/   The /r/ sound is made with the tip of the tongue slightly curled back in the mouth. Pronounce the word 'red' and prolong the initial consonant. You should feel the tip of the tongue in a curled-back position. You may also feel some backward movement of the tongue and some rounding of the lips. Upon pronunciation of the vowel sound in 'red', the tongue uncurls. Because the tongue is curled back during the pronunciation of the /r/ sound, it is referred to as a *retroflex* consonant.

There is some disagreement regarding the precise characterization of /r/. Some authors describe the tongue as 'bunched' rather than curled back or retroflexed in its articulation. Furthermore, rather than calling it an alveolar sound, these authors prefer to consider it a *palatal* or *central* sound. Much of the disagreement may be based on dialect differences. For pedagogical purposes, we have found the characterization of /r/ as a retroflex sound to be most useful.

While many of the world's languages contain /r/ sounds, the particular way in which the /r/ is produced can differ greatly from language to language. For example, in Polish the /r/ is produced as a trill; that is, the tip of the tongue touches the tooth ridge repeatedly. In some dialects of German and French, /r/ is not a tooth ridge sound but rather a *uvular* sound, a sound produced at the back of the mouth (i.e., at the uvula).

The substitution of these different /r/-like sounds for the English /r/ contributes to a foreign accent. However, this type of substitution does not necessarily interfere with comprehensibility; thus, it may not be worthwhile to overemphasize it in class.

Speakers of Mandarin, Japanese, and Korean often have difficulty making the distinction between the /r/ and the /l/ sounds of English. Instead of pronouncing the word 'arrive', for example, we may think that a Japanese speaker is pronouncing 'alive', substituting the /l/ for the /r/. One way of helping students to make the distinction between these two sounds is to tell them that the /l/ sound is made with the tip of the tongue touching the tooth ridge while the /r/ sound is made with the tip of the tongue touching no part of the mouth.

Semi-vowels (glides)

Other consonant sounds of English produced with little turbulence in the airstream are the initial sounds of the words 'wet' and 'yet'. The phonetic symbols for these sounds are identical to the English letters /w/ and /y/. These two sounds are often called *semi-vowels* because they are made with a relatively wide opening in the mouth. The difference between semi-vowels and vowels will be discussed later in this chapter (see page 35).

In the pronunciation of /w/, the lips are rounded and, at the same time, the back of the tongue approaches the soft palate. Pronounce the word 'wet', prolonging the first sound of this word. You should feel the lips coming together and rounding slightly. It is difficult to feel the back of the tongue approaching the soft palate but, in fact, this narrowing occurs as well.

In the pronunciation of /y/, the blade of the tongue approaches the hard palate. Pronounce the word 'yet', prolonging the first sound of this word. You should be able to feel the tongue coming close to the hard palate.

The consonant /h/

Although /h/ is traditionally described as a consonant, it is difficult to classify in terms of manner of articulation. Because the /h/ sound is most easily understood in relation to its following vowel, we shall postpone discussion of this sound to the section on 'Vowels' (see page 35).

Voicing

The third way in which consonants can differ from each other is in terms of *voicing*. In order to understand voicing, consider the pronunciation of the initial consonants in the words 'sue' and 'zoo'. 'Sue' is pronounced with a /s/, while 'zoo' is pronounced with a /z/. These two sounds are identical in terms of place of articulation (tooth ridge sounds) and manner of articulation (fricatives). However, they differ in terms of voicing. The /s/ is a voiceless sound and the /z/ is a voiced sound. In order to hear this difference, say a long /s/ sound followed immediately by a long /z/ sound. Say each of them alternately—[ssssziiiiissssziiii]. Now put your fingers on your Adam's apple as you pronounce this sequence of sounds and notice that with the /s/ sound, there is no vibration at the Adam's apple, whereas with the /z/ sound, there is vibration. The vibration of the /z/ can be heard even more distinctly if you plug your ears while pronouncing the /s/ and /z/ alternately.

The vibration that is heard with the voiced /z/ sound is caused by the vocal cords. Sounds that are made with the vocal cords vibrating are voiced and sounds made with no vibration of the vocal cords are voiceless. The vocal cords are bands of muscle attached to the walls of the larynx (voicebox). (See Figure 2.1 above for the location of the larynx.) When they are held close together, the air passing from the lungs into the mouth causes them to vibrate. When they are apart, the air passing through causes no vibration.

A common problem among many ESL students of various language backgrounds involves not voicing certain consonants in English when they occur at the end of a word. A Polish speaker, for example, may pronounce a word like 'leave' as 'leaf', substituting a /f/ sound for a /v/ sound. The only difference between these two sounds involves the state of the vocal cords; /f/ has no vibration of the vocal cords and is therefore voiceless; /v/ is accompanied by vibration of the vocal cords and is voiced. Notice that this is a critical error as it could interfere with the Polish speaker's comprehensibility.

All of the stops, fricatives, and affricates we have discussed so far come in voiced/voiceless pairs. The nasals, liquids, semi-vowels, and vowels of English are all voiced.

With pairs of fricatives, it is easy to determine which is voiced and which is voiceless because they can be prolonged. There are eight fricative sounds in English; four of these are voiced and four are voiceless. The phonetic classification of the eight fricatives of English is provided in Table 2.6.

Table 2.6: Classification of fricatives in terms of voicing

	labiodental	interdental	alveolar	alveopalatal
voiceless	f (fish)	θ (think)	s (sale)	ʃ (pressure)
voiced	v (veal)	ð (these)	z (zone)	ʒ (pleasure)

Photocopiable © Oxford University Press

The stop consonants also come in voiced/voiceless pairs. With stop consonants, however, it is a little more difficult to feel the vibration of the vocal cords that accompanies voicing. This is because stops cannot be prolonged. (See 'Positional variation': 'Aspiration', page 40, and 'Vowel lengthening', page 44, for a more detailed discussion of differences between voiced and voiceless stops.) The phonetic classification of the six stop consonants of English is provided in the chart below in Table 2.7.

Table 2.7: Classification of stops in terms of voicing

	bilabial	alveolar	velar
voiceless	p (pay)	t (tell)	k (coal)
voiced	b (buy)	d (dent)	g (gold)

Photocopiable © Oxford University Press

The two affricates of English are made at the same place of articulation but are distinguished in terms of voicing. The affricate /tʃ/, as in 'chug', is voiceless and /dʒ/, as in 'jug', is voiced.

Table 2.8: Classification of affricates in terms of voicing

	alveopalatal
voiceless	tʃ (chug)
voiced	dʒ (jug)

Photocopiable © Oxford University Press

Languages can differ greatly in terms of voiced consonants. Some languages do not have any voiced fricatives and others do not have any voiced stops. Vietnamese is interesting because at the beginning of a word there is a voiced stop /b/, but the voiceless counterpart /p/ does not occur. Vietnamese speakers may substitute either a /b/ or an /f/ when attempting to produce the English sound /p/. Thus, the word 'put' may be pronounced as 'foot' and the name 'Peter' may be pronounced as 'beater'.

Summary

We have described the formation of English consonants by referring to three features of their pronunciation. We have discussed where they are produced in the mouth (place of articulation), how they are produced (manner of articulation), and whether they are voiced or voiceless (voicing). From the examples given above, you have seen that ESL students can make errors that involve each of these features of pronunciation. You have also seen that some knowledge of these features can aid you in identifying and correcting the problems students are having with particular sounds. While being able to produce sounds in isolation is not all that is involved in improving pronunciation, the correction of mispronounced sounds that interfere with students' comprehensibility can go a long way in improving students' performance and confidence in speaking English.

Below we provide a consonant chart that incorporates all three aspects of articulation in one chart. This is the type of chart you will find in most books on the phonetic classification of sounds.

Table 2.9: Consonant chart
vcls = voiceless   *vd* = voiced

		bilabial	labiodental	interdental	alveolar	alveopalatal	velar
stops	*vcls*	p			t		k
	vd	b			d		g
fricatives	*vcls*		f	θ	s	ʃ	
	vd		v	ð	z	ʒ	
affricates	*vcls*					tʃ	
	vd					dʒ	
nasals		m			n		ŋ
retroflex					r		
lateral					l		
semi-vowels		w				y	w

For ease of reference, a classification of the consonants of English in terms of place of articulation, manner of articulation, and voicing is provided below in Table 2.10.

Table 2.10: Classification of the consonants of English in terms of place of articulation, manner of articulation, and voicing

place of articulation

both lips (bilabial): p, b, m, w
lower lip and upper teeth (labiodental): f, v
tip of tongue and teeth (interdental): θ, ð
tip of tongue and tooth ridge (alveolar): t, d, n, s, z, l, r
blade of tongue and hard palate (alveopalatal): ʃ, ʒ, tʃ, dʒ, y
back of tongue and soft palate (velar): k, g, ŋ, w

manner of articulation

stops: p, b, t, d, k, g
fricatives: f, v, θ, ð, s, z, ʃ, ʒ
affricates: tʃ, dʒ
nasals: m, n, ŋ
liquids: l, r
semi-vowels: w, y

voicing

voiceless	*example*	*voiced*	*example*
p	put	b	boot
t	tin	d	dive
k	cape	g	gone
f	foot	v	vote
θ	think	ð	them
s	sink	z	zoo
ʃ	ship	ʒ	measure
tʃ	choose	dʒ	gem
		m	move
		n	nose
		ŋ	sing
		l	lose
		r	race
		w	win
		y	yes

The description of English vowels

In this section we describe the articulatory characteristics of English vowels. Vowels, unlike consonants, exhibit a great deal of dialect variation. This variation can depend on factors such as geographical region, social class, educational background, age, and gender. (Of course, these factors exhibit an effect on all aspects of pronunciation, not just on the pronunciation of vowels. It is just that with the vowels the variation in English is the most noticeable.) The vowels we describe below are those of General American English, that is, the English used in the national media in the USA and by a large number of North American speakers. Occasionally, we will point out specific examples of dialect variation in the pronunciation of vowels; it is important to remember, however, that your vowel system may not be identical to the one we are describing, particularly in the low, back region of the mouth. If you are not a speaker of North American English, the differences may be even greater.

Vowels are differentiated from consonants by the relatively wide opening in the mouth as air passes from the lungs out of the body. This means that there is relatively little obstruction of the airstream in comparison to consonants. Different vowel sounds result from different positions of the tongue and lips. In describing vowels, it is necessary to discuss four characteristics:

1 Tongue Height—whether the tongue is high or low in the mouth.
2 Frontness/Backness of Tongue—whether the front or the back of the tongue is involved.
3 Tenseness/Laxness—whether the muscles are tense or lax.
4 Lip Rounding—whether the lips are rounded.

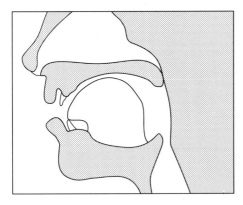

Figure 2.14: The position of the tongue in the pronunciation of the high front vowel in the word 'beat'

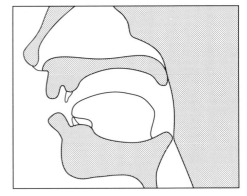

Figure 2.15: The position of the tongue in the pronunciation of the low front vowel in the word 'bat'

Tongue height

Pronounce the vowel sound in the word 'beat' followed immediately by the vowel sound in the word 'bat'. You will feel your jaw dropping and your tongue lowering as you move to the vowel in 'bat'. Now pronounce the two vowels in the reverse order. This time you will feel your tongue and jaw rising as you move to the vowel in 'beat'.

Pronounce the vowels in 'beat', 'bit', 'bait', 'bet', and 'bat' in sequence. Notice that your tongue lowers and your jaw drops as you move from one vowel to the next. The vowels in 'beat' and 'bit' are both considered to be *high vowels* because they are made with the tongue raised above its rest position. The vowels of 'bait' and 'bet' are considered to be *mid vowels* because the tongue is neither high nor low in the mouth. The vowel of 'bat' is considered to be a *low vowel* because it is made with the tongue below its rest position.

If you pronounce the vowel of the word 'boot' immediately followed by the vowel of 'pot', you will again feel your tongue and your jaw dropping as you did with the vowels of 'beat' and 'bat'.

Now pronounce the vowels of the following words in sequence, feeling the tongue gradually lowering with each vowel: 'boot', 'book', 'boat', 'bought', 'pot'. The same relationship that exists among the previous sequence of vowels also exists with these five vowels: your tongue lowers and your jaw drops as you move from one vowel to the next. The vowels in 'boot' and 'book' are both considered to be high vowels. The vowels in 'boat' and 'bought' are mid vowels and the vowel in 'pot' is a low vowel.

It should be noted that for many American and most Canadian speakers of English, the words 'pot' and 'bought' are pronounced with the same vowel, the low vowel of 'pot'. Thus, the overwhelming majority of North American English speakers will pronounce pairs such as 'caught' and 'cot' in the same way. For others, the word 'caught' is pronounced with the mid vowel as in 'bought' and the word 'cot' is pronounced with the low vowel as in 'pot'. Speakers with this distinction will pronounce words such as 'taught', 'augment', 'awful', 'ought', 'talk', 'flaw', 'dawn', and 'saw' with the mid vowel of 'bought', and words such as 'not', 'Don', 'rock', 'got', 'top', and 'stop' with the low vowel of 'pot'. In contrast, speakers without this distinction will pronounce all of these words with the same vowel, the low vowel of 'pot'.

high	beat	boot
	bit	book
mid	bait	boat
	bet	bought
low	bat	pot

Table 2.11: Classification of English vowels by tongue height

Frontness/backness of tongue

In pronouncing the sequences of vowels in the chart above, you may have noticed that a different part of the tongue was raised or lowered with the vowels in the first column, as opposed to the vowels in the second column. Say the vowel in 'beat' followed immediately by the vowel in 'boot'. Both of these are high vowels because the tongue is raised above its rest position. However, the vowel of 'beat' is made with the front part of the tongue high in the mouth, while the vowel of 'boot' is made with the back part of the tongue high in the mouth. Thus, the vowel of 'beat' is referred to as a high *front vowel* and the vowel of 'boot' is referred to as a high *back vowel*. (See Figures 2.14 and 2.16.)

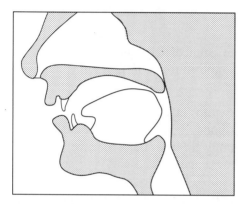
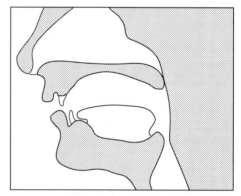

Figure 2.16: The position of the tongue in the pronunciation of the high back vowel in the word 'boot'

Figure 2.17: The position of the tongue in the pronunciation of the low back vowel in the word 'pot'

This same difference exists between the vowels of 'bat' and 'pot'. Say the vowel of 'bat' immediately followed by the vowel of 'pot'. Both of these vowels are low vowels. The vowel of 'bat' is made with the front of the tongue low in the mouth, while the vowel of 'pot' is made with the back part of the tongue low in the mouth. Thus, we say that the vowel of 'bat' is a low front vowel and the vowel of 'pot' is a low back vowel. (See Figures 2.15 and 2.17.) There is considerable variation in the pronunciation of the vowel of 'pot'. For many speakers of North American English, it is a low back vowel while for many other speakers, it is a low vowel but more centralized. For this reason, in our charts we have not placed it as far back as the other back vowels.

The vowel sounds in the words 'beat', 'bit', 'bait', 'bet', and 'bat' are front vowel sounds. The vowel sounds of 'boot', 'book', 'boat', 'bought', and 'pot' are back vowel sounds. Pronounce the vowels of 'beat', 'bit', 'bait', 'bet', and 'bat' in sequence again, comparing them to the vowels of 'boot', 'book', 'boat', 'bought', and 'pot'. With the first sequence, the front part of the tongue gradually lowers in the mouth, while with the second sequence, the back part of the tongue lowers.

There are also vowels in English made with neither the front nor the back part of the tongue. These are referred to as *central vowels*. Pronounce the vowel of 'but'. The tongue is neither high nor low in the mouth when this vowel is pronounced. In addition, neither the front nor the back part of the tongue is involved. This is called a *mid central vowel*. The position of the tongue for this vowel is very close to the position that the tongue occupies when it is at rest.

Another vowel sound made with the tongue in the mid central position is the initial vowel sound /ə/ in a word such as 'machine'. This vowel is called *schwa*. The schwa is the most frequently occurring vowel in English and plays a major role in the English stress system. It will be discussed in more detail in Chapter 5, 'Word stress and vowel reduction' (see page 63).

	front	**central**	**back**
high	beat		boot
	bit		book
mid	bait	machine	boat
	bet	but	bought
low	bat	pot	

Table 2.12: Classification of English vowels by height and frontness

Tenseness/laxness

Another way in which vowels can differ is in terms of muscle tension in the mouth. We say that vowels produced with extra muscle tension are *tense* and that vowels produced without this tension are *lax*. Compare the vowels of 'beat' and 'bit'. Both of these vowels are made with the front part of the tongue high in the mouth. They differ in the degree of muscle tension with which they are produced. You should feel that your facial muscles are more tense in the pronunciation of 'beat' than in 'bit'. This causes a greater spreading of the lips in 'beat'. An effective way of detecting the difference in tenseness is to sing both vowels at a high pitch. The tense vowel (the vowel of 'beat') will feel as if it is being produced with much more effort than the lax one (the vowel of 'bit').

There are three tense/lax vowel pairs in English: the vowels of 'beat' and 'bit', 'bait' and 'bet', and 'boot' and 'book'. In all of these pairs, it is the first member that is tense. The tense vowels are pronounced with the tongue slightly higher in the mouth than their lax counterparts. In addition, the front tense vowels are pronounced with the tongue further forward than their lax counterparts; the back tense vowel is pronounced with the tongue further back than its lax counterpart. The tense vowels are longer and also involve some tongue movement during their pronunciation (see description of Off-glides on page 33).

The vowel sound in 'boat' is also a tense vowel but there is no directly corresponding lax vowel. For those speakers who have the 'caught/cot' distinction discussed above, the vowel sound of 'bought', which might be considered the corresponding lax vowel, is, in fact, somewhat tense. A survey of North American introductory linguistics textbooks shows considerable variation in the treatment of the mid vowel of 'bought'. Some authors consider the vowel to be the lax counterpart of the mid vowel in 'boat' whereas others consider it to be tense and low. This is probably because there is a good deal of dialectal variation in the pronunciation of this vowel.

Table 2.13 shows how English vowels can be classified by tenseness. It is useful to remember, however, that in many dialects the vowel in 'bought' is lower and more centralized.

Table 2.13: Classification of English vowels by tenseness

		front	central	back
high	*tense*	beat		boot
	lax	bit		book
mid	*tense*	bait		boat
	lax	bet	but	bought

Photocopiable
© Oxford University Press

Lip rounding

In addition to tongue height, frontness/backness, and muscle tension, *lip rounding* is also important in the articulation of vowels. If you pronounce the vowel in the word 'boot' and compare it to the vowel in the word 'beat', you will feel that your lips are rounded in the first case, but spread apart in the second. English has four vowels made with lip rounding: the back vowels in 'boot', 'book', 'boat', and 'bought'. (Note that the vowel in 'bought' is rounded only for those speakers who have the 'caught'/'cot' distinction.) Compare the vowels of these three words to the vowels of 'beat', 'bit', 'bait', and 'bet', paying attention to the formation of your lips. Your lips are spread in the pronunciation of the last four vowels.

Phonetic symbols for vowels

We have seen that vowels can be described in terms of four basic character-istics. For example, the vowel in a word such as 'beat' is made with the front part of the tongue high in the mouth. The lips are unrounded and the facial muscles are relatively tense. Thus, it is referred to as a high, front, tense, unrounded vowel.

In Table 2.14 and Figure 2.18 below we present the phonetic symbols for each of the vowel sounds discussed above. The symbols for vowels rarely correspond to English spelling because there are many more vowel sounds in English than there are vowel letters.

		front (unrounded)	central (unrounded)	back (rounded)
high	*tense*	iy (beat)		uw (boot)
	lax	ɪ (bit)		ʊ (book)
mid	*tense*	ey (bait)	ə (machine)	ow (boat)
	lax	ɛ (bet)	ʌ (but)	ɔ (bought)
low		æ (bat)	a (pot)	

Table 2.14: The vowels of English

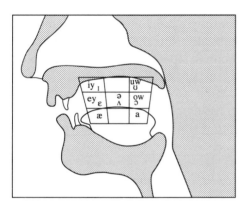

Figure 2.18: The vowel chart in relation to the inside of the mouth

Off-glides

Notice that the symbols used here to represent the tense vowels of English, /iy/, /ey/, /uw/, and /ow/, have two parts. The front vowels /iy/ and /ey/ are composed of the pure vowels /i/ and /e/ followed by the semi-vowel /y/. The back vowels /uw/ and /ow/ are composed of the pure vowels /u/ and /o/ followed by the semi-vowel /w/. These semi-vowels are usually referred to as *off-glides* and reflect the fact that there is movement of the tongue during the pronunciation of each of the tense vowels. In many languages of the world, these tense vowels are not followed by off-glides, but are pure vowels. Thus, when ESL students pronounce the tense vowels of English, they often omit the semi-vowel, producing vowels that sound to the English ear more like the lax counterparts of the tense vowels, that is, /ɪ/, /ɛ/, and /ʊ/.

Complex vowels (diphthongs)

There are three complex vowel sounds (or *diphthongs*) in English: the vowel sounds of 'bough', 'buy' and 'boy'. These are considered to be complex vowel sounds because they consist of a vowel followed by a semi-vowel, either /y/ or /w/. The phonetic symbols used in this book for these complex vowels are: /aw/ as in 'bough', /ay/ as in 'buy', and /oy/ as in 'boy'. As we saw, the tense vowels, /iy/, /ey/, /ow/, and /uw/, are also represented with semi-vowels because they involve movement of the tongue. We are not classifying the tense vowels as diphthongs because there is less tongue movement with these vowels than with the diphthongs /ay/, /aw/, and /oy/.

The vowel /ər/

Pronounce the following words:

sir	fur
fern	journey
heard	mirror

All of these vowel-plus-/r/ combinations are pronounced in the same way. We will represent this sound phonetically with the symbol combination /ər/. Although we are using two symbols to represent this sound, it is really a single sound and should be taught as such. This vowel sound can be described as an r-coloured mid central vowel. In other words, it has characteristics of both the schwa (/ə/, as in machine) and the /r/ sound. It is like the schwa in that it is a mid central vowel and like the /r/ in that the tongue curls back slightly.

Figure 2.19: The diphthongs and /ər/ on the vowel chart

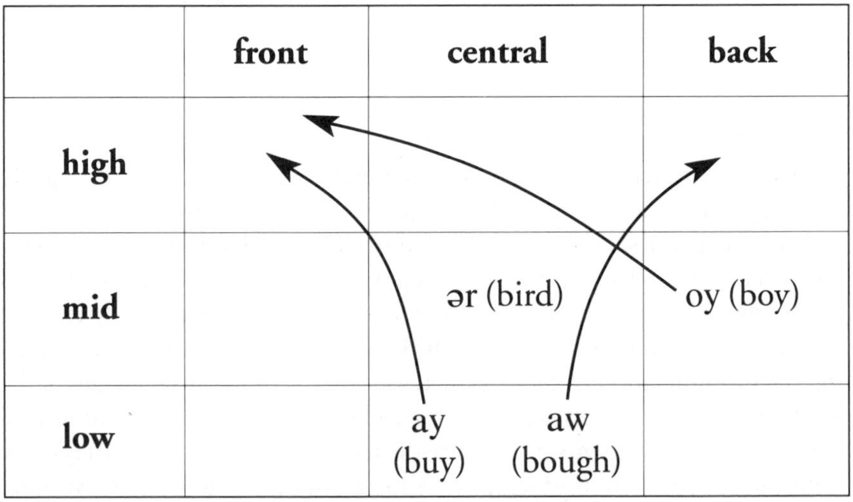

	front	central	back
high			
mid		ər (bird)	oy (boy)
low		ay (buy) aw (bough)	

The consonant /h/

Now that we have introduced all the vowel sounds of English, it is possible to describe the consonant /h/. When you produce an /h/, you breathe out and the tongue and lips assume the position of whatever vowel follows it. Thus, /h/ is made differently depending on the nature of the following vowel. Consider how you pronounce /h/ in the words below:

> heat   hat   hoot   hot

In these words, the /h/ takes on the position of the vowels /iy/, /æ/, /uw/, and /a/, respectively. We can thus see why /h/ is often described as a voiceless vowel. The mouth is in the position of the following vowel, but there is no vibration of the vocal cords as there is with vowels.

Semi-vowels (glides)

In our description of the semi-vowel /w/, we stated that the lips are rounded and the back of the tongue approaches the soft palate. In fact, the tongue and lips are in approximately the same position in the pronunciation of the high, back vowel /uw/. The primary difference between /w/ and /uw/ is that /uw/ occupies the centre of a syllable whereas /w/ occupies a peripheral position in a syllable.

Similarly, the semi-vowel /y/ and the high, front vowel /iy/ are produced with the tongue in approximately the same position. Again, the primary difference between the two sounds is that /iy/ occupies a central position in a syllable. This is, more generally, the difference between vowels and semi-vowels.

If students have difficulties in pronouncing words such as 'would' and 'year', ESL teachers can exploit the similarity between the semi-vowels and their corresponding vowels. Most frequently the difficulty with such words arises because students omit the word-initial semi-vowels. Teachers can tell students to make two identical vowels in succession and to emphasize the second of the identical vowels.

Exercises

Transcription

Throughout the rest of this book, you will find examples of words and sentences transcribed using phonetic symbols. As we have now introduced most of the phonetic symbols you will encounter, we provide some examples of transcribed words in the exercises that follow in order to familiarize you with this type of representation.

1 a. Give the phonetic symbol for the first sounds in the following words.

Example: bomb /b/

a city	**e** physics	**i** pneumonia	**m** quick
b cake	**f** shoot	**j** zone	**n** what
c thick	**g** Thames	**k** usually	**o** English
d choice	**h** knee	**l** jug	

b. Give the articulatory description for each of these first sounds.

Example: bomb /b/ voiced bilabial stop

2 a. Give the phonetic symbol for the final sound in the following words.

Example: rock /k/

a ridge	**e** is	**i** bomb	**m** garage
b sonic	**f** moth	**j** gauge	**n** bathe
c wife	**g** relax	**k** traipse	**o** though
d made	**h** log	**l** dogs	

b. Give the articulatory description for each of these sounds.

Example: rock /k/ voiceless velar stop

3 a. Give the phonetic symbol for the vowel sound in the following words.

Example: meat /iy/

a head	**f** I	**k** late	**p** meat
b fun	**g** May	**l** Don	**q** boat
c ham	**h** dawn	**m** toy	**r** ice
d strange	**i** hill	**n** food	
e thing	**j** took	**o** stop	

b. Give the articulatory description for each of these sounds.

Example: meat /iy/ high front tense unrounded vowel

4 Write the English words represented in the phonetic transcriptions below.

Example: /krawd/ crowd

a /kæt/	**d** /fɪŋgər/	**g** /mayn/	**j** /pərpəl/
b /wərðiy/	**e** /baks/	**h** /plaw/	**k** /ʃʊd/
c /kruwz/	**f** /bɛgz/	**i** /pley/	**l** /dʒʌdʒ/

5 Write the following words in phonetic transcription.

Example: lunge /lʌndʒ/

a church	**d** thrive	**g** huge	**j** pew
b compass	**e** yelled	**h** stop	**k** feud
c campus	**f** caught	**i** awful	**l** possess

6 For each error provided below describe what the student has done wrong in articulatory terms.

Consonant errors

Example: A Cantonese speaker pronounces 'thought' as 'fought'.

Answer: The Cantonese speaker has substituted a voiceless labiodental fricative for a voiceless interdental fricative. This is an error in place of articulation.

a. A Polish speaker pronounces 'log' as 'lock'.
b. A Canadian French speaker pronounces 'those' as 'doze'.
c. A Korean speaker pronounces 'rip' as 'lip'.
d. A Greek speaker pronounces 'sheet' as 'seat'.
e. A Vietnamese speaker pronounces 'march' as 'marsh'.
f. A Spanish speaker pronounces 'vowel' as 'bowel'.
g. A Cantonese speaker pronounces 'right' as 'white'.
h. A Portuguese speaker pronounces 'mass' as 'mash'.
i. A Spanish speaker pronounces 'chip' as 'ship'.
j. A German speaker pronounces 'grieve' as 'grief'.

Vowel errors

Example: A Japanese speaker pronounces 'live' so that it sounds like 'leave'.

Answer: The Japanese speaker has substituted a high front tense unrounded vowel for a high front lax unrounded vowel. This is an error in the tense/lax distinction.

k. A Cantonese speaker pronounces 'man' so that it sounds like 'men'.
l. An Italian speaker pronounces 'cut' so that it sounds like 'cot'.
m. A French speaker pronounces 'full' so that it sounds like 'fool'.
n. A Spanish speaker pronounces 'met' so that it sounds like 'mate'.
o. An Arabic speaker pronounces 'bought' so that it sounds like 'boat'.

3 ENGLISH SOUNDS IN CONTEXT

Peter Avery and Susan Ehrlich

Positional variation

Contrastive sounds of English

In our description of English consonants and vowels, we introduced the sounds in English that contrast; that is, those sounds that can be substituted for one another in words to cause a change in meaning. For example, in English, /θ/ contrasts with /s/. We can show this by constructing what are termed *minimal pairs*. These are pairs of words that differ in meaning on the basis of a change in only one sound. The following list of minimal pairs illustrates that /θ/ and /s/ contrast in English.

/θ/	/s/
thank	sank
think	sink
bath	bass
math	mass

In the previous section, 'Individual sounds of English', we presented the articulatory characteristics of the *contrastive* sounds of English. This information can be used to help your students who are having difficulty making the appropriate contrasts of English.

In linguistics, the study of how sounds pattern in languages is called *phonology*. Phonologists study how individual sounds in a particular language can vary depending on their position within a word or sentence. For example, /p/ in English is pronounced differently in 'pot' and 'spot', even though English speakers perceive these variations of /p/ to be the same sound. These variants, then, cannot create a meaning difference (as can /θ/ and /s/, for example) and are said to be *non-contrastive* sounds of English. Because such variants differ on the basis of their position within a word or sentence, they are called *positional variants*. In this section, we will introduce some of the major positional variants of English and show their relevance in understanding the pronunciation problems of second language learners.

Non-contrastive sounds of English

Aspiration

Have a paper handkerchief handy before reading this section. Take the paper handkerchief, hold it about three inches from your mouth and say the word 'pit' rather loudly. When you release the /p/ sound, a burst of air will blow the paper handkerchief away from your mouth. Now say the word 'spit' while holding the paper handkerchief in the same position. This time when you release the /p/ sound, there will be no burst of air and the paper handkerchief will remain in the same position. In both words we have the same consonant, /p/, but it is pronounced rather differently. This is a good example of positional variation, as a sound is pronounced differently depending on the position of the sound within a word.

Try the experiment with the paper handkerchief using the following words:

Table 3.1: Examples of positional variation

the sound /p/		the sound /t/		the sound /k/	
pie	spy	tie	sty	key	ski
pool	spool	tool	stool	cool	school
pat	spat	too	stew	cold	scold
pear	spare	tore	store	core	score

Photocopiable © Oxford University Press

When you say the words in the first, third, and fifth columns, there should be a noticeable burst of air on the release of the initial consonant. With the words in the second, fourth and sixth columns, there is no such burst of air.

This burst of air is called *aspiration* and is characteristic of the voiceless stop consonants /p/, /t/, and /k/ in English when they occur at the beginning of a word. Note that /p/, /t/, and /k/ share certain articulatory features. They are all stops, that is, they involve a complete blockage of the airstream, and they are all voiceless. This is typical of positional variation. It is rarely restricted to a single sound, but rather is a characteristic of sounds that share articulatory features.

The difference between the aspirated and unaspirated /p/, /t/, and /k/ is not contrastive in English. That is, there are no minimal pairs that contrast aspirated and unaspirated /p/, /t/, and /k/. To the English speaker the aspirated and unaspirated versions are really one and the same sound and, thus, are positional variants.

Sounds that are positional variants in one language may contrast in another language. As we have seen, in English the aspirated and unaspirated versions of /t/ are positional variants. Substituting one for the other does not cause the meaning of a word to change—it is merely an incorrect pronunciation of the word. In some languages, the difference between an aspirated and an unaspirated /t/ sound can cause a difference in meaning. For example, Vietnamese has both an aspirated and an unaspirated /t/ sound at the beginning of words. These are not just variants of the same sound; they represent two different sounds in the language, just as /t/ and /d/ represent two different sounds in English. Therefore, substituting the aspirated /t/ for the unaspirated /t/ in Vietnamese will change the meaning of a word. The following list illustrates this point. The phonetic symbol for the aspirated /t/ is a /t/ written with a raised h: /tʰ/.

Unaspirated /t/ (as in 'sty')			Aspirated /tʰ/ (as in 'tie')		
Vietnamese spelling	*Phonetic transcription*	*Meaning*	*Vietnamese spelling*	*Phonetic transcription*	*Meaning*
tua	[tua]	tassel	thua	[tʰua]	lose
tu	[tu]	repair	thu	[tʰu]	mackerel
tinh	[tɪn]	smart	thinh	[tʰɪn]	silent

We can see that the aspirated and unaspirated /t/ are potentially contrastive sounds in a language. In English, these two sounds pattern together and are perceived as the same sound. In Vietnamese, these two sounds are contrastive and thus are perceived as different sounds.

Flapping

Pronounce the following words in as natural a way as possible, listening to how you pronounce the /t/ in each word:

cottage	pretty	butter	total
Peter	attic	putting	city

If you are a speaker of North American English, your pronunciation of the /t/ in a word such as 'putting' sounds like the /d/ in 'pudding' and these two words are pronounced in exactly the same way. The sound that you are using is not the same as the /d/ sound in a word such as 'down', however. While it is a voiced sound and is articulated at the tooth ridge like a /d/, it is much shorter than a /d/. The tongue touches the tooth ridge and is quickly pulled back. This sound is called a *flap* and its occurrence is one of the major differences between North American and British English. The phonetic symbol we use for a flap is a capital D: /D/.

When /t/ is pronounced as a flap, it is a positional variant of the /t/ sound. It only occurs between vowels when the preceding vowel is stressed. Compare the pronunciation of the words below, which contain aspirated and flapped /t/'s in similar positions:

Flapped /t/	Aspirated /t/
patio	potential
meteor	meticulous
platter	platonic
citizen	citation

A word ending with a *t* may be pronounced as a flap if the following word begins with a vowel. In rapid or informal speech, the italicized *t*'s of the following sentences are usually pronounced as flaps:

I go*t* a charge ou*t* of that.
The ligh*t* at the end of the tunnel.
The police sho*t* a*t* him.
He cu*t* a lo*t* of wood yesterday.
Shu*t* up.
Ge*t* ou*t* of here.

The flap is also a positional variant of the /d/ sound when it occurs between a stressed and an unstressed vowel. This creates many *homophones* (words that sound the same) between words that have a flapped /t/ and a flapped /d/. The following set of words illustrates this:

Flapped /t/	Flapped /d/
putting	pudding
latter	ladder
debtor	deader
bitter	bidder
litre	leader

Many people feel that the flap, especially when used with words spelled with a *t*, is the result of lazy or sloppy speech. However, both the flapped /t/ and /d/ are part of standard North American English and not the result of lazy speech. Native speakers of North American English often adjust their speech when speaking to non-native speakers by pronouncing /t/ instead of a flap in words spelled with a *t*. For example, in pronouncing a word such as 'city', they will say [sɪtiy] rather than the more common [sɪDiy]. However, our students are not always exposed to such adjusted speech. We remember an advanced student telling us that he could not understand a man who came to his door to read the 'water meter'. The student mimicked the pronunciation of the flaps in these words, producing a native-like pronunciation of 'water meter'—[waDər miyDər]. However, he had no idea what these common words meant when pronounced in this way, especially under the pressure of the communicative situation. Thus, we can see the importance of teaching our students about the flap.

You should not insist on having students pronounce flaps because using a /t/ where native speakers use a flap results in very little loss in comprehensibility. However, students should be given extensive practice in the recognition of flaps. They are very frequent in the spoken language and the ability to recognize words that contain flaps is very important in improving students' comprehension of natural speech.

Glottalization

Glottalized /t/

Pronounce the following words, concentrating on the pronunciation of the /t/ sound:

button	mutton
mountain	fountain
certain	curtain

In the speech of many North Americans, the pronunciation of the /t/ in these words is much different from the pronunciation of the flapped /t/ as in 'city', the aspirated /t/ as in 'top', or the unaspirated /t/ as in 'stop'. This sound is referred to as a glottalized /t/. It is a *glottalized* /t/ because the air moving out from the lungs is momentarily blocked at the glottis (see Figure 2.1 on page 12) by the coming together of the vocal cords. In the words above, the /t/ sound is pronounced at the tooth ridge and at the glottis simultaneously.

This positional variant of the /t/ sound only occurs before unstressed syllables containing /n/. A word such as 'baton' has an aspirated /t/ rather than a glottalized /t/ because the syllable containing the /n/ is stressed.

The glottalized /t/ often occurs in sentences when a word that ends with a /t/ is followed by a word that begins with a consonant. Consider the pronunciation of the /t/ in the following sentences when spoken fairly rapidly:

John bought the book for you.
Bill ate four hamburgers.
Susan saw Pete running down the street.

The glottal stop

A *glottal stop* is a non-contrastive sound of English that involves blockage of the air at the glottis. It differs from glottalized /t/ in that the tongue does not touch the tooth ridge in its production. In some British dialects of English, the glottal stop occurs as the middle consonant of a word such as 'bottle'. Thus, in these dialects, it is a positional variant of /t/. In North American English, the glottal stop occurs in the expression of dismay, 'Uh-oh'; it precedes the vowels in both syllables.

Many Cantonese speakers of English substitute glottal stops for word-final stops such as /t/ and /d/ and this gives their speech a staccato-like rhythm.

Vowel lengthening

One other important example of positional variation in English concerns the length of vowels. A vowel is longer when it occurs before a voiced consonant than it is before a voiceless one. Pronounce the following pairs of words and you will notice the difference in vowel length:

Shorter vowel (before voiceless consonant)	**Longer vowel** (before voiced consonant)
beat	b e a d
back	b a g
bat	b a d
race	r a i s e
loose	l o s e
cap	c a b

ESL learners often have difficulty in distinguishing between voiced stops (/b/, /d/, /g/) and voiceless ones (/p/, /t/, /k/) in word final position. Teaching these students to lengthen vowels before voiced stops will often help them with the voiced/voiceless distinction.

Light and dark /l/

A further example of positional variation in English involves the /l/ sound. Say the word 'leaf' very slowly prolonging the /l/ sound: 'l-l-l-leaf'. Now say the word 'feel', again prolonging the /l/: 'feel-l-l-l'. During the pronunciation of the /l/ in 'leaf', the tip of your tongue should be touching the tooth ridge. When you pronounce the word 'feel', the tip of your tongue need not touch the tooth ridge. However, the back of your tongue is raised so that it is near the soft palate. In some dialects of English, the /l/ sounds in these two words are pronounced rather differently, but native speakers consider them to be one and the same sound. The /l/ in 'leaf' is referred to as a light /l/ and the /l/ in 'feel' as a dark /l/. The light /l/ occurs before a vowel and the dark /l/ occurs after a vowel. Identify which /l/ you use in the following list of words.

leak	pull
late	pal
plate	milk

The /l/ sounds in 'leak', 'late', and 'plate' are examples of a light /l/, and those in 'pull', 'pal', and 'milk' are examples of a dark /l/. If the dialect of English you are teaching has both a dark and light /l/, notice that you cannot substitute a light /l/ for a dark /l/ or a dark /l/ for a light /l/ without making the word sound somewhat odd.

When sounds differ in the way light /l/ and the dark /l/ do, learners generally have quite different problems with the two variants and each must be practiced separately. Cantonese learners, for example, confuse the light /l/ with /n/ and the dark /l/ with /w/.

Alternatively, learners may use a light /l/ in positions where most English speakers use a dark /l/. This is the case with German learners.

r-coloring

We have seen that consonants can affect the pronunciation of a vowel. Thus, a vowel will be longer before a voiced consonant than before a voiceless one. The consonant /r/ also affects the pronunciation of vowels. The following list contains the vowels that occur before /r/.

/i/ as in 'beer'
/e/ as in 'bear'
/ə/ as in 'burr'
/a/ as in 'bar'
/u/ as in 'boor'
/o/ as in 'bore'

The tense/lax vowel distinction that is apparent in words such as 'beat' and 'bit' is lost when vowels precede /r/. Thus, /iy/ and /ɪ/ do not both occur before /r/. What occurs is a vowel between /iy/ and /ɪ/. The same holds true for the other tense/lax vowel pairs. When you pronounce each of the words in the list above, you should concentrate on the tongue position during the pronunciation of the vowel and the following /r/ sound. Notice that during the production of the vowel the tongue curls slightly and is pulled back in the mouth. This pronunciation of vowels when followed by /r/ is referred to as *r-coloring*.

If your ESL students are unable to pronounce these /r/ sounds, inform them that there are many dialects of English, for example British English, where the /r/ is not pronounced after vowels. This will usually make them feel a little better about their difficulty.

Implications for teaching

Production

Students may transfer the sound patterns of their native languages into English and produce positional variants that are appropriate to the native language but inappropriate to English. Consider the case of Spanish learners of English. Spanish speakers generally have difficulty in pronouncing the /ð/ sound in a word such as 'this' or 'the'. However, in many dialects of Spanish the /ð/ sound does, in fact, exist as a positional variant of /d/. The /d/ occurs at the beginning of a word and the /ð/ occurs after vowels. In speaking English, a Spanish speaker may transfer the sound patterns of Spanish onto English. Thus, a word such as 'mad' may be pronounced as [mæð]. When teachers tell Spanish-speaking students to substitute a /d/ for the incorrect /ð/, they will often get a look of disbelief. As /ð/ and /d/ are positional variants in Spanish, the Spanish students believe that the sound they have produced is a /d/. That is, these two sounds are perceived as being one and the same sound.

A similar situation exists for Korean learners of English. Korean speakers generally have difficulty in distinguishing between the English /r/ and /l/ sounds. However, the /r/ and /l/ sounds do exist in Korean as positional variants. The /r/ sound occurs between two vowels and the /l/ sound occurs at the beginning or end of a word.

When an /l/ sound in English is found between vowels in a word such as 'filing', the Korean speaker may impose the sound pattern of Korean onto English and produce a word that sounds more like 'firing'. As with the Spanish speakers, it is difficult to bring this to the consciousness of Korean learners because they usually believe that they have produced an /l/ sound in words such as 'filing'. They are not aware that they have produced an /r/, which is a positional variant of the /l/ sound in Korean.

Just as the positional variants of the /t/ sound in English are not part of the consciousness of English speakers, so too the positional variants of the /d/ sound in Spanish or of the /l/ sound in Korean are not part of the consciousness of Spanish or Korean speakers. Thus, it is very difficult to correct errors that arise as a result of positional variation in sounds. It must be pointed out to the students exactly what sound they are producing and under what circumstances they are producing this sound. If Spanish speakers can become conscious of their use of the /ð/ sound or if Korean speakers can become conscious of their use of the /r/ sound, the information will help these learners to make these sounds in the appropriate positions in English.

Perception

If learners of English are unable to produce the appropriate variants of a given sound, misinterpretation or incomprehensibility may result. For example, if a learner substitutes an unaspirated /p/, /t/, or /k/ for the initial sound of words such as 'plot', 'tot', and 'cot', native English speakers may hear the voiced stops /b/, /d/, and /g/, understanding the words to be 'blot', 'dot', and 'got'. Thus, it appears to the English teacher that the learner is not contrasting voiced and voiceless stops in initial position. However, this error is not the result of learners failing to make the voiced/voiceless distinction between stop pairs, but rather the result of learners not producing the appropriate positional variants of voiceless stops. Thus, in correcting this error, the teacher should not focus on the difference between voiced and voiceless stops, but rather on the difference between aspirated and unaspirated stops.

Conclusion

Sounds pattern differently in different languages   What are positional variants in one language may be contrasting sounds in another. In English, aspirated and unaspirated /t/ are positional variants while in Vietnamese these are contrasting sounds. In English /d/ and /ð/ are contrasting sounds while in Spanish they are positional variants.

Level of awareness   Native speakers are usually unaware of the differences between positional variants. English speakers are generally unaware of the difference between aspirated and unaspirated /p/, /t/, or /k/, just as Spanish speakers are unaware of the difference between /d/ and /ð/.

Production of sounds in different positions   Pronunciation teachers must ensure that sounds are practised in all positions. It is possible that a student will be able to produce a sound correctly in one position without being able to produce it correctly in another position.

Grammatical endings

Grammatical endings are suffixes that add grammatical information such as tense or number to nouns or verbs. In this section, we look at the pronunciation of grammatical endings in English, using some of the concepts introduced in the section on individual sounds.

The regular past tense

Read the following words aloud:

A	B
roped	robbed
liked	lagged
laughed	lived
missed	realized
wished	judged
watched	hummed
	fanned
	winged
	feared
	rolled

These words are all examples of the regular past tense, which is spelled *-ed*. Notice, however, that the past tense ending is pronounced differently in columns A and B. Furthermore, in neither case is it pronounced as two sounds but rather it is pronounced as a single consonant sound.

The past tense ending of the words in column A is pronounced as /t/; in column B, it is pronounced as /d/. Is the choice of /t/ or /d/ just random or is there some regularity that will allow us to predict the pronunciation of the past tense? As these are all examples of the regular past tense ending, we would expect that the choice of /t/ or /d/ would be predictable. By examining the phonetic characteristics of the sounds surrounding these past tense endings, we will show the way in which the choice is predictable.

Recall that the difference between /t/ and /d/ is a difference in voicing. Both are pronounced with the tip of the tongue touching the tooth ridge, but the /t/ is voiceless and the /d/ is voiced. If the final sound of the verb to which the past tense is attached is voiceless, the past tense is pronounced as /t/. This is the case with the verbs in column A. For example, 'rope', which ends with the voiceless sound /p/, has the past tense pronounced as /t/. If the final sound of the verb to which the past tense is attached is voiced, the past tense is pronounced as /d/. This is the case with the verbs in column B. For example, 'rob', which ends in the voiced sound /b/, has the past tense pronounced as /d/.

Now pronounce the following verbs:

> wanted
> deleted
> handed
> surrounded

With these verbs the past tense ending is not pronounced as a /t/ or a /d/, but as a vowel plus the /d/ sound. Again, these are perfectly regular verbs and the pronunciation of the past tense ending is entirely predictable. If the verb to which the past tense is attached ends with a /t/ or a /d/, the past tense is pronounced as /əd/.

Notice that the past tense ending of a verb that ends with a vowel is pronounced as /d/. This is because all vowels are voiced. To confirm this for yourself, pronounce the words below:

> flowed
> glued
> prayed

The following rule is applicable to all verbs that have the regular past tense ending:

Past tense rule

A If a verb ends with /t/ or /d/, the past tense is pronounced /əd/.
   Otherwise,
B If a verb ends with a voiced sound, the past tense is pronounced /d/.
C If a verb ends with a voiceless sound, the past tense is pronounced /t/.

The plural, possessive, and third person singular

The plural

Read the following lists of plural noun forms aloud:

A	B
ropes	robes
cats	cads
docks	dogs
reefs	reeves
cloths	clothes
	gems
	pawns
	kings
	cars
	halls

We have a single spelling, *s*, for the plural form, but two different pronunciations. The plural is pronounced as /s/ in column A and as /z/ in column B. As with the past tense ending, these two sounds are made at the same place in the mouth. The only difference is that the /s/ is voiceless and the /z/ is voiced. Also, like the past tense ending, the choice of /s/ or /z/ is predictable on the basis of the phonetic characteristics of the sounds surrounding the plural ending. If the final sound to which the plural is attached is voiceless, the plural is pronounced as /s/. This is the case in column A where all the nouns end in voiceless sounds. If the final sound of the noun to which the plural is attached is voiced, the plural is pronounced as /z/. This is the case in column B where all of the nouns end with voiced sounds.

Now consider the following plural forms:

mazes
marshes
houses
churches
judges

With these forms the plural is not pronounced /s/ or /z/, but /əz/. If you have trouble hearing the final sound as a /z/, try pronouncing the words with /s/ at the end, making the /s/ very strong. This should sound strange. Now try pronouncing them with /z/, making the /z/ very strong. This should not sound strange at all.

There are six different sounds after which the plural is pronounced /əz/: /s/, /z/, /ʃ/, /ʒ/, /tʃ/, and /dʒ/. All of these sounds are rather high-pitched sounds and are referred to as *sibilants* because of this characteristic.

You should be able to predict that the plural is pronounced /z/ after nouns that end with vowels since all vowels are voiced and the plural suffix is voiced after voiced sounds. Pronounce the following nouns that end with a vowel.

 spas
 plays
 dues
 bows

The following rule is applicable to all nouns that have the regular plural ending:

Plural rule

A If a noun ends with /s/, /z/, /ʃ/, /ʒ/, /tʃ/, or /dʒ/ (a sibilant sound), the plural is pronounced /əz/. Otherwise,
B If a noun ends with a voiced sound, the plural is pronounced /z/.
C If the noun ends with a voiceless sound, the plural is pronounced /s/.

Third person singular and possessive

The Plural Rule is also applicable to the third person singular present tense ending and the possessive ending. Pronounce the following words to confirm this.

Table 3.3: Pronunciation of third person singular and possessive

third person singular			possessive		
/s/ *voiceless*	/z/ *voiced*	/əz/ *sibilant*	/s/ *voiceless*	/z/ *voiced*	/əz/ *sibilant*
hopes	lobs	misses	Jack's	Doug's	Thomas's
laughs	believes	realizes	Ralph's	Dave's	Liz's

As we can see, the third person singular present tense and the possessive are pronounced in exactly the same way as the plural.

Contractions

There are two other situations in which the Plural Rule is applicable. Consider the sentences below where 'is' and 'has' occur in their contracted forms:

Contraction of 'is'	**Contraction of 'has'**
Pat's leaving early.	Pat's already left.
This book's quite interesting.	This book's been selling well.
The dog's a bit thirsty.	The dog's been acting strangely.
Ilsa's not here yet.	Ilsa's been late three times.

In saying these sentences note how the contracted form of 'is' or 'has' is pronounced. Note the parallel between the pronunciations of the contracted forms and the plural, possessive, and third person singular endings.

Grammatical endings in the pronunciation classroom

Grammatical endings can be used to make your students aware of the important difference between voiced and voiceless consonants. Even students at a relatively low level of proficiency have some knowledge of the past tense and plural endings. Provide your students with a list of verbs or nouns and ask them how they would pronounce the past tense or plural form. They usually catch on very quickly to the distinction between voiced and voiceless sounds.

Conclusion

In this section we have seen how the pronunciation of grammatical endings such as the past tense and plural differ depending on the sound that precedes them. We have also seen that the pronunciation of the grammatical ending is entirely predictable. Two relatively simple rules tell us how these suffixes will be pronounced. Rules of this nature are very common in languages in general. That is, the pronunciation of sounds will vary depending on the phonetic context in which they occur and these variations can be stated by a rule.

What is interesting about these variations in sounds is that native speakers are not usually aware of them until they are pointed out. Most of us consider the regular past tense ending to be *ed* until it is pointed out to us that it is actually more often pronounced as a /t/ or a /d/. (This is, of course, partly the influence of the spelling system.) This variation in the pronunciation of grammatical endings is similar to the variation in the pronunciation of positional variants in that it is below the level of consciousness of native speakers and it is entirely predictable based on phonetic context.

Exercises

1 For each of the errors described in question 6 in the previous chapter (page 37), provide three minimal pairs that contrast the incorrect sound with the correct sound. With the consonant errors, try to find minimal pairs that contrast these sounds *word-initially*, *word-medially*, and *word-finally*. (Note: This may not always be possible.)

2 a. In Japanese, /s/ and /ʃ/ are positional variants; /ʃ/ occurs before high front vowels and /s/ occurs before all other vowels. On the basis of this positional variation, how would you predict Japanese learners would pronounce the following pairs of words?

seat	sheet
sip	ship
seep	sheep
seed	she'd
sin	shin

b. Similarly, /t/ and /tʃ/ are positional variants in Japanese; /tʃ/ occurs before high front vowels and /t/ occurs before all other vowels. On the basis of this positional variation, provide examples of pairs of English words that Japanese learners may have difficulty distinguishing. How would you predict these pairs of words would be pronounced?

3 In Spanish, the voiced stops /b/, /d/, and /g/ occur as their fricative counterparts after vowels. Thus, the positional variant of /b/ is the voiced bilabial fricative /ß/, the positional variant of /d/ is the voiced interdental fricative /ð/, and the positional variant of /g/ is the voiced velar fricative /γ/. On the basis of this positional variation, provide examples of English words in which /b/, /d/ and /g/ may be pronounced as /ß/, /ð/, and /γ/, respectively. How might English speakers interpret these mispronounced words?

4 Consider how a Polish speaker might pronounce the following words:

Target word	Pronunciation
cab	/kæp/
rise	/rays/
bad	/bæt/
leave	/liyf/
bag	/bæk/
dock	/dak/
ridge	/rɪtʃ/
vine	/vayn/
side	/sayt/
judge	/dʒʌtʃ/
zone	/zown/
doze	/dows/

a. Describe the incorrect substitutions the learner is producing in the above words.
b. What generalization can you make regarding the learner's pronunciation problem? Hint: Think about the class of sounds that is mispronounced and the position in which these sounds are mispronounced.

5 Pronounce each of the following words and provide the phonetic symbol(s) that represent(s) the sound(s) of the grammatical ending. In each case explain why the ending is pronounced as it is.

a reached	g stopped	m Ralph's
b churches	h handed	n rags
c lunged	i tables	o stated
d opened	j fixes	p paths
e elbows	k garages	q passes
f Jim's	l played	r robed

4 THE SHAPE OF ENGLISH WORDS

Peter Avery and Susan Ehrlich

Syllable types

Many pronunciation problems result from ESL students' inability to produce the different syllable types of English. A consideration of these syllable types and how they differ from those of other languages will help in understanding these difficulties.

Some examples of the syllable types of English are provided below:

Word	Transcription	Syllable type
see	[siy]	C(onsonant) V(owel)
sit	[sɪt]	CVC
spit	[spɪt]	CCVC
spits	[spɪts]	CCVCC
sprint	[sprɪnt]	CCCVCC

The word 'see' has a CV syllable, the most common syllable type among the languages of the world. This is referred to as an *open syllable* because it ends with a vowel. The word 'sit' has a CVC syllable, also common among the languages of the world. This is referred to as a *closed syllable* because it ends with a consonant. The word 'spit' has a CCVC syllable and begins with the *consonant cluster* /sp/. The word 'spits' has a CCVCC syllable with consonant clusters at the beginning and the end. A consonant cluster at the beginning of a word is an *initial cluster* and a consonant cluster at the end of a word is a *final cluster*. The word 'sprint' has a CCCVCC syllable. In this case the initial cluster has three consonants and the final cluster has two consonants.

Open and closed syllables

English allows a wide variety of syllable types. These include both open syllables and closed syllables. Some languages, such as Japanese, have predominantly open syllables. Japanese words of more than one syllable are always CV–CV–CV–CV as illustrated below:

Japanese word	Meaning	Syllables
ha	tooth	CV
naka	centre	CV–CV
wakarimasu	(I) understand	CV–CV–CV–CV

When learning English, Japanese speakers frequently experience difficulty in pronouncing closed CVC syllables and may add a vowel to the end of a closed syllable to make the word conform to the Japanese pattern. Thus, a word with a closed syllable such as 'sit' may be pronounced as 'sito' with two open syllables (CV–CV).

In Italian, closed syllables do not occur at the end of a word; consequently, many Italian learners of English will add a vowel to words which end with closed syllables. The word 'big' may thus be pronounced as 'bigə'.

In addition to restrictions on open and closed syllables, languages may also have restrictions on the segments which can occur at the beginning or end of a syllable. For example, no syllable in English can begin with /ŋ/ (the final sound of 'sing'). Thus, an English speaker learning a language with syllables beginning with /ŋ/ would undoubtedly encounter some difficulty.

In both Cantonese and Vietnamese, there are open and closed syllables, but only the voiceless stops /p/, /t/, and /k/ and nasals /m/, /n/, and /ŋ/ are permitted in syllable-final position. Compare this to English where almost any consonant sound can occur in syllable-final position. For Cantonese and Vietnamese speakers, a word such as 'bad', with a voiced stop /d/ in syllable-final position, may be difficult to pronounce. Cantonese and Vietnamese speakers may substitute the voiceless stop /t/ at the end of the syllable, pronouncing 'bad' as 'bat'. Alternatively, such speakers may insert a vowel (usually a schwa) at the end of the word, producing 'badə'. In both cases, the pronunciation results from a difference between the types of closed syllables allowed in the native and second languages.

Consonant clusters

An important aspect of restrictions on syllable types involves consonant clusters and specifically the limited number of permitted combinations of consonants in initial and final clusters. A famous example which illustrates this limitation involves the distinction between the two nonsense words 'blick' and 'bnick'. While the word 'blick' does not exist in English, it does seem to be a possible word of English. If we were to invent a new product, we could call it a 'blick'. If, on the other hand, we were to name our new product 'bnick', it is likely that native speakers would consider this to be a very odd word. The initial cluster /bl/ is familiar to English speakers from words such as 'blue', 'black', and 'blank', while the initial cluster /bn/ does not occur in English and would probably be very difficult for English speakers to pronounce. This is not to say, however, that some other language could not have a consonant cluster such as /bn/.

In English, the only consonant which can precede an /n/ in an initial cluster is /s/. We have many words which begin with /sn/, such as 'snow', 'snooze', and 'sneer', but no words beginning with /pn/ or /kn/ (those spelled *pn* or *kn*, such as 'pneumonia' or 'knee' are pronounced without the /p/ or /k/). These clusters do occur in other languages. For example, in French, the word *pneu* ('tire') is pronounced with a /pn/ cluster, and in Russian, *kniga* ('book') is pronounced with a /kn/ cluster.

The permissible initial and final consonant clusters of English are listed in the tables below. You should give your students some practice in using words which contain the full range of consonant clusters, as an inability to produce many of these clusters can lead to incomprehensibility.

Initial clusters

The following tables illustrate the possible initial two-consonant clusters of English:

Table 4.1: Initial two-consonant clusters beginning with a stop consonant

lips		tooth ridge		velum	
cluster	*example*	*cluster*	*example*	*cluster*	*example*
pl	play			kl	clean
pr	pray	tr	tree	kr	cream
py	pure	ty	tune	ky	cute
		tw	twin	kw	queen
bl	blue			gl	gleam
br	brew	dr	dream	gr	green
by	beautiful	dy	due		
		dw (rare)	dwindle	gw (rare)	Gwen

Note that the clusters /ty/, /dy/, /sy/, and /ny/ are not used in most dialects of North American English. Therefore, 'tune' is pronounced [tuwn], 'due' is pronounced [duw], 'suit' is pronounced [suwt] and 'news' is pronounced [nuwz].

Photocopiable © Oxford University Press

Table 4.2: Initial two-consonant clusters beginning with a fricative

lips and teeth		between teeth		tooth ridge		hard palate	
cluster	*example*	*cluster*	*example*	*cluster*	*example*	*cluster*	*example*
fl	flew			sl	slow		
fr	fry	θr	three			ʃr	shriek
fy	few			sy	suit		
		θw (rare)	thwart	sw	switch		
				sp	spit		
				st	stone		
				sk	school		
				sm	smile		
				sn	snow		
				sf	sphere		
vy (rare)	view						

Table 4.3: Clusters beginning with a nasal

lips		tooth ridge	
cluster	*example*	*cluster*	*example*
my	music	ny	news

Table 4.4: Clusters beginning with /h/

cluster	*example*
hy	huge
hw	whether

Note that for many speakers of North American English, there is no /h/ at the beginning of words spelled *wh*. Thus 'whether' and 'weather' are pronounced in exactly the same way.

There are few initial clusters of three consonants in English. They all begin with an /s/ followed by /p/, /t/, or /k/ followed in turn by /r/, /l/, /y/, or /w/.

Table 4.5: Initial clusters of three consonants in English

cluster	*example*	*cluster*	*example*	*cluster*	*example*
spl	splice			skl (rare)	sclerosis
spr	spring	str	string	skr	screw
spy	spew	sty	stew	sky	skew
				skw	squirt

'Stew' is usually pronounced [stuw] not [styuw] in North American English. See note above on two-consonant clusters.

Final clusters

The consonants that occur in final clusters are not necessarily the same as those which occur in initial clusters. We do not find a three-consonant combination like /spr/ at the end of a syllable. We do find final clusters which would be impossible to pronounce as initial clusters, such as /ps/ in 'lapse' or /ld/ in 'hold'. The following tables illustrate the possible final clusters in English. No words which contain grammatical endings have been included in the tables.

Table 4.6: Final clusters of two consonants beginning with a nasal

lips		tooth ridge		velum	
mp	bump	nt	rant	ŋk	think
m(p)f	triumph	nd	hand		
		ns	tense		
		nθ	tenth		
		ntʃ	wrench		
		ndʒ	strange		

Note that the two-consonant cluster /ns/ is pronounced as a three-consonant cluster /nts/. Therefore, the words 'tents' and 'tense', and 'prince' and 'prints' are pronounced in the same way.

Table 4.7: Final clusters of two consonants beginning with a liquid

l		r		l		r	
cluster	*example*	*cluster*	*example*	*cluster*	*example*	*cluster*	*example*
lp	help	rp	harp	lθ	wealth	rθ	hearth
lb (rare)	bulb	rb	curb	ls	else	rs	course
lt	welt	rt	art	lʃ	Welsh	rʃ	marsh
ld	old	rd	cord	ltʃ	belch	rtʃ	arch
lk	milk	rk	cork	ldʒ	bulge	rdʒ	barge
		rg	morgue	lm	film	rm	arm
lf	elf	rf	scarf	ln	kiln	rn	barn
lv	shelve	rv	serve			rl	girl

Table 4.8: Final clusters of two consonants beginning with a fricative or stop

fricative		stop	
cluster	*example*	*cluster*	*example*
sp	wasp	pt	apt
st	trust	pθ	depth
sk	ask	ps	lapse
ft	rift	tθ (rare)	eighth
fθ	fifth	ts	ritz
		kt	act
		ks	tax
		dz	adze

Table 4.9: Final clusters of three consonants in English

stop		nasal		liquid	
cluster	*example*	*cluster*	*example*	*cluster*	*example*
kst	text	mpt	exempt	lts	waltz
ksθ	sixth	mps	glimpse	rps	corpse
		nts	prince	rts	quartz
		nst	against	rst	first
				rld	world
				rlz	Charles
				r(p)θ	warmth

The addition of grammatical endings creates many more final consonant clusters than are listed above. The past tense ending /t/ when added to 'glimpse' creates the four-consonant cluster /mpst/ and the plural ending /s/ when added to 'text' creates the four-consonant cluster /ksts/. Very difficult clusters created by the addition of the plural ending are /sps/, /sts/, and /sks/ found in words such as 'wasps', 'fists', and 'whisks'. Final clusters such as /kts/ in 'acts' and /pst/ in 'lapsed' may be very difficult for learners of English.

Difficulty with consonant clusters

Learners employ two general strategies in dealing with consonant clusters which they find difficult to pronounce. One is to insert vowels between the consonants; the other is to delete one of the consonants. Both of these strategies serve to simplify the syllable structure of the English word by making the word conform to the pattern of the native languages of the learners. For example, there are no consonant clusters in Japanese. When first learning to pronounce a word like 'street', with an initial three-consonant cluster, Japanese speakers will often insert a vowel between each consonant of the cluster and produce 'sutorito'. The word then conforms to the Japanese pattern, with four open syllables CV–CV–CV–CV.

Speakers of different languages may employ different strategies of insertion when faced with a difficult cluster. Spanish does not allow any initial clusters which begin with an /s/. Spanish speakers will insert the vowel /e/ at the beginning of a word such as 'speak' or 'street' producing 'espeak' and 'estreet'. Arabic does not allow initial three-consonant clusters. Arabic speakers, like Japanese speakers, will insert a vowel to break up the cluster in a word such as 'street', producing 'sitreet' or even 'istreet'. When correcting these two problems, the teacher would probably use different techniques with Spanish and Arabic students. It would be useful to have Spanish students begin the word 'street' with a prolonged /ssss/ so that they could avoid using the initial /e/. However, this technique may not work with Arabic speakers who are inserting a vowel after the initial /st/ of 'street'. In their case, it would probably be better to use a two-word combination such as 'this treat'. Have the students combine the words, pronouncing 'thistreet' and eventually eliminate the 'thi' from 'this', producing 'street'.

Like Japanese, Cantonese and Vietnamese do not have any consonant clusters. However, in pronouncing English words with initial or final consonant clusters, Cantonese and Vietnamese speakers tend to delete one of the consonants of the cluster rather than insert a vowel. A CCVC word like 'green' may be pronounced as a CVC word—'geen', without the /r/. A CVCC word like past may also be pronounced as a CVC word—'pat' or even 'pa'. Again, the words conform to the pattern of the learners' native languages.

In pronouncing difficult final consonant clusters, learners most often simplify the cluster through the deletion of one or more of the consonants. This should not be surprising when you consider that English speakers deal with many final clusters in the same way. Consider your own pronunciation, in informal speech, of the italicized words in the sentences below:

1 *Last one* out please close the window. Phonetically: [læs wʌn . . .]
2 This sweater was *hand-made*. Phonetically: [. . hæn meyd]

The words in italics contain final clusters which are usually simplified by native speakers. 'Last' is pronounced as 'las' without a final /t/, and 'hand' is pronounced as 'han' without a final /d/. These deletions are very common in the speech of native speakers but do not occur randomly. For example, the final /t/ of the word 'last' or /d/ of 'hand' is much less frequently deleted if the following word begins with a vowel sound as in the phrases 'the last announcement' and 'hand out'. Unlike native speakers, learners of English may simplify consonant clusters inappropriately, leading to misunderstanding or incomprehensibility. As an ESL teacher, you should focus on cluster simplifications that are inappropriate to English and not on cluster simplifications that occur in the speech of native English speakers.

Learners of English may employ a number of strategies in overcoming problems with difficult sound combinations. Often they do not realize that they are inserting or deleting sounds in attempting to pronounce such combinations. It is the task of the pronunciation teacher to make students aware of their specific pronunciation errors and to give them an opportunity to correct them.

Exercises

1 The following list contains nonsense words, some of which are possible English words and some of which are not. Identify those which are possible English words and those which are not. In each case, explain your reasoning.

a	/ptæd/	b	/plɪŋ/
c	/kniy/	d	/stratp/
e	/ŋɪt/	f	/mrayn/
g	/slan/	h	/klawp/
i	/strɛθp/	j	/dlɪŋk/
k	/frɛnt/	l	/smowp/

2 In Vietnamese, words are normally of the shape CV or CVC, being composed of one syllable. Consonant clusters are normally simplified by the deletion of a consonant; if /s/ is included in the cluster, it will always be deleted. In Japanese, on the other hand, words are polysyllabic of the shape CV, CVCV, CVCVCV, etc, the only exception being that a syllable can end with a nasal consonant if it is followed by another consonant. Japanese speakers generally insert the vowel /u/ when a new word does not conform to the expected pattern. However, /o/ is inserted after /t/ or /d/ and /i/ is inserted after /tʃ/ or /dʒ/. Given this information, how would you predict a Vietnamese and a Japanese learner would pronounce the following words? Explain.

cream	stripped	pride
fit	mind	extra
match	mistake	edge
confirm	past	company

3 Consider the following errors produced by speakers of two different dialects of Arabic:

Egyptian Arabic		Iraqi Arabic	
/filoor/	floor	/ifloor/	floor
/bilastik/	plastic	/ibleen/	plane
/θirii/	three	/iθrii/	three
/tiransilet/	translate	/isnoo/	snow
/silayd/	slide	/istadi/	study
/firɛd/	Fred	/ifrɛd/	Fred
/tʃildiren/	children	/tʃilidren/	children

a. Notice that English consonant clusters have been simplified by both groups of speakers. Describe the different strategies used by the Egyptian and Iraqi speakers. (Ignore the vowel and consonant errors.)

b. How would you go about trying to correct these errors? Would you use the same technique for both groups of speakers? or different techniques? Which group would be easier to correct? Why?

(Acknowledgement: The data for this problem are taken from Selinker and Gass 1984)

5 WORD STRESS AND VOWEL REDUCTION

*Ilsa Mendelsohn Burns, Peter Avery,
and Susan Ehrlich*

What is stress?

Another important dimension of English pronunciation is *stress*. In this section, we will represent stress with dots: the larger the dot, the heavier the stress; the smaller the dot, the lighter the stress.

Listen to yourself as you pronounce the following two-syllable words:

● ·   ● ·   ● ·
cabbage   cotton   sentence

Even though each word contains two occurences of the same vowel letter, there are some important differences in the pronunciation of the two vowels in each of the words. What are these differences?

1 The first vowel in each word is louder than the second; we can hear it more easily than the second. In fact, it wouldn't sound too unnatural if we were to scream it out: 'cabbage!'. Try it.
2 The first vowel in each word is longer than the second. It wouldn't sound terribly strange if we were to really lengthen it: 'ca-a-a-bbage'. Try it.

The long, loud vowels that we find in the first syllables of these three words are *stressed* vowels. Stress involves making vowels longer and louder. When teaching students about stress in English, it is a good idea to exaggerate both of these properties. This is because in many other languages, stress involves simply making vowels louder or saying them at a higher pitch. Therefore, even if your students understand the concept of stress, they may still need to be taught that, in English, stressed vowels are both lo-o-o-onger and louder.

Schwa

Now, let us look at some common two-syllable words.

Table 5.1

spelling	a	e	i	o	u
stress	● ·	● ·	● ·	● ·	● ·
group A	atlas distant palace	college illness socket	tulip cousin promise	anchor purpose ribbon	lettuce minute circus
stress	· ●	· ●	· ●	· ●	· ●
group B	advice canoe machine	escape dessert reveal	disease divide ignore	offend contain tonight	suggest subtract support

Photocopiable © Oxford University Press

When you pronounce these words, notice that all the words in Group A are stressed on the first syllable and those in Group B are stressed on the second syllable. Now concentrate on the vowel of each word that is not stressed. In spite of the many vowel letters represented in these unstressed syllables, they are all pronounced in almost exactly the same way. This may be difficult to hear at first. In comparison to vowels made in stressed syllables, these vowels are much shorter and quieter. As a result, they are often described as *reduced vowels* in contrast to the vowels of stressed syllables which are described as *full vowels*. Pay close attention to the unstressed *a*, *e*, *i*, *o*, and *u*: 'atlas', 'college', 'promise', 'purpose', 'lettuce'. The vowel sound that you use in the unstressed syllables is called *schwa*. We previously described the schwa as a mid central vowel (see 'Individual sounds': 'Vowels', page 31). In general, *unstressed* vowels in English are pronounced as schwa and, because of this, the schwa is the most frequently occurring vowel sound in English. Recall that the schwa is represented by the phonetic symbol /ə/.

If you have difficulty hearing the schwa in the two-syllable words above, consider the following pair of words:

● · ·   · ● ··
Canada   Canadian

'Canada' is stressed on the first syllable while 'Canadian' is stressed on the second. Compare the pronunciation of the first vowel in each word. Notice that when this vowel is stressed, it is pronounced as /æ/. However, when this vowel is unstressed, it is pronounced as /ə/, schwa.

Now consider the second syllable in this pair of words. When the vowel in the second syllable is unstressed, as in 'Canada', it is pronounced as /ə/, schwa. When the same vowel is stressed, as in 'Canadian', it is pronounced as /ey/.

Other word pairs exhibit this same alternation:

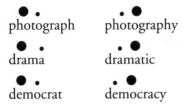

photograph	photography
drama	dramatic
democrat	democracy

The first vowels of these pairs of words are full in the first column where they are stressed, and reduced to schwa in the second column where they are unstressed. Similarly, the second vowels of these pairs of words are full in the second column where they are stressed, and reduced to schwa in the first column where they are unstressed.

ESL students, generally, have to be taught explicitly to reduce unstressed vowels to schwa. One reason for this is that their native languages may not have reduced vowels in unstressed syllables. For example, Spanish speakers have a difficult time in learning to reduce vowels to schwa because, in Spanish, unstressed vowels are not shortened and reduced to the extent that they are in English. This affects both the pronunciation of individual words and the overall rhythm of sentences. Furthermore, the English spelling system has no way of representing the schwa and thus students may give the reduced, unstressed vowels the sound value that they associate with the vowel letter used in the word they are attempting to pronounce.

In helping your students to become more aware of the effect of stress and unstress on vowels, you might want to give them a list of common English words such as those provided above. Try two-syllable words first, having them pay close attention to two things:

a. which syllable is stressed
b. how the vowel in the unstressed syllable is pronounced relative to the stressed vowel.

Be careful that you are actually pronouncing the vowels in unstressed syllables as schwa. If you try to say the words from our lists in isolation, there is a danger that you will pronounce them in a manner different from the way they are normally pronounced in sentences. For example, the first vowel in a word such as 'advice' is pronounced as schwa in normal speech. In order to confirm this for yourself, pronounce the word in the context of the following sentence.

He gave me some good advice.

It is extremely important for both you and your students to recognize that pronouncing unstressed vowels as schwa is not lazy or sloppy. All native speakers of Standard English (including the Queen of England, the Prime

Minister of Canada, and the President of the United States!) use schwa. Furthermore, the speech of your students will be more natural and easier for others to understand if they can master the use of schwa. In the next section, 'Connected speech', we discuss the importance of schwa to the overall rhythm of English sentences.

Major and minor stress

Very often in words with more than one syllable, all the vowels in the unstressed syllables are pronounced as schwa. We have already seen this to be true in two-syllable words. Now consider the three-syllable words below. The first group is stressed on the first syllable; the second is stressed on the second syllable.

List A	List B
● ● ●	● ● ●
accident	addition
calendar	diploma
elephant	completion
instrument	proportion
oxygen	opinion
vegetable	conclusion

Notice in saying these words that all of the vowels in the unstressed syllables, regardless of how they are spelled, are pronounced as schwa. The difference between List A and List B is only that the words in List A are stressed on the first syllable and the words in List B are stressed on the second syllable.

Now try pronouncing the following two-syllable words. Pay attention to the way in which the italicized syllable is pronounced.

ath*lete*
con*tact*
boy*cott*

Both syllables in these words are stressed but the first syllable receives stronger stress than the second. Because the second syllable receives some stress, it is not pronounced as schwa. We say that the first syllables of these words receive *major stress* and that the second syllables receive *minor stress*. What we have been calling stressed syllables up to this point can be more accurately described as syllables with major stress.

Now pronounce the three-syllable words below. Try to determine where the major stress occurs in these words and where the minor stress occurs.

● •●
acrobat
celebrate
telephone

The first syllable of all three words receives major stress, the second syllable is unstressed and the final syllable receives minor stress. Notice that it is only the second syllable, the one that is unstressed, that is reduced to schwa. Thus, our generalization about unstressed syllables reducing to schwa does *not* apply to syllables receiving minor stress.

Placement of word stress

Given the relationship between stress and the pronunciation of vowels in English, ESL students may want to know if there is any *rule* for the placement of stress. Unfortunately, there are no hard and fast rules. Thus, stress patterns must often be learned with each vocabulary item. However, in the sections that follow, we provide a few generalizations regarding the placement of stress in English.

Two-syllable words

The major stress on two-syllable words is more likely to fall on the first syllable if the word is a noun, and on the second syllable if the word is a verb. If you look carefully at the two-syllable words on page 68, you will see that most of the words in group A, which are stressed on the first syllable, are nouns, while most of the words in group B, which are stressed on the second syllable, are verbs. More than 90 per cent of all English nouns of two syllables are stressed on the first syllable, and more than 60 per cent of all English verbs are stressed on the second syllable. Try to have your students come to this conclusion themselves. One way to do this is to have them volunteer two-syllable words. You can then help them to discover that the vast majority of nouns are stressed on the first syllable while many verbs are stressed on the second syllable.

A good example of the difference in stress on nouns and verbs involves related noun-verb pairs in English. These are words that function as nouns when stressed on the first syllable, and as verbs when stressed on the second syllable. Consider the following two sentences, paying attention to the placement of stress in the italicized words.

a. The unhappy customer may *insult* the manager.
b. That's an *insult*.

In (a), the verb 'insult' receives major stress on the second syllable. In (b), the noun 'insult' receives major stress on the first syllable. There are many noun-verb pairs of this type. Here are some more examples:

Nouns	Verbs
● ● (or ●)	● ●
produce	produce
pervert	pervert
record	record
convert	convert
present	present
conflict	conflict
perfect	perfect
conduct	conduct
project	project
contrast	contrast
contract	contract

Three-syllable words

With words of three syllables, the major stress usually falls on the first or second syllable. In list A below, major stress falls on the first syllable; in list B, major stress falls on the second syllable.

List A	List B
● ● ●	● ● ● ●
instrument	commercial
calendar	vanilla
curious	develop
sentiment	astonish
document	opponent

In Lists A and B, all of the syllables without major stress are unstressed and therefore, the vowels of these syllables are pronounced as schwa. With many three-syllable words stressed on the first syllable, the final syllable receives minor stress. Some examples are provided below:

● ● ●
artichoke
hurricane
appetite
crocodile
porcupine
congregate

Compounds

In compound words, stress placement is very regular. Consider the words 'drug' and 'store', which form 'drugstore' when combined. Notice where the stress falls on this compound; the first word receives major stress and the second word receives minor stress. All of the compounds listed below have this same stress pattern. These compounds are sometimes written as one word and sometimes as two separate words. The way in which they are written, however, does not affect their stress pattern.

airplane	bedtime	eyelid
armchair	birthplace	farmhouse
backache	doorbell	file clerk
bookstore	haircut	gold-dust
classroom	hair-style	gold mine

In order to illustrate further the stress patterns of compounds, it is helpful to consider the differences between adjective-noun phrases and adjective-noun compounds. In the adjective-noun phrases below, major stress falls on the noun and minor stress falls on the adjective.

> That's a black board. (a board that is black)
> He works in a green house. (a house that is green)
> I saw a black bird. (a bird that is black)

In the adjective-noun compounds below, however, major stress falls on the adjective and minor stress falls on the noun.

> That's a blackboard. (a board for writing on—green or black)
> He works in a greenhouse. (a place to grow plants)
> I saw a blackbird. (a kind of bird)

The difference between adjective-noun phrases and adjective-noun compounds illustrates the importance of stress in determining meaning. For this reason, it is beneficial to have students distinguish between phrases and compounds on the basis of stress.

Suffixes

With certain suffixes in English, the placement of major stress is predictable. Sometimes this results in what is termed a stress shift. For example, the related words:

photograph   photography   photographic

all receive major stress on a different syllable. This change in stress is caused by the addition of the suffixes *-y* and *-ic*.

The following rules describe the effects of particular suffixes on stress placement. Most of the examples we provide below are words of Greek and Latin origin. These words will often be familiar to Portuguese, Spanish, Italian, French, and Greek students because they exist in their native languages. This familiarity can cause problems for such students because the stress patterns will almost always be different in English than in the students' native languages.

-ity

Major stress is always on the syllable before the suffix *-ity*:

	●	●
Notice the changes:	possible	possibility
	able	ability
	festive	festivity
Other examples:		activity
		community
		diversity
		maturity
		responsibility
		university

-ic

Major stress is always on the syllable before the suffix *-ic*:

	●	●
Notice the changes:	democrat	democratic
	magnet	magnetic
	alcohol	alcoholic
Other examples:		antiseptic
	athlete	athletic
		cosmetic
	economy	economic
	mechanism	mechanic
		apologetic

-ical

Major stress is always on the syllable before the suffix *-ical*:

	●	●
Notice the changes:	alphabet	alphabetical
	history	historical
	psychology	psychological
Other examples:	theory	theoretical
		chemical
		electrical
		identical
	politics	political
		technical

-tion

Major stress is always on the syllable before the suffix *-tion*:

	●	●
Notice the changes:	accuse	accusation
	perspire	perspiration
	communicate	communication
Other examples:	administer	administration
	appreciate	appreciation
	invite	invitation
	explain	explanation
	populace	population
	participate	participation

Conclusion

Devoting class time to these rules of stress placement can benefit your students as it can save them the trouble of memorizing the stress patterns of many vocabulary items. Once your students have discovered the correct placement of major stress in words such as the ones above, ensure that they pronounce the vowels in the unstressed syllables as schwa.

Exercises

1 Consider the stress patterns of the following word pairs:

Noun	Verb
graduate	graduate
alternate	alternate
duplicate	duplicate
moderate	moderate
syndicate	syndicate
estimate	estimate

What is the difference between the pronunciation of the final vowels in the nouns and the verbs? What is the stress pattern of the nouns? What is the stress patterns of the verbs?

2 Consider the following word pairs:

Noun	Adjective
government	governmental
instrument	instrumental
development	developmental
department	departmental

What is the difference between the pronunciation of *-ment* in the nouns and the adjectives? What is the stress pattern of the nouns? What is the stress pattern of the adjectives?

3 In Polish, major stress generally falls on the second-to-last syllable of a word. Thus, a Polish speaker might pronounce the words below in the following way (we use italics to indicate where the stress is placed):

*be*lieve	*at*las
*con*ceive	Can*a*da
*ta*ble	*mus*tard
econom*i*cal	cig*a*rette
econ*o*mics	*mid*get
div*i*dend	*pa*per
ab*an*don	*pic*ture
app*re*hend	dis*a*gree
ac*ro*bat	dil*em*ma

Determine which of these words is stressed correctly and which is stressed incorrectly.

4 Consider the pronunciation of the following words when the suffix *-y* is added:

Group 1

democrat	democracy
aristocrat	aristocracy
photograph	photography
diplomat	diplomacy

Group 2

literate	literacy
secret	secrecy
pirate	piracy
consistent	consistency
private	privacy
confederate	confederacy

In Group 1, stress shifts upon the addition of the suffix *-y* whereas in Group 2, stress does not shift. What generalization can you make regarding the effect of the suffix *-y* on stress? Describe any changes to the vowels of Group 1 which are associated with the stress shift.

6 CONNECTED SPEECH

Peter Avery, Susan Ehrlich, and Douglas Jull

The *segmental* aspects of the English sound system—consonants and vowels—are often distinguished from the *suprasegmental* aspects—rhythm, stress, and intonation. In this section, we describe the rhythm, stress, and intonation patterns of English phrases and sentences, and some of the modifications of segments that occur as a result of these patterns. If our students are to develop fluent, natural English, we must consider these aspects of pronunciation as they are essential to the production of connected speech.

Rhythm, sentence stress, and intonation

The stress-timed rhythm of English

English is a *stress-timed* language. In a stress-timed language, there is a tendency for stressed syllables to occur at regular intervals. The amount of time it takes to say a sentence in a stress-timed language depends on the number of syllables that receive stress, either major or minor, not on the total number of syllables. Unlike English, many languages of the world are *syllable-timed*. This means that the amount of time required to say a sentence depends on the number of syllables, not on the number of stresses.

Figure 6.1: The rhythm of a syllable-timed language

Figure 6.2: The rhythm of a stress-timed language

The stress-timed nature of English can be illustrated by the sentences below:

B i r d s	e a t	w o r m s.
The b i r d s	e a t	w o r m s.
The b i r d s	e a t	the w o r m s.
The b i r d s	will e a t	the w o r m s.
The b i r d s	willhave e a t en	the w o r m s.

Figure 6.3   **Photocopiable** © Oxford University Press

When you say each of these sentences, the same three syllables are stressed—'birds', 'eat', and 'worms'. Although the sentences become increasingly longer in terms of the number of syllables, it takes approximately the same amount of time to say them. You can test this yourself. Use your index finger to tap out a regular rhythm on the edge of a table, keeping the beats constant, at about one beat per second. Say the sentences above, so that the three stresses in each sentence coincide with a tap. In doing this, you should notice that the unstressed words are greatly reduced in comparison to the stressed ones. It is as though the unstressed words must be sandwiched together in order to allow the stressed syllables to recur at regular intervals. In the examples above, all the vowels in the unstressed syllables are pronounced as schwa. As was discussed in the section on word stress, this is a reduced vowel. As it is a reduced vowel, it takes much less time to pronounce than a full vowel. It is the reduction associated with the schwa that is in large part responsible for the characteristic rhythm of English.

Languages such as Spanish, French, Cantonese, and Polish are syllable-timed languages. ESL students who speak a syllable-timed language will often assign equal weight to each syllable in English sentences, regardless of whether the syllable is stressed or unstressed. This may give their speech a staccato-like rhythm that can adversely affect the comprehensibility of their English.

Placement of stress in sentences

Content versus function words

For students to produce sentences that have the appropriate stress patterns and thus the appropriate English rhythm, it is necessary that they know which words of a sentence are stressed and which are not stressed.

English words can be divided into two groups: *content words* and *function words*. Content words are those words that express independent meaning. Included in this group are:

1 Nouns
2 Main Verbs
3 Adverbs
4 Adjectives
5 Question Words (e.g. why, when, what)
6 Demonstratives (this, that, these, those)

Content words are usually stressed.

Function words are words that have little or no meaning in themselves, but which express grammatical relationships. Function words include:

1 Articles (a, an, the)
2 Prepositions (e.g. at, to, of)
3 Auxiliaries (e.g. will, have and forms of the verb be)
4 Pronouns (e.g. her, him, it, them)
5 Conjunctions (e.g. and, or, as, that)
6 Relative pronouns (e.g. that, which, who)

Function words are usually unstressed, unless they are to be given special attention.

Placement of main stress in sentences

While all content words receive major word stress, one content word within a particular sentence will receive greater stress than all the others. We refer to this as the *major sentence stress*. In most cases the major sentence stress falls on the last content word within a sentence. Consider the pronunciation of the sentences below:

Susan bought a new sweater at Creeds.

I walked home in the rainstorm.

Peter likes your suggestion.

In each of these sentences, the stressed syllable of the final content word receives the major sentence stress.

With individual words, we distinguished between three levels of stress: major, minor, and unstress. With sentences, we must distinguish between four levels of stress: major sentence stress, major word stress, minor word stress, and unstress. Thus, in the sentence 'I walked home in the rainstorm', 'I', 'in', and 'the' are function words and are unstressed; 'walked', 'home', and 'rainstorm' are content words and receive major word stress; and 'rainstorm', in addition, receives the major sentence stress. As 'rain' is the syllable of this content word that receives major word stress, it is also the syllable that receives major sentence stress. This makes 'rain' both louder and longer than 'walked' and 'home'. Since 'rainstorm' is a compound, 'storm' receives minor word stress.

In some cases major sentence stress will not fall on the major stressed syllable of the final content word of a sentence. That is, when a speaker wishes to direct the hearer's attention to some other content word in the sentence, this word will receive major sentence stress. Consider the following dialogue:

                ● · · ● · ●

Speaker A What did you buy at Creeds?

             ● · ● · ● ● · · ●

Speaker B I bought a new sweater at Creeds.

Notice that the second sentence does not receive major sentence stress on 'Creeds', but rather on the stressed syllable of 'sweater'. This is the element of the sentence that Speaker B is directing Speaker A's attention to. We call this element the *information focus* of the sentence. Generally, it is the stressed syllable of the content word representing information focus that receives major sentence stress. Most often, the information focus occurs at the end of a sentence. Indeed, a more natural response to Speaker A's question above would be: 'I bought a new sweater', or simply 'A new sweater'.

Contrastive stress

It is also possible for major sentence stress to function contrastively. Consider the following short dialogues. In the first, the contrast takes the form of a contradiction. In the second, the contrast takes the form of a choice between alternatives. (We use capital letters to represent contrastive stress.)

Speaker A I hear that Susan bought another second-hand sweater.
Speaker B No, she bought a NEW sweater.

Speaker A Did Susan buy a new sweater or a second-hand one?
Speaker B She bought a NEW sweater.

We might expect the major sentence stress in Speaker B's responses to fall on 'sweater' because it is the final content word of both sentences. However, notice that it is the contrasted information in Speaker B's responses that receives major sentence stress, i.e., the fact that the sweater is new. This contrastive stress can be even heavier and louder than the normal major sentence stress, particularly in sentences where a contradiction is being made.

Intonation

What is intonation?

Intonation is often called the melody of language since it refers to the pattern of *pitch* changes that we use when we speak. If you listen to someone speaking, you will notice that there are many changes in pitch. These pitch changes are called *intonation patterns* and play an important role in conveying meaning. Some languages, like Cantonese, Mandarin, and Vietnamese, use pitch to distinguish word meanings. For example, in Mandarin, the word *na* said with a rising pitch means 'to take'. Said with a falling pitch, it means 'to pay taxes'. Languages that use pitch to signal a difference in meaning between words are referred to as tone languages. English does not use pitch in this way. Nevertheless pitch changes do contribute significantly to the meaning of English sentences. These changes in pitch in English occur over entire clauses or sentences and different pitch patterns can signal very different meanings for the same sentence.

In the following sections, we introduce some of the basic intonation patterns of English. We represent these patterns with arrows.

Final intonation

Rising-falling intonation   Listen to yourself when you say the following sentence:

Susan bought a new sweater.

Notice that the pitch of your voice rises at the major sentence stress, the first syllable of the word 'sweater', and falls over the second syllable of this word. The pitch of the entire sentence is referred to as the *intonation pattern*. The pattern in this sentence is *rising-falling*. It is the most common intonation pattern in English and is characteristic of simple declarative sentences, commands and questions that begin with a *wh*-word, such as 'who', 'what', 'when', 'where', 'why', or 'how'. Say the sentences below, concentrating on the pitch change at the word receiving major sentence stress.

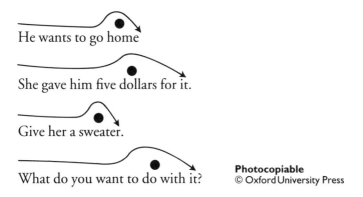

He wants to go home

She gave him five dollars for it.

Give her a sweater.

What do you want to do with it?

In each case, the pitch rises at the major sentence stress and falls over the remaining part of the sentence. This descent in pitch can be rather abrupt, especially when it must be accomplished over just one syllable as is the case with 'home' in the first sentence. When the voice falls to the bottom of the pitch range, it usually indicates that the speaker has finished speaking.

Rising intonation   Listen to the pitch of your voice when you say the following sentence:

Did Susan buy a new sweater?

Notice again that the pitch of your voice rises at the major sentence stress. However, rather than a sharp decline in pitch level after the stressed syllable, as with the rising-falling intonation pattern, the voice continues to rise. The intonation pattern in this case is *rising* and is characteristic of questions that require a simple yes or no answer.

In order to familiarize yourself with this pattern, say the following sentences, concentrating on the pitch of your voice. We represent this intonation pattern with a rising arrow.

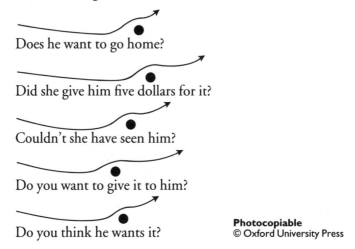

Does he want to go home?

Did she give him five dollars for it?

Couldn't she have seen him?

Do you want to give it to him?

Do you think he wants it?

This intonation contour is used to express doubt. That is, the speaker is not sure what the answer to the question is and would like the information supplied. We can turn a simple statement into a yes/no question through the use of rising intonation. For example, if we say:

John left town

with a rising intonation, we are not making a statement. We are expressing some doubt regarding the truth of the statement, indicating to the listener that a response is required. Thus, we can see that intonation patterns can contribute to sentence meaning in English.

Non-final intonation

Rising-falling intonation
Complex sentences often have two separate intonation patterns. An example of such a sentence is provided below.

Because of his athletic ability, he was given a scholarship.

Here the pitch rises and falls on the word 'ability', and also on the word 'scholarship'. On 'scholarship', the pitch drifts to the bottom of the pitch range, while on 'ability', the pitch does not fall nearly as far. The intonation contour on the first half of the sentence is a *non-final rising-falling contour*. The following sentences usually have two intonation contours—the non-final contour on the first phrase and the final contour on the second. We represent these contours slightly differently, as shown by the arrows. The arrow on the non-final contour does not go as far down as it does for the final contour. (We indicate that there should be two separate contours by the use of //.)

When John left the house // it was raining.

The man you say you met yesterday // has left town.

After we have dinner // we'll go to a movie.

Thus, a fall at the end of the sentence to the lowest pitch possible indicates that our thought is complete, and a fall that is not to the bottom of the pitch range indicates that we still have more to say. It is very useful to bear this in mind when listening to your students' pronunciation. Our experience is that if a student does not have a large enough drop in pitch in ending a sentence, native speakers will expect that there is more to come. This can lead to embarrassing silences and communication breakdowns.

Continuation rise   Say the following sentence.

Susan bought a new sweater, new shoes, and a new dress.

This intonation contour of this sentence is termed a *continuation rise* and is often used with lists. The pitch of the voice rises slightly on each noun of the list, indicating that we are not yet finished speaking. On the final noun of the list, we find the familiar rise-fall. Pronounce the following sentences in order to familiarize yourself with this pattern.

He bought apples, peaches, pears, and oranges.

I'll have two pencils, a black pen, and some ink.

We went to Paris, Brussels, Amsterdam, and London.

I saw Esther, Jane, Neil, and Susan.

Some complex sentences display a continuation rise on the first half rather than a rise-fall.

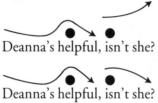

If you want to get ahead, you have to work hard.

In this sentence, the intonation may rise slightly on the word 'ahead'. Following a slight pause, we find the rising-falling contour on the next clause.

Tag questions

Tag questions can display either final rising-falling or final rising intonation contours. Their meaning will differ depending on which of these contours is used. Pronounce the following tag questions with the intonation contours indicated:

Deanna's helpful, isn't she?

Deanna's helpful, isn't she?

The first sentence, with a rising contour, indicates that the speaker genuinely does not know whether Deanna is helpful and wants the listener to provide this information. The second sentence, with a rising-falling contour, indicates that the speaker believes that Deanna is helpful and is merely eliciting confirmation from the listener.

Tag questions with rising-falling intonation are very often used to begin conversations. For example, in attempting to begin a conversation with a stranger, one might say:

Lovely day, isn't it?

In uttering this sentence, the speaker is not demanding an answer to a question but rather opening the lines of communication.

Speaker attitude

Speaker attitude can be signalled through the use of pitch variation in intonation patterns. For example, if we raise our pitch, we may be indicating surprise; if we lower our pitch, we may be indicating anger. If we expand our pitch range (that is, if our high pitches become higher and our low ones become lower), we may be indicating deference. If we narrow our pitch range, we may be indicating boredom.

Given the role of intonation in conveying speaker attitude, there is great potential for ESL students to be misunderstood if their intonation patterns are too dissimilar from the English ones. For example, many languages of the world display less pitch variation than English. Thus, learners who speak these languages may unwittingly convey boredom or lack of interest through the use of too narrow a pitch range.

Modifications of sounds in connected speech

The characteristic stress and intonation patterns of English have a profound effect on the pronunciation of sounds in connected speech. In particular, the fact that function words in English are generally unstressed and reduced makes them almost unrecognizable to beginning ESL students. In this section, we provide specific information regarding the ways in which sounds are modified in connected speech. In addition, we discuss the ways in which words are linked to one another in phrases and sentences. Such information is not only important in helping students to improve their production of spoken English, but is also essential in helping students to improve their comprehension.

The pronunciation of function words

Strong forms and weak forms

When function words are spoken in isolation, they are stressed; that is, they are pronounced in their strong form. In connected speech, where function words are normally unstressed, they are pronounced in their weak form. In the following list of words, compare the pronunciation of the strong forms to the pronunciation of the weak forms.

	Strong form	Weak form
can	[kæn]	[kən]
will	[wɪl]	[wəl], [əl]
have	[hæv]	[əv], [v]
to	[tuw]	[tə]
he	[hiy]	[iy]
them	[ðɛm]	[ðəm], [əm]
and	[ænd]	[ən], [n]

Note: In many cases where we find schwa + /n/, the resulting sound is closer to what is termed a syllabic nasal. We consistently transcribe this as /ən/. We do however agree that there is really no vowel articulation in this sound.

Below we list the specific ways in which strong forms of function words are modified in connected speech.

1 The vowel is reduced to schwa in function words such as 'to', 'them', 'the', 'a', 'and', 'as', and 'of'.

    Examples: He went to the store.   [hiy wɛnt tə ðə stor]
                Give them a break.   [gɪv ðəm ə breyk]
                Apples and oranges.   [æpəlz ənd orəndʒəz]
                As sweet as sugar.   [əz swiyt əz ʃʊgər]
                A cup of coffee.   [ə kʌp əv kafiy]

2 An initial consonant can be lost, as with the pronouns 'he', 'him', 'her', and 'them'.

    Examples: Where did he go?   [wer dɪd iy gow]
                Have you seen him today?   [hæv yuw siyn əm tədey]
                I watched her do it.   [ay watʃt ər duw ɪt]
                I watched them last night.   [ay watʃt əm læst nayt)

3 Some function words lose their final consonants. This is particularly true of 'of' and 'and'.

    Examples: A cup of coffee.   [ə kʌp ə kafiy]
                A lot of nonsense.   [ə lat ə nansɛns]
                Cream and sugar.   [kriym ən ʃʊgər]
                Now and then.   [naw ən ðɛn]

Words and phrases

Due to the reduction of function words in phrases, some phrases can sound like single words. Consider the following sentences:

    All of her seams ripped.   [al əv ər siymz rɪpt]
    Oliver seems ripped.   [aləvər siymz rɪpt]

When spoken at a normal conversational rate, the phrase 'all of her' and the name 'Oliver' are pronounced in the same way. In both cases, the first syllable has major stress and the second and third syllables are unstressed. The function words 'of' and 'her' occur in their weak forms. The vowels are reduced to schwa and the initial consonant of 'her' is deleted. (For speakers who have the distinction beteween /a/ and /ɔ/, the initial vowels in these sentences may be different.)

Below we give further examples of comparable phrases and polysyllabic words. Say each word and phrase at a normal conversational rate and notice that both are pronounced in a similar way.

approximate	confederate	orthopedic
a box of it	can better it	or to feed it
justifiable	opinion	alphabetize
just as viable	a pinion	half of her size

Acknowledgement: Some of these examples are taken from Woods (1979).

If your students are having difficulty in reducing function words in sentences, it is a good idea to give them pairs of words and phrases like the ones above. Have them concentrate on pronouncing both members of the pair with the same rhythm. This type of exercise can aid students in understanding the extreme reduction that function words undergo in connected speech.

Contractions

Auxiliary verbs, such as 'will' and 'have', and some forms of the verb 'be', often display both the loss of a consonant and the loss of a reduced vowel. The resulting forms are referred to as *contractions*. Contractions always involve the loss of the initial consonant of the auxiliary verb. In written form the vowel is also lost. Whether the vowel is lost in spoken form depends on the preceding sound.

Contractions with 'will' and 'have'   The auxiliary verbs 'will' and 'have' are contracted to the single consonants /l/ and /v/ if the preceding word ends with a vowel sound, as in the (A) sentences below. If the preceding word ends with a consonant, they are usually pronounced as /əl/ and /əv/, as in the (B) sentences below.

	Written form	Spoken form
A	They'll arrive soon.	[θeyl ərayv suwn]
	They've finished.	[θeyv fınıʃt]
B	John'll arrive soon.	[dʒanəl ərayv suwn]
	The men have finished.	[ðə mɛn əv fınıʃt]

Contractions with 'would' and 'had'   When contracted, the auxiliaries 'would' and 'had' are both pronounced as /d/ or /əd/ depending on the preceding sound, as was the case with 'will' and 'have'. 'Would' and 'had' are contracted to the single consonant /d/ if the preceding word ends with a vowel, as in the (A) sentences below. If the preceding word ends with a consonant, they are usually pronounced as /əd/, as in the (B) sentences below.

	Written form	Spoken form
A	I'd like to see you.	[ayd layk tə siy yuw]
	He'd never seen it before.	[hiyd nɛvər siyn ət bəfor]
B	The boss would like to see you.	[ðə bas əd layk tə siy yuw]
	Bob had never seen it before.	[babəd nɛvər siyn ət bəfor]

Contractions with 'is' and 'has'   When 'is' and 'has' are contracted they are also indistinguishable. As was pointed out in the section on 'Grammatical endings' (page 50), the pronunciation of these forms follows the Plural Rule.

Pronounced as /əz/ after the sibilant sounds /s/, /z/, /ʃ/, /ʒ/, /tʃ/, and /dʒ/:

The boss is mad.	[ðə bas əz mæd]
The church has been closed.	[ðə tʃərtʃəz bɪn klowzd]

Pronounced as /s/ after the voiceless consonants /p/, /t/, /k/, /f/, /θ/:

What's the problem?	[wʌts ðə prabləm]
My cat's been sick.	[may kæts bɪn sɪk]

Pronounced as /z/ after vowels and the voiced consonants /b/, /d/, /g/, /v/, /ð/, /m/, /n/, /ŋ/, /l/ and /r/:

The dog's outside.	[ðə dagz awtsayd]
Who's been asking anyway?	[huwz bɪn æskɪŋ ɛniywey]

Contractions with 'not'   Contractions are also formed with auxiliary verbs and 'not'. Because contractions with 'not' are stressed, the strong form of the auxiliary is used.

Written form	Spoken form	Compare
She can't hear me.	[ʃiy kænt hir miy]	She can hear me. [ʃiy kən hir miy]
He hasn't left.	[hiy hæz ənt lɛft]	He's seen them. [hiyz siyn ðəm]
He isn't leaving.	[hiy ɪzənt liyvɪŋ]	He's leaving. [hiyz liyvɪŋ]

ESL students often avoid using contracted forms. This is partly because of the final consonant clusters that are created through contraction. The pronunciation teacher should assure students that contractions are a normal part of spoken English, and should provide practice in using them.

Linking

In connected speech, words within the same phrase or sentence often blend together. Connecting groups of words together is referred to as *linking*. When words are properly linked, there is a smooth transition from one word to the next. Below we provide information concerning the linking of sounds.

Linking consonants to vowels

When a word that ends with a consonant is followed by a word that begins with a vowel, the consonant seems to become part of the following word. This is especially true when the word beginning with a vowel is a function word.

C(labial) + V	C(dental) + V	C(alveolar) + V	C(palatal) + V	C(velar) + V
stop‿it	with‿it	washed‿it	cash‿out	back‿out
grab‿it	breathe‿it	played‿on	camouflage‿it	drag‿out
came‿in		run‿around	march‿in	sing‿it
laugh‿about		pass‿out	rage‿on	
leave‿early		carves‿up		
		fool‿around		
		fair‿enough		

C = consonant   V = vowel

Linking consonants to consonants

When a word that ends with a stop consonant is followed by a word that begins with a consonant, the stop consonant is usually not released. That is, the tongue or lips will move to the place of articulation of the stop consonant and then move immediately to the place of articulation for the next consonant. Read the following examples, noting how the consonant at the end of the first word in each pair is pronounced.

p + t	t + k	p + d	g + b
stop‿trying	pet‿crocodile	lap‿dog	big‿boy

t + tʃ	d + dʒ	g + k	t + d
fat‿chance	bad‿judge	log‿cabin	let‿down

t + l	p + s	g + z	k + ʃ
pet‿lizard	keep‿speaking	big‿zoo	deck‿shoes

Linking identical consonants

Very often the consonant that ends one word is identical to the consonant that begins the next word. When this happens, the two consonants are usually pronounced as one long consonant. Pronounce the following short phrases to see that this is the case.

p + p	t + t	k + k	b + b	d + d	g + g
ripe‿plum	hurt‿Tom.	black‿cat	grab‿Bill	played‿darts	big‿girls

f + f	θ + θ	s + s	ʃ + ʃ	r + r	l + l
if‿Fred	with‿thanks	ice‿skating	push‿Shirley	far‿reaches	fall‿leaves

Linking vowels to vowels

When a word that ends with a tense vowel such as /iy/, /ey/, /uw/, or /ow/ is followed by a word that begins with a vowel, the words are usually linked by the semi-vowel ending the tense vowel.

iy + V	ey + V	uw + V	ow + V
be‿on time	pay‿up	blue‿angel	grow‿up
he‿isn't here	lay‿it here	flew‿in	row‿over
see‿it's done	way‿up north	stew‿it	blow‿out

Linking vowels to semi-vowels

When a word ends with a tense vowel, such as /iy/, /ey/, /uw/, or /ow/, and the next word begins with the same semi-vowel that ends the tense vowel, these will be linked like identical consonants.

iy + y	ey + y	uw + w	ow + w
be‿yourself	pay‿yourself	do‿we?	blow‿wind blow
free‿union	stay‿united	who‿wouldn't	go‿west
see‿Europe	say‿yes	blue‿water	show‿window

Deletion of consonants

In Chapter 4, 'The shape of English words', we mentioned that, in connected speech, final consonant clusters are often simplified (see page 96). This simplification depends on the following sound and on the nature of the cluster. If the following word begins with a vowel, then the final consonant of the cluster will be linked to that following vowel and, therefore, cannot be deleted as the examples below show.

Cluster	Example	Pronunciation
nd	hand out	[hænd awt]
st	last offer	[læst afər]
st	next up	[nɛkst ʌp]
ft	left out	[lɛft awt]

If the following word begins with a consonant, the final consonant is usually unreleased and can even be deleted as the examples below show.

Cluster	Example	Pronunciation when simplified
nd	band shell	[bæn ʃɛl]
ft	left field	[lɛf fiyld]
st	past president	[pæs prɛzədənt]
st	next month	[nɛks mʌnθ]

Consonants are also deleted in words that have suffixes or are compounds:

Cluster	Example	Pronunciation
nd	kindness	[kaynnəs]
ft	softness	[safnəs]
st	postman	[powsmən]
st	textbook	[tɛks bʊk]

Clusters created by the addition of grammatical endings, however, are not usually simplified:

Cluster	Example	Pronunciation
nd	canned peaches	[kænd piytʃəz]
ft	laughed hard	[læft hard]
st	missed chances	[mɪst tʃænsəz]
st	taxed me	[tækst miy]

Assimilation

The linking of consonants to consonants often causes a change in the place of articulation of the first consonant. This is know as *assimilation* because the first consonant becomes more like (i.e., assimilates to) the second one.

Assimilation of nasals

One very striking example of assimilation occurs with the final nasal consonants of function words. In the examples below, the final /n/ sound of a function word assimilates in place of articulation to a following stop consonant. This is particularly true in casual speech.

Written form	Spoken form	Assimilation
I can believe it.	[ay kəm bəliyv ət]	n → m
I can go.	[ay kəŋ gow]	n → ŋ
There's nothing on my plate.	[ðərz nʌθɪŋ am may pleyt]	n → m
I saw him in Korea.	[ay sa əm ɪŋ kəriyə]	n → ŋ

As the transcription indicates, the final nasal sound of the function words 'can', 'on', and 'in' changes its place of articulation to that of the initial consonant of the following word. That is, the tooth ridge sound /n/ changes to the bilabial sound /m/ before the initial bilabial sounds /b/ of 'believe' and /p/ of 'plate'. Similarly, it changes to the velar sound /ŋ/ before the initial velar sounds /k/ of 'Korea' and /g/ of 'go'.

When the negative *n't* is attached to an auxiliary verb, the /t/ is often changed to a short transitional sound at the same place of articulation as the following consonant and the /n/ assimilates to this consonant.

Written form	Spoken form	Assimilation
I can't believe it.	[ay kæmp bəliyv ət]	nt → mp
I can't go.	[ay kæŋk gow]	nt → ŋk
I don't believe it.	[ay domp bəliyv ət]	nt → mp

Palatalization

Consider the pronunciation of the following sentence:

Did you tell him what you saw?   [dɪdʒə tɛl əm watʃə sa]

Several things happen in the pronunciation of this sentence:

1 The final /d/ of 'did' and the initial /y/ of 'you' are pronounced as the consonant /dʒ/.
2 The vowel of the word 'you' is reduced to schwa. The two words 'did' and 'you' are often pronounced as a single syllable: /dʒə/.
3 The word 'him' is reduced to /əm/, the initial consonant being dropped and the vowel being reduced to schwa.
4 The final /t/ of 'what' and the initial /y/ of 'you' are pronounced as the consonant sound /tʃ/.
5 Again the vowel of the word 'you' is reduced to schwa.

We have discussed the reduction of function words in a previous section. Our interest here is the change of /d/ + /y/ to /dʒ/ and of /t/ + /y/ to /tʃ/. Assimilation of this nature is referred to as *palatalization*. It is called palatalization because the tooth ridge sounds /t/ and /d/ are pronounced further back in the mouth, closer to the hard palate, in the same place as the semi-vowel /y/ is pronounced. Palatalization occurs regularly with words such as 'did' and 'what' when they occur before words that begin with the semi-vowel /y/. It is also common for /s/ and /z/ to be pronounced as /ʃ/ and /ʒ/ when they occur before a word beginning with /y/. For example, the following phrases all display palatalization in casual speech:

Spelling	Palatalized form
not yet	[natʃɛt]
Where did you go?	[werdɪdʒəgow] or even [werdʒgow]
this year	[ðɪʃyir]
Where's Union station?	[werʒyuwnyənsteyʃən]
Would you mind?	[wʊdʒəmaynd]
Could you move	[kʊdʒəmuwv]
Please yourself.	[pliyʒyərsɛlf]

High frequency phrases: 'wanna', 'gonna', and 'dunno'

Certain English phrases undergo sound modifications because of their high frequency in the spoken language.

'Wanna' and 'gonna'   When 'want' and 'going' are followed by 'to' in verb + infinitive constructions, they are usually pronounced [wanə] and [gənə], respectively:

I want to leave.	[ay wanəliyv]
She is going to leave soon.	[ʃiyz gənə liyv suwn]

Because these contracted forms blend in with the overall rhythm of English sentences, we do not often notice their use. As a result, native speakers may consider them to be lazy or sloppy. However, if you listen carefully to the speech of native speakers, you will notice that these contracted forms are more commonly used than the uncontracted forms.

'Dunno' The common expression 'I don't know' is frequently pronounced as 'I dunno', causing some confusion for beginning ESL students.

The type of modification present in the pronunciation of 'wanna', 'gonna', and 'dunno' is familiar in many words and expressions that are used with high frequency in the spoken language. The word 'Toronto', for example, is pronounced by those who use it very frequently as 'tranow'. The modification of this word is very similar to the modification of 'don't know'.

When our ESL students use 'wanna', 'gonna', and 'dunno', they often sound unnatural. This unnaturalness stems from the fact that the overall rhythm of the sentence is incorrect and the contracted forms stand out. We should probably not insist on having our students produce these forms until their spoken English is fairly advanced. We should, however, introduce these forms for recognition to even basic students as they appear frequently in spoken English.

Summary

Developing fluent and comprehensible speech in our ESL students is the primary goal of training in the spoken language. Extensive work on the aspects of connected speech discussed in this section will not only contribute to students' ability to produce fluent and comprehensible speech, but also to their ability to comprehend the spoken language. We have seen that differentiation between stressed and unstressed syllables, the reduction of function words, the linking of words and phrases, etc., all combine to give English its characteristic rhythm. In attempting to increase your students' fluency and comprehensibility, it is essential that all of these aspects of connected speech be practised in the ESL classroom.

Exercises

1 Read each of the sentences below at a normal conversational speed. Describe how the pronunciation of the function words in these sentences is different from their pronunciation in isolation.

   a. Do you want a cup of coffee?
   b. Would you like cream and sugar?
   c. Where did he go last night?
   d. Give her a hand.
   e. He can go to the store but she can't.
   f. She can't go to the store but he can.

2 Read the dialogues below and determine where the major sentence stress falls in each of the sentences.

a. In a Restaurant
Customer: I'd like a hamburger.
Waiter: Do you want cheese on your hamburger?
Customer: No, just a plain hamburger.
b. Discussing a Trip
Speaker A: Last week, I flew to San Francisco.
Speaker B: Oh, what kind of plane were you on?
Speaker A: I was on a DC-9 from Toronto to Detroit and a 747 from Detroit to San Francisco.
In these dialogues, major sentence stress does not always fall on the last content word of the sentence. Explain the reason in each case.

3 Transcribe the sentences below, first as though the words were spoken in isolation, and then as they would be pronounced in connected speech.

Example:	Would you give him a hand?
In isolation	/wʊd yuw gɪv hɪm æ hænd/
In connected speech	/wʊdʒə gɪ vɪm əhænd/

a. What did he do last night?
b. Give her some help.
c. Could you tell me what you're doing?
d. Are you going to be coming to the party tomorrow?

4 Tape and transcribe phonetically two minutes of natural conversation between native speakers of English. Describe the differences between a written and spoken transcript of this tape.

5 In English, polite requests generally have a rising intonation pattern as in:

Would you close the window?

Many languages of the Indian subcontinent use a rising-falling intonation pattern for requests of this nature, producing a pattern as shown below:

Would you close the window?

How might a speaker of Indian English be perceived by native speakers of American English if she or he used a rising-falling pattern in this context?

PART TWO

The identification and correction of specific pronunciation problems

INTRODUCTION

In this part of the book, we describe many of the pronunciation problems that the ESL teacher will encounter. In Chapter 7, we discuss common pronunciation problems and in Chapter 8, the specific problems of fourteen language groups. The list of problems is in no way meant to be exhaustive.

For the most part, our emphasis has been on segmental rather than suprasegmental problems. This does not mean that the segmental problems are more important, only that they are more simply described. All second language learners require extensive work on the suprasegmental aspects of English pronunciation. Many of the articles in the final section provide activities dealing with the suprasegmental aspects of English.

Each of the problems described in the following chapters is followed by tips on correction. These tips are ways of teaching students to make a sound or a sound distinction in isolation. The teacher must remember that the mere ability to produce a sound or to hear a difficult distinction in isolation does not guarantee that the problem has been overcome; it is only the first step. Several of the articles in the final part of this volume give excellent techniques for contextualized sound practice. Many of the activities found in Chapter 9 are usual for practising consonant and vowel distinctions in a communicative context. Those in Chapters 11 and 12 are useful for practising suprasegmental aspects of English.

7 COMMON PRONUNCIATION PROBLEMS

Peter Avery and Susan Ehrlich

Pronunciation teachers do not usually find themselves in a classroom populated with students who share a common native language. This is often a source of great despair. Teachers feel that the pronunciation problems of two or more given language groups are so different that working on the difficulties of one group leads to the exclusion of the others. While it is true that many pronunciation problems vary according to the native languages of the learners, it is also true that many problems of a more general nature can be found. For example, learners from most language backgrounds have difficulty with the English *th* sounds. This is simply because these sounds are not common in the languages of the world. Thus, practising these sounds with a class of learners usually benefits everyone.

In this chapter we introduce some common pronunciation problems. A description of each problem will be followed by tips on correction. The tips are not necessarily presented in sequential order. Teachers should choose the tips that are most suitable for the needs of their students.

English vowels

ESL students generally have difficulty producing English vowel distinctions. This is because there are more vowels in English than in most other languages. Many of the world's languages (e.g. Spanish and Japanese) have only five vowels. In Tables 7.1 and 7.2 below, the English vowel systems is presented along with a typical five-vowel system.

Table 7.1

	front	central	back
high	iy		uw
	ɪ		ʊ
mid	ey	ə	ow
	ɛ	ʌ	ɔ
low	æ	a	

Table 7.2

	front	central	back
high	i		u
mid	e		o
low		a	

Comparing the English vowel system to a typical five-vowel system reveals several potential problem areas. For example, the tense/lax vowel pairs of English, /iy/ vs. /ɪ/, /ey/ vs, /ɛ/, /uw/ vs. /ʊ/, do not exist in a five-vowel system as there is no tense/lax distinction. The low front vowel /æ/ and the central vowels /ʌ/ and /ə/ do not exist in a five-vowel system. Furthermore, the English vowel /a/ is further back than the low vowel of a typical five-vowel system. Notice also that in English there are five front vowel sounds and, depending on one's dialect, four or five back vowel sounds, whereas in the five-vowel system, there are only two vowels made in both the front and back part of the mouth. Therefore, the small differences in tongue positioning between the five front vowels and the five back vowels of English may pose problems for second language learners who are accustomed to making only two distinctions in tongue height in the front and back of the mouth.

Problem   Tense vs. lax vowels

/iy/ vs. /ɪ/ as in 'beat' and 'bit'
/ey/ vs. /ɛ/ as in 'bait' and 'bet'
/uw/ vs. /ʊ/ as in 'boot' and 'book'

The distinction between tense and lax vowel pairs of English almost always creates problems. Second language learners often produce the two vowels of each pair identically, using neither the tense nor the lax vowel, but a vowel between the two. Failure to make these distinctions can lead to misunderstandings. Words such as 'sleep', 'taste', and 'stewed' may be heard by English speakers as 'slip', 'test', and 'stood' respectively.

Learners from some language backgrounds (e.g. French and Arabic) are reported to have difficulty with the distinction between /ow/ and /ɔ/, at least in dialects that have the /ɔ/. It is our understanding that this problem is most prevalent for those learners who are being taught British English, where there are even more vowel distinctions in the low back part of the mouth than in any North American dialect. We therefore ignore the /ow/ vs. /ɔ/ problem in the text, though we do think that teachers should check to make sure that pairs such as 'boat' and 'bought' are not confused.

Before working on the tense/lax distinction, we recommend that you begin by concentrating on the four tense vowels of English, the vowels /iy/, /ey/, /uw/, and /ow/ as in 'beat', 'bait', 'boot', and 'boat'. Students generally produce a pure form of the vowel without the following semi-vowel, /y/ or /w/. Thus, the vowel they produce is shorter than the equivalent in English and has no tongue movement during its production.

Tips for teaching tense vowels

1 Exaggerate your pronunciation of each vowel sound in 'bee', 'bay', 'boo', and 'bow'. In saying /iy/ and /ey/, be sure that you spread your lips. Tell the student to smile when pronouncing these vowels. With /uw/ and /ow/, be sure that your lips are rounded.

2 To emphasize that all these vowels are long, pretend you are stretching an imaginary elastic band.

3 Work on each vowel in isolation. Begin with /ey/ as this vowel involves more tongue movement than the other tense vowels. Have the students produce a very long /ey/: [eeeeyyyy]. Repeat the procedure for the other three vowels.

4 Do linking exercises in which a tense vowel is followed by a word beginning with another vowel. In linking the two vowels, students are more likely to produce the desired semi-vowel, /y/ or /w/, as part of the tense vowel.

I see it.	[ay siyɪt]
I play at it.	[ay pleyæt ɪt]
A blow out.	[əblowawt]
They blew it.	[ðey bluwɪt]

5 Have students concentrate on lengthening the vowels. It is good to begin with single-syllable words that end with these vowels: 'bee', 'pay', 'boo', 'low'. Construct sentences in which the word containing the tense vowel is heavily stressed. For example, create short dialogues like the following.

Teacher Did you say you live on Bloor Street?
Student No, I said *Bay* Street.
Teacher You said you came last June, didn't you?
Student No, I said I came last *May*.

The heavy stress will result in the vowel being much longer and the semi-vowel being more noticeable. Note that the length contrast between the tense and lax vowels is relative to the phonetic environment. For example, the /iy/ in 'beat' may be shorter than the /ɪ/ in 'bid' because the final voiced consonant of 'bid' serves to lengthen the vowel (see section on 'Vowel lengthening' in 'English sounds in context', page 44). It is wise to keep this in mind when having students lengthen the tense vowels.

6 When you use words of more than one syllable to illustrate tense vowels, choose words in which the tense vowels receive major stress: 'peacock', 'payment', 'poodle', and 'motion'. Do not use words like 'happy', 'birthday', 'curfew', or 'bellow' as examples, as the tense vowels in these words do not receive major stress. As a result, they are pronounced without much lengthening.

Tips for teaching lax vowels
1 Illustrate the lax vowels by relaxing your body when producing them. Be sure that your mouth is relaxed. Your lips should not be too spread for /ɪ/ and /ɛ/ or too rounded for /ʊ/.

2 To emphasize that these vowels are short, bring your hands together quickly in a clapping motion.

3 Have the students pronounce words that contain these vowels, concentrating on relaxing the facial muscles.

/ɪ/	/ɛ/	/ʊ/
sit	said	book
lip	mess	push
bid	red	hood
window	fender	wooden

4 Students should practise the lax front vowels, /ɪ/ and /ɛ/, in minimal pairs.

/ɪ/	/ɛ/
rid	red
pin	pen
pit	pet
mint	meant

5 Point out that the lax vowels do not occur at the end of a word in English.

Tips for teaching the tense/lax distinction
1 After you have taught the tense and lax vowels separately, have students distinguish between them in minimal pairs. Be sure that you do both recognition and production activities. In this way, students can determine which member of the pair gives them the most difficulty.

/iy/	/ɪ/	/ey/	/ɛ/	/uw/	/ʊ/
meat	mitt	mate	met	stewed	stood
lead	lid	late	let	Luke	look
sheep	ship	waist	west	pool	pull
reason	risen	main	men	cooed	could

2 Work on the tense/lax distinction should also be done with minimal pair sentences.

/iy/ vs. /ɪ/	Don't sleep on the subway platform.
	Don't slip on the subway platform.
/ey/ vs. /ɛ/	They're going to taste that wine.
	They're going to test that wine.
/uw/ vs. /ʊ/	I read Luke. (a book of the Bible)
	I read *Look*. (a magazine)

Problem /ɛ/ vs. /æ/ vs. /ʌ/ vs. /a/ as in 'bet', 'bat', 'but', and 'pot'
Great confusion arises with the /ɛ/, /æ/, /ʌ/, and /a/ of 'bet', 'bat', 'but', and 'pot'. Some learners produce all four vowel sounds in a similar manner. More commonly they produce two or perhaps three vowel sounds instead of

four. The vowel charts given at the beginning of this chapter show that all four of these English vowels are made relatively low in the mouth. A five-vowel system, on the other hand, has only one low vowel. Some learners may also have difficulty making the distinction between /ɔ/ and /a/ as in 'bought' and 'pot'. Because there are many speakers of North American English who themselves do not make this distinction, we advise teachers not to be overly concerned with it.

Tips for teaching /ɛ/ vs. /æ/ as in 'bet' and 'bat'

Students often pronounce these two vowels in exactly the same way. Most commonly, students fail to lower their tongue and jaw far enough in attempting to produce the /æ/ sound.

1 It is a good idea to have the students move through the entire set of front vowels: /iy/ /ɪ/ /ey/ /ɛ/ /æ/. Do this several times so that they can feel the mouth gradually opening as the sequence is produced. Tell the students that the tip of the tongue is against the bottom teeth in the pronunciation of /æ/.

2 It often helps if the teacher demonstrates the contrast between /ɛ/ and /æ/ by exaggerating the dropping of the jaw with /æ/. Have the students imitate this.

3 The teacher should emphasize that /æ/ is peculiar to English. We have found it useful to describe /æ/ as an ugly sound and then to produce a long exaggerated version of the vowel.

4 Many words with emotional overtones are pronounced with the vowel /æ/. Examples of such words are 'mad', 'bad', 'glad', 'sad', and 'happy'. Students can express emotional states using these words, e.g. 'I feel mad!'

5 Practise comprehension and production of the vowels using minimal pairs.

/ɛ/	/æ/
pen	pan
men	man
denser	dancer
send	sand
lend	land

6 Have the students say sentences such as those below.

```
    æ  æ  æ          æ
The fat cat sat on the mat.
```

```
    ɛ  ɛ      ɛ  ɛ              ɛ
I bet Esther bet ten dollars on the Jets.
```

```
    æ    ɛ      ɛ   æ            æ    ɛ
The fat men put ten baskets on the black desk.
```

Tips for teaching /ʌ/ vs. /a/ as in 'but' and 'pot'

The vowel /ʌ/ is made with the tongue in its rest position, in the centre of the mouth, while /a/ is made with the back part of the tongue low in the mouth.

1 Explain that the vowel /ʌ/ is the sound produced if you were to be punched in the stomach.

2 Pronounce the sequence /ʌa/, pointing out that the mouth is more open with the pronunciation of /a/.

3 Practise comprehension and production of the vowels in minimal pairs.

/ʌ/	/a/
hut	hot
colour	collar
hunt	haunt
sung	song

4 Have students say sentences such as those below.

   a   a a   a
John got lost in the shop.

   ʌ   ʌ   ʌ
Young love is fun.

   ʌ   a   a   ʌ   a   ʌ
Young John lost his love on Monday.

General tips for teaching vowels

It is good to keep in mind that it is probably the entire vowel system that is causing your students difficulty. When students learn to make a distinction between vowels such as /ɛ/ and /æ/, it may be a result of distorting the pronunciation of /ɛ/ rather than a result of learning to make the /æ/ correctly. This distortion may, in turn, lead to the loss of the distinction between /ɛ/ and /ɪ/. Thus, working on isolated vowel distinctions has its limitations. It can be useful to work on all the front vowels at one time, for example, so that all the front vowel distinctions are made.

The ability to produce difficult vowel distinctions in isolation is not necessarily extended to connected speech. Therefore, it is essential that pronunciation work be contextualized. When working on vowels, try to develop hand signals to represent difficult vowel contrasts. For example, stretch an imaginary elastic band to indicate the tense vowels; bring the hands together quickly to indicate the lax vowels; lower your jaw to indicate the vowel /æ/. If students recognize these signals, the teacher can use them during more communicative tasks. See Chapter 9 for communicative activities and Chapter 14 for the use of mnemonic devices in developing the ability to self-correct.

English Consonants

For the most part, we have organized the common consonant problems according to particular articulatory features. This is because learners usually have difficulty with a set of sounds that share these articulatory features rather than with isolated sounds.

Problem   Aspiration: /p/, /t/, and /k/

Students fail to aspirate the voiceless stops /p/, /t/, and /k/ at the beginning of a word. Therefore, 'plot', 'tot', and 'cot' may sound like 'blot', 'dot', and 'got'.

Tips

1 A good way to begin teaching aspiration is to make the students aware that aspiration is the puff of air that accompanies the release of the consonant. This is easily demonstrated with a match or a piece of paper using the consonant /p/. Exaggerate the pronunciation of the word 'pot'. Have the students hold a piece of paper close to their mouth and say the word after you, making sure that a burst of air blows the paper away from them. Repeat the procedure for /t/. The consonant /k/ is less amenable to this type of treatment because the air has very little force left by the time it reaches the lips. However, once the students have understood exactly what aspiration is, they can quite easily aspirate /k/.

2 Tell the students that the puff of air that accompanies these voiceless stops is much like the /h/ sound in a word such as 'hot'. Have students practise words beginning with /h/ and then have them place a voiceless stop in front of these words. For example:

hot	p(h)ot	t(h)aught	c(h)ot
hi	p(h)ie	t(h)ie	k(h)ind
he	p(h)ea	t(h)ea	k(h)ey

Problem   Voicing of fricatives

/v/ as in 'vote' or 'love'
/ð/ 'then' or 'breathe'
/z/ 'zoo' or 'rose'
/ʒ/ 'beige' or 'measure'

Many students are unable to distinguish voiced and voiceless fricatives. Most commonly, they will be able to produce voiceless fricatives but not voiced ones. For example, /f/ may be substituted for /v/ so that a word such as 'leave' is pronounced as 'leaf'. Similarly, /s/ may be substituted for /z/, so that a word such as 'peas' is pronounced as 'peace'.

Tips

1 As vowels are always voiced, they can be useful in teaching students to voice fricatives. Have students place their fingers lightly on their throat

while making a prolonged /a/. Point out that they should feel some vibration of the vocal cords when the vowel is pronounced. Next, have them produce /a/ followed by /z/ concentrating on maintaining the voice: [aaazzzaaazzz]. While pronouncing this sequence, students should feel their throats, put a hand on the top of their head, or cover their ears with their hands. If there is sufficient voicing of the consonant, they should feel the vibration. Repeat the procedure for the other voiced fricatives: /v/, /ð/ as in 'this', and /ʒ/ as in 'beige'.

2   Once students are able to voice the fricatives, provide comprehension and production practice of the voiced/voiceless distinction using minimal pairs.

/f/	/v/	/θ/	/ð/	/s/	/z/	/ʃ/	/ʒ/
fan	van	thigh	thy	sue	zoo	Aleutian	allusion
safer	saver	ether	either	ceasing	seizing	mesher	measure
leaf	leave	teeth	teethe	face	phase		

3   Point out that vowels are longer before voiced fricatives than before their voiceless counterparts. Making the vowel longer before voiced fricatives will help students to distinguish between minimal pairs such as below.

Before voiceless consonant	**Before voiced consonant**
(shorter vowel)	(longer vowel)
leaf	leave
teeth	teethe
peace	peas

4   Practise the pronunciation of the plural in English. This grammatical ending involves a difference between the voiceless fricative /s/ and the voiced fricative /z/ (see Chapter 3, 'Sounds in context': 'Grammatical endings', page 47).

Problem   Voicing of Final Stop Consonants: /b/, /d/, and /g/

Many ESL students will not voice final stops, but will substitute a voiceless stop for a voiced one. Thus, 'cub' may sound like 'cup'. It is more difficult to demonstrate the voiced/voiceless distinction with stops than with fricatives because stops cannot be prolonged. However, final voicing does affect the pronunciation of preceding vowels; they are longer before voiced consonants than before voiceless consonants. This fact is helpful in teaching final voiced consonants.

If students are having difficulty in voicing final stops, they will probably have difficulty with final voiced fricatives also. Be sure you also practise voiced fricatives in the final position.

Tips

1   Use minimal pairs such as those below, pointing out that the vowels are longer before voiced stops than before voiceless ones.

Before voiceless consonant (shorter vowel)	Before voiced consonant (longer vowel)
tap	tab
pat	pad
back	bag

2 In producing the final sounds in the minimal pairs above, have students release (that is, aspirate lightly) the voiceless stops /p/, /t/, and /k/, but keep the articulators together for /b/, /d/, and /g/.

3 As students may be able to produce voiced stops at the beginning of words, practise linking words with final voiced stops to function words that begin with vowels. The voiced stops should seem to begin the following function words as shown below.

Don't rub it.   [downt rʌ bɪt]
He's mad at me.   [hiyz mæ dət miy]
A bag of it.   [ə bæ gəvɪt]

Problem   Initial consonant clusters

Many students have difficulty producing some of the initial consonant clusters of English. This is especially true when stops, /p/, /t/, /k/, /b/, /d/, and /g/ are followed by /l/ or /r/, as in words such as 'brew', 'blue', 'drew', and 'glue'.

Tips

1 If students cannot pronounce initial clusters, have them insert a short schwa-like vowel between the consonants, for example, 'bəlue'. They should say the word repeatedly, increasing their speed, until the inserted vowel disappears.

bəlue → bᵊlue → bᵊlue → bᵊlue → blue

2 If students have difficulty with initial consonant clusters, they may have more success pronouncing the same sequence of consonants in separate words. For example, students may be able to produce the /dr/ sequence in the phrase 'bad rift', but be unable to produce the /dr/ cluster in the word 'drift'. Students can practise the cluster across separate words, gradually dropping more and more of the first word.

bad rift → ad rift → d rift → drift

3 Have students produce syllables with initial consonant clusters of increasing complexity.

pit	top	cat	pay	go
spit	stop	scat	spay	glow
split	strap	scrap	spray	grow

See 'The shape of English words' (pages 55–6) for lists of initial consonant clusters.

Problem   Final consonant clusters

Final consonant clusters such as /kt/ as in 'worked', /ʃt/ as in 'washed', /dʒd/ as in 'judged', and /ld/ as in 'filed' are often difficult for learners to produce. The addition of grammatical endings produces many word-final clusters, and an inability to produce such clusters is often misinterpreted as a grammatical problem.

Tips

1 Difficult final consonant clusters can be practised using two words. For example, to practise the final cluster /ld/ as in 'field', use the phrase 'feel down'. The students can gradually eliminate more and more of the second word.

    feel down → feel dow → feel d → field

2 Practise consonant clusters created through the addition of grammatical endings. This will help students understand the importance of such clusters in conveying meaning. For example, contrast the following two sentences.

    I watch a lot of TV
    I watched a lot of TV

3 Have students produce syllables with final consonant clusters of increasing complexity.

bread	class	car	feel	tax (/ks/)
brand	clasp	card	field	taxed (/kst/)
brands	clasps	cards	fields	texts (ksts/)

See Chapter 4, 'The shape of English words' (pages 57–8) for lists of final consonant clusters.

4 Native speakers of English often simplify final consonant clusters in connected speech. This occurs mainly with the final clusters /st/ and /nd/ when followed by a word beginning with a consonant, e.g.:

    Hand me the book. → han me the book.
    Post the letter. → pos the letter.

Because students have difficulty with consonant clusters, it is important to convey to them that the simplification of clusters in certain contexts is characteristic of connected speech. For a description of cluster simplification, see 'The shape of English words' (page 59).

Problem   /θ/ and /ð/ as in 'think' and 'this'

Almost without exception, /θ/ and /ð/ are problematic for ESL students. The particular native language of a student usually determines which sounds will be substituted: /t/, /s/, or /f/ for /θ/; and /d/, /z/, or /v/ for /ð/. In general, a voiceless sound will be substituted for the voiceless /θ/ and a voiced sound for the voiced /ð/.

Tips

1 As these sounds are fricatives, make sure that students produce them without stopping the airstream. It is helpful to have students place their tongue between their teeth. It is not vital that the tongue protrude between the teeth a great deal, but if no contact is made with the teeth, the sounds will not be produced correctly. For students from some cultural backgrounds, it is embarrassing to protrude the tongue; this should be kept in mind if you are having the students exaggerate the articulation of these sounds.

2 Most of the ordinal numbers contain the /θ/ sound: 'third', 'fourth', 'fifth', etc. Therefore, practising the date or birth dates provides useful practice with the /θ/ sound.

3 Try tongue twisters such as the one below to practise producing these sounds.

ð   θ   θ   θ   ð   ð   θ   ð   θ   ð
Those three thugs think that they threw those things there.

Problem   English /r/

ESL students generally require work in learning to produce the English /r/. Most languages have an /r/ sound, but the particular way in which /r/ sounds are pronounced varies greatly from language to language. Learners commonly produce the English /r/ as a trill, a sound made when the tip of the tongue touches the tooth ridge repeatedly. Alternatively, learners may produce the English /r/ as a uvular sound, a sound made when the back of the tongue approaches the uvula (See Figure 2.1, page 21). As /r/ is a high frequency sound in English, learners are usually aware of their mispronunciation of the English /r/ and often ask for instruction in the correct pronunciation. Recall that it is made with the tip of the tongue curled back and the lips rounded.

Tips

1 Have students pronounce a prolonged [aaaaaa], gradually curling the tip of the tongue back. Make sure that they do not touch the tooth ridge with the tip of the tongue and that their lips become slightly rounded. Then have them uncurl the tongue and unround the lips so that the sequence [aaarrraaa] is produced.

2 Point out that the /r/ sound is made with the tip of the tongue curled back and not touching the tooth ridge. This is useful information for those students who are producing a trill.

3 Contrast /r/ with the flap sound /D/ in words such as 'putting' and 'pudding' (See 'Positional variation': 'Flapping', page 41). Point out that the tongue touches the tooth ridge momentarily in pronouncing a flap, but does not touch the tooth ridge at all in pronouncing /r/.

Flap	/r/
putting	purring
leading	leering
heating	hearing
skating	scaring

Stress, rhythm, and intonation

All students will need practice in English stress, rhythm, and intonation. These are key elements of English pronunciation and, if mastered, can greatly increase the comprehensibility of learners' speech. In all contextualized pronunciation practice, the teacher should be sure that students are producing appropriate English stress and intonation patterns. For some excellent activities dealing with these aspects of pronunciation, see Chapters 9, 11, and 12 as well as Judy Gilbert's *Clear Speech* (see bibliography).

Problem   Stress

A stressed or accented syllable is one that is more prominent than the surrounding syllables. It is generally agreed that stress (or prominence) may be marked by three variables: length, pitch, and loudness. Each of these variables may be present or absent to different degrees in different languages. The most important marker of stress in North American English is length, but stress is also accompanied by greater loudness or clarity on the stressed syllable and also a rise in pitch. Unstressed syllables, on the other hand, are very short and unclear in English and they are generally reduced to schwa. Some languages may indicate the prominence of a syllable through pitch. This is the case in Japanese and many other languages which are referred to as pitch-accent languages. Learners whose languages have different acoustic manifestations of stress from English may have difficulty in mastering the acoustic properties of the English stress system. For this reason it is important that teachers emphasize the length (and loudness) aspects of English stress.

Tips

1 Develop mnemonic devices for indicating stress. For example, the teacher could indicate stressed syllables with a quick downward hand motion.

2 Use exaggeration of both length and loudness in order to focus students' attention on stressed syllables. Remember that if students speak a language that indicates stress differently from American English, they may have difficulty hearing stressed syllables.

Problem   Word stress

Stress in English can fall on almost any syllable of a word. In many other languages, word stress regularly falls on the same syllable. Students who speak such languages may have difficulty in changing the location of the stress for different vocabulary items.

Tips

1 When teaching new vocabulary items, always ensure that the students know how to stress the item properly (see Chapter 11).

2 Give students related sets of words that display different stress patterns and have them practise shifting the major stress, e.g.:

    ●   ●   ●

photograph   photography   photographic

3 A variation on the above tip involves using nonsense words and having students shift the stress. When nonsense words are used they should resemble English words which show the pattern in question, e.g.:

    cortoplate   cortoplaty   cortoplatic

4 For activities that aid students' recognition of word-level stress patterns, see Chapter 12.

Problem   Rhythm

The characteristic rhythm of English is closely bound up with the correct pronunciation of stressed and unstressed syllables. Vowels in unstressed syllables are reduced and vowels in stressed syllables are longer and spoken with greater volume. Many ESL students fail to differentiate sufficiently between stressed and unstressed vowels, producing full vowels in unstressed syllables. The particular full vowel used may be influenced by the spelling. Thus, a learner who does not reduce unstressed vowels may pronounce a word such as 'campus' (/kæmpəs/) as /kæmpus/, and 'canoe' (/kənuw/) as /kænuw/.

Tips

1 A very good technique for teaching rhythm involves the recitation of rote-learned lists: numbers, the days of the week, the months of the year, the alphabet, etc. The teacher can vary the rhythm of the recitation task by having students group the members of the list in different ways. For example, students can group the numbers in fours or fives or tens. They can do the days of the week as a single group or as two or three groups and the months of the year can be recited in groups of three, four, or six. The advantage of using overlearned items is that the students can focus on achieving the appropriate rhythm and do not need to worry too much about meaning.

2 Nursery rhymes are also excellent for practising rhythm. Nursery rhymes such as 'Mary had a little lamb' and 'Jack and Jill went up the hill' are very useful in practising rhythm.

3 For other tips and techniques, see Chapters 11, 12, and 13. For more details on stress and unstress in words and sentences, see Chapters 5 and 6.

Problem   Intonation

Students should practise all the characteristic intonation patterns of English: final rising as used in yes-no questions; final rising-falling as used in statements, commands and wh-questions; non-final rising-falling as used in complex sentences; and non-final rising as used in lists.

Sometimes the pitch level of the learner's voice does not fall or rise far enough with final rising-falling or final rising intonation. This can result in English speakers misinterpreting the intent of the learners' utterances. For example, if a learner's voice does not fall far enough in uttering a statement, an English speaker may misinterpret the statement as a question, or assume that the learner has not finished speaking.

Tips
Always include intonation practice in the pronunciation class. Any dialogues or sentences can be used for this work. For tips and techniques, see Chapters 11, 12, and 15. For more details on intonation see Chapter 6, 'Connected speech' (page 76).

Problem   Linking

Students often fail to link words properly in connected speech. Failure to link words results in choppy speech.

Tips
1 Do linking exercises in which words ending in consonants are linked to following words that begin with vowels. It is best if the following word is an unstressed function word.

    Put the book on top of the shelf.
    He taught us a lot about language.
    Breathe in and breathe out.
    Sit at the back of the room.
    He made a lot of money.
    Pass out the books.
    He decided it wasn't enough time.

2 See Chapter 11 for a discussion of the relationship between pausing and linking, and activities that contrast the two.

3 See Chapter 6, 'Connected speech': 'Linking' (page 84), 'Assimilation' (page 130), and 'Palatalization' (page 87) for specific details on the linking of other sounds. See Chapter 9 for further activities.

Problem   Contractions

Students generally have difficulty with contractions. Very often this is because contractions create difficult sound combinations.

Tips

1 Include contracted forms when working on individual sounds. For ex-ample, include 'I'll' in work on the dark /l/, 'I've', and 'he's' in work on the voicing of fricatives, and 'he'd' in work on the voicing of final stop consonants. Contractions that create consonant clusters should be included in work on clusters. For example, the contraction 'it's' has the final cluster /ts/, and the contraction 'wrist's' (as in 'My wrist's sore') has the final cluster /sts/.

2 See Chapter 9 for further activities involving contractions.

8 PROBLEMS OF SELECTED LANGUAGE GROUPS

Peter Avery and Susan Ehrlich

Arabic

There are many dialects of Arabic (e.g. Egyptian Arabic, Iraqi Arabic, Moroccan Arabic, etc.), not all of which are mutually intelligible. Most speakers of Arabic, however, are familiar with a standard dialect used in the mass media. The problems described below are common to most dialects of Arabic.

Consonants

Problem   /p/ vs. /b/

Arabic does not have a /p/ sound and learners may substitute /b/ for /p/. Thus, 'Pompeii' sounds like 'Bombay'.

Tips

1 Focus on the aspiration of /p/ in trying to get students to make the distinction between /p/ and /b/ in initial position. See 'Common problems': 'Aspiration', page 101.

2 Use minimal pairs such as those below:

pie	bye	mopping	mobbing
pet	bet	cop	cob
pride	bride	rope	robe
nipple	nibble		

Problem   /v/ vs. /f/

Arabic does not have a contrastive /v/ sound, although the sound does occur as a positional variant of /f/ before voiced stops and fricatives. Learners tend to substitute /f/ for /v/ in other positions.

Tips

See 'Common problems': 'Voicing of fricatives', page 101.

Problem   /θ/ and /ð/

Speakers of some dialects of Arabic may substitute /t/ and /d/ for /θ/ and /ð/ respectively, while speakers of other dialects may substitute /s/ and /z/.

Tips
See 'Common problems': '/θ/ and /ð/', page 104.

Problem   /ŋ/ as in 'sing'

Arabic speakers tend to pronounce /ŋ/ as /n/ or /ŋg/.

Tips
Practise minimal pairs that contrast /n/ and /ŋ/.

stun	stung
run	rung
win	wing
sin	sing
sinner	singer
winner	winger

Problem   /tʃ/ and /dʒ/ as in 'church' and 'judge'

Arabic does not have affricates and, thus, Arabic speakers potentially have problems with English /tʃ/ and /dʒ/. Because the sequence /t + ʃ/ occurs word-internally in Arabic, learners will have little difficulty with the voiceless affricate. The voiced affricate poses greater difficulty and /tʃ/ will often be substituted in its place.

Tips
1 Point out to the students that they are substituting a voiceless sound for its voiced counterpart. Since voiced stops and fricatives occur in Arabic, Arabic learners should be able to produce the voiced affricate when made aware of their substitution.
2 Tell students that /dʒ/ is a combination of the familiar voiced sounds /d/ and /ʒ/ and that it can be pronounced as a consonant cluster.

Problem   English /r/

The English /r/ may be pronounced as a trill.

Tips
See 'Common problems': 'English /r/', page 105.

Problem   Consonant clusters

Arabic has no clusters of more than two consonants, and in word-initial position there are no clusters at all, at least in most dialects. Arabic learners tend to insert vowels to break up English clusters, even with clusters created by the juxtaposition of words. The position of the inserted vowels will vary depending on the dialect of Arabic spoken by the learner. (See 'The shape of English words': Exercise 3 (page 61).)

Tips
See 'Common problems': 'Initial consonant clusters' (page 103) and 'Common problems': 'Final consonant clusters' (page 104).

Vowels

Problem   Tense vs lax vowels: /iy/ vs. /ɪ/, /ey/ vs. /ɛ/, /uw/ vs. /ʊ/

While Arabic has contrasts between long and short vowels, the tense/lax distinction of English does pose problems for Arabic learners (including the /ow/ vs. /ɔ/ distinction in some dialects of English).

Tips
See 'Common problems': 'Tense vs. lax vowels', page 96.

Problem   /ɛ/ vs. /æ/ vs. /ʌ/ vs. /a/

Arabic has only one low vowel, /a/, and thus, Arabic learners encounter difficulty with all of these vowel distinctions.

Tips
See 'Common problems': '/ɛ/ vs. /æ/ vs. /ʌ/ vs. /a/', page 98.

Problem   /ɛ/ vs. /ɪ/

Arabic learners may have difficulty distinguishing between /ɛ/ and /ɪ/ as in 'bet' and 'bit', producing a vowel which is between the two.

Tips
1 Point out that the tongue is higher in the mouth in the production of /ɪ/ than it is for /ɛ/.
2 Use minimal pairs such as the following:

/ɛ/	/ɪ/
set	sit
bell	bill
mess	miss
bless	bliss

Stress, rhythm, and intonation

Problem   Word stress

Word stress in Arabic is fairly regular relative to English word stress. This can pose difficulties for Arabic learners who may expect English word stress to be as regular as it is in Arabic.

Tips
See 'Common problems': 'Word stress', page 106.

Problem   Vowel reduction

While Arabic is a stress-timed language, unstressed vowels are not reduced to the extent that they are in English.

Tips
See Chapter 5, 'Word stress and vowel reduction' (page 63) and 'Common problems': 'Rhythm', page 107.

Chinese

Chinese refers to a large group of languages spoken primarily in China, Taiwan, Hong Kong, and Singapore. While many of these languages are not mutually intelligible, they are all tone languages (that is, a change in pitch can cause a change in meaning). Our focus is on Cantonese and Mandarin. Cantonese is spoken in Hong Kong and Canton, while Mandarin is the national language of the People's Republic of China, and of Taiwan. The major difference between Cantonese and Mandarin is one of rhythm: Cantonese is a syllable-timed language while Mandarin is a stress-timed language. The shape of words in Chinese is radically different from the shape of words in English as Chinese lacks consonant clusters in both initial and final position. Most of the problems described below are common to both Cantonese and Mandarin.

Consonants

Problem   Word-final voiceless stop consonants: /p/, /t/, and /k/

In Chinese, the voiceless stop consonants /p/, /t/, and /k/ occur at the end of a word but these consonants are never released in final position and are much shorter than their English equivalents. This means that even when Chinese speakers pronounce these consonants in final position, English speakers may have difficulty hearing them. Thus, a word such as 'beat' may sound like 'bee'.

Tips
1 Have students release the final voiceless stop consonants in words such as

'top', 'taught', and 'back'. A small puff of air, similar to aspiration, should accompany the release of the consonants. Practise these words in sentence final position where they receive major sentence stress. This may involve some exaggeration of your own speech because these consonants are not always released in English in this position.

Put it up on *top*.
I didn't know that you *taught*.
Do you mind sitting near the *back*?

2 Do linking exercises in which words ending in voiceless stops are followed by words beginning with vowels. See 'Common problems': 'Linking', page 108.

Problem Voiced vs. voiceless stops in word-final position: /b/, /d/, /g/ vs. /p/, /t/, /k/

As Chinese has no voiced stops at the ends of words, Chinese speakers need practice in distinguishing between voiced and voiceless stops in this position. For example, words such as 'cap' and 'cab' may sound identical, with a short unreleased /p/ at the end of both words.

Tips
Once Chinese speakers have practised releasing voiceless stops at the ends of words (as outlined above), begin exercises that have them distinguish between voiced and voiceless stops. For tips see 'Common problems': 'Voicing of final stop consonants', page 102.

Problem Voiced fricatives and affricates: /v/, /ð/ as in 'bathe', /z/, /ʒ/ as in 'beige', and /dʒ/ as in 'judge'

As voiced fricative and affricate sounds do not exist in Chinese, Chinese speakers generally require practice in producing them. Often voiceless fricatives and affricates are substituted for the appropriate voiced ones.

Tips
See 'Common problems': 'Voicing of fricatives', page 101.

Problem /l/ vs. /n/ as in 'light' and 'night'

In some Cantonese dialects, /l/ and /n/ may be freely substituted for each other in word-initial position. This means that words such as 'light' will sometimes be correctly pronounced as 'light' and at other times as 'night'.

Tips
Point out that /n/ is made with air escaping through the nose and that /l/ is made with the air escaping around the sides of the tongue. Give the students word combinations such as 'night light' and 'slow snow' to provide practice in distinguishing between the two sounds.

Problem   /l/ vs. /w/ as in 'mole' and 'mow'

Chinese speakers will produce a sound more like a /w/ than a dark /l/ after a vowel. Thus 'mole' will be pronounced as 'mow', 'goal' as 'go', and 'old' as 'ode'. Words such as 'feel' and 'veal' may sound like 'few' and 'view'.

Tips

Have students produce the vowel /ow/. During the pronunciation of this vowel, they should raise their tongue until it touches the tooth ridge. At the same time the lips should be unrounded. This should result in the production of dark /l/. Then practise distinguishing between words such as 'mole' and 'mow', 'goal' and 'go', and 'cold' and 'code'.

Problem   Word-final nasals: /m/, /n/, /ŋ/

Word-final nasal sounds are much shorter in Chinese than in English. As a result, English speakers may not be able to identify the nasal that has been produced, thus, confusing words such as 'sin' and 'sing'. Chinese speakers must learn to lengthen word-final nasal sounds. In addition, the /n/ and /ŋ/ sounds are often confused by Chinese speakers.

Tips

1 Practise nasals in word-final position with words such as the following:

/m/	/n/	/ŋ/
seem	seen	sing
came	cane	
ram	ran	rang
some	sun	sung

2 Chinese (particularly Cantonese) speakers may have particular difficulty in pronouncing the final /n/ sound in words such as 'noun', 'down', 'frown', and 'clown'. This can be practised by building up words:

now → noun   dow → down

Problem   /r/ vs. /w/ and /l/

Chinese speakers often pronounce word-initial /r/ as /w/. This can lead to confusion between words such as 'right' and 'white'. Alternatively, they may substitute /l/ for /r/, particularly in initial consonant clusters.

Tips

Explain that the tongue must be curled back slightly and that there is a slight backward movement of the tongue during the pronunciation of the /r/. In contrasting /r/ with /l/, point out that the tongue has no contact with the tooth ridge in the production of /r/, whereas with /l/, it does.

Problem   /w/ vs. /v/ as in 'west' and 'vest'

Chinese speakers often confuse /w/ and /v/. At the beginning of words, they produce what sounds like a /w/, pronouncing a word such as 'west' as 'vest'.

Tips

Point out the different articulations of /w/ and /v/. Give the students practice in making the distinction using minimal pairs such as those below.

/w/	/v/
west	vest
wine	vine
whale	veil

Problem   /y/ in word-initial position

Cantonese learners will produce the following pairs of words in approximately the same way:

east	yeast
ear	year

To the English ear, 'east' sounds like 'yeast' and 'yeast' sounds like 'east'. The Cantonese speaker tends to insert a short /y/ sound before the vowel /iy/ at the beginning of a word such as 'east'. The same short /y/ sound is also used in pronouncing 'yeast'. This /y/ sound is not long enough to sound like the /y/ of 'yeast' and English speakers, therefore, hear 'east'. When this /y/ sound is used in a word such as 'east', however, it is clearly audible because it is not expected and the word 'yeast' is heard.

Tips

Point out that there is no /y/ in 'east' and have students lengthen the /y/ of 'yeast'. It is probably most important to practise words beginning with the vowel /iy/: 'eat', 'ear', 'east', 'easy', 'eel', 'Easter'.

Problem   /θ/ and /ð/ as in 'think' and 'this'

Chinese students will often substitute either /t/ or /f/ for /θ/ in 'think' and /d/ for /ð/ in 'this'. In word-final position /f/ is usually substituted for both /ð/ and /θ/, with Chinese speakers producing 'wif' instead of 'with'.

Tips

See 'Common problems': /θ/ and /ð/, page 104.

Problem   Consonant clusters

Chinese has no consonant clusters in initial or final position. Chinese speakers must, therefore, learn to produce a large variety of new syllable types that contain consonant clusters.

Tips

See Chapter 4, 'The shape of English words' for lists of initial and final consonant clusters. See also 'Common problems': 'Initial consonant clusters', page 103, and 'Final consonant clusters', page 104.

Vowels

Problem   Tense vs. lax vowels: /iy/ vs. /ɪ/, /ey/ vs. /ɛ/, /uw/ vs. /ʊ/

The distinction between tense and lax vowels does not exist in Chinese. Chinese speakers produce vowel sounds that are between the tense and lax vowels of English.

Tips
See 'Common problems': 'Tense vs. lax vowels,' page 96.

Problem   /ɛ/ vs. /æ/ as in 'bet' and 'bat'

Chinese speakers have difficulty distinguishing between /ɛ/ and /æ/. This problem is particularly severe before nasals, as in 'ten' and 'tan', 'bend' and 'band'.

Tips
See 'Common problems': '/ɛ/ vs. /æ/ vs. /ʌ/ vs. /a/', page 98.

Stress, rhythm, and intonation

Problem   Word stress

As Chinese words generally consist of only one syllable, Chinese speakers may have difficulty in producing the longer words of English with appropriate stress patterns.

Tips
Always include some practice in the production of longer words in the pronunciation class. See 'Common problems': 'Stress' and 'Word stress' (page 106) for activities.

Problem   Rhythm

Cantonese is a syllable-timed language which means that each syllable of an utterance will receive equal weight, giving Cantonese learners' speech a staccato-like rhythm. Because Mandarin is a stress-timed language, Mandarin learners will experience less difficulty with English rhythm.

Tips
See 'Common problems': 'Rhythm', page 107, for activities.

Problem   Contractions

Chinese students often have difficulty with contractions because of the difficult consonant clusters that are created.

Tips
See 'Common problems': 'Contractions', page 108.

Problem   Linking

Chinese students often fail to link words. They tend to separate words through the use of pauses or the insertion of additional sounds at the ends of words. This makes their speech sound very choppy.

Tips
See Chapters 11 and 13 in Part Three for useful exercises on rhythm and linking. See also 'Common problems': 'Linking', page 108.

Problem   Intonation

Chinese speakers may have difficulty with the characteristic intonation patterns of English because pitch functions differently in Chinese. In particular, Cantonese speakers may use a non-final intonation contour rather than a final intonation contour. In English, a final contour indicates the completion of a turn at speaking, while a non-final contour indicates that the speaker has more to say.

Tips
Include practice in all aspects of English intonation in the pronunciation class. See Chapters 11 and 12 in Part Three for activities that provide intonation practice. See also 'Connected speech': 'Intonation', page 76.

Farsi

Farsi, sometimes referred to as Persian, is spoken mainly in Iran and Afghanistan. It is a member of the Indo-European group of languages (as is English), but has had considerable influence from Arabic.

The pronunciation problems of Farsi speakers are generally not too severe, the most striking aspect of a Farsi accent being related to the rhythmic differences between Farsi and English.

Consonants

Problem   /w/ vs. /v/

Farsi speakers tend to substitute a /v/-like sound for /w/, pronouncing 'vest' instead of 'west'.

Tips
Point out the different articulations of /w/ and /v/. The lower teeth and upper lip should not come together for the pronunciation of the /w/ sound.

Problem   /θ/ and /ð/ as in 'think' and 'this'

Farsi does not have the interdental fricatives /θ/ and /ð/. Farsi speakers generally substitute /t/ for /θ/ and /d/ or even /t/ for /ð/.

Tips
See 'Common problems': '/θ/ and /ð/', page 104.

Problem   English /r/

The English /r/ may be pronounced as a trill.

Tips
See 'Common problems': 'English /r/', page 105.

Problem   Initial consonant clusters

Farsi speakers tend to insert a vowel between consonants in order to break up a cluster, pronouncing a word such as 'plight' so that it sounds like 'polite'. With clusters beginning with /s/, Farsi speakers insert the vowel prior to the /s/, producing 'esnow' instead of 'snow'.

Tips
See 'Common problems': 'Initial consonant clusters', page 103.

Vowels

Problem   Tense vs. lax vowels: /iy/ vs. /ɪ/, /ey/ vs. /ɛ/, /uw/ vs. /ʊ/

The distinction between tense and lax vowels does not exist in Farsi. Farsi speakers produce vowel sounds that are between the tense and lax vowels of English.

Tips
See 'Common problems': 'Tense vs. lax vowels', page 96.

Problem   /ɛ/ vs. /æ/ vs. /ʌ/ vs. /a/

Farsi speakers may confuse /ɛ/ and /æ/ as in 'bed' and 'bad', producing a vowel which sounds more like /æ/ in a word such as 'bet'. They also have difficulty producing /ʌ/ and English speakers tend to hear the substituted vowel as /a/.

Tips
See 'Common Problems': '/ɛ/ vs. /æ/ vs. /ʌ/ vs. /a/', page 98.

Stress, rhythm, and intonation

Problem   Word stress

Stress generally falls on the final syllable of a word in Farsi. This means that Farsi speakers must learn to produce stress on non-final syllables in English words.

Tips
See 'Common problems': 'Word stress', page 106.

Problem   Rhythm

Farsi is a syllable-timed language and has no reduced vowel equivalent to the English schwa. This combined with the tendency to place stress on the final syllable can lead to a rhythm uncharacteristic of English. Thus, it is important for the teacher to work extensively on the rhythmic pattern of English.

Tips
See 'Common problems': 'Rhythm', page 107.

French

French and English share many vocabulary items because many French words were borrowed into English after the Norman Conquest. However, differences between the stress systems of French and English result in quite different pronunciations of many of the shared vocabulary items, causing difficulty for French learners. While there are many dialects of French (e.g. Parisian, Canadian, Belgian, etc.) most of the problems described below are common to all dialects.

Consonants

Problem   Aspiration of /p/, /t/, and /k/

French speakers may not aspirate the voiceless stops /p/, /t/ and /k/ in word-initial position.

Tips
See 'Common problems': 'Aspiration', page 101.

Problem   /tʃ/ and /dʒ/

Because /tʃ/ and /dʒ/ do not exist in French, French speakers often substitute /ʃ/ and /ʒ/, respectively.

Tips
1 Have students place the tip of the tongue at the tooth ridge as if they were about to make a /t/ or a /d/ and then release the sound as a /ʃ/ or /ʒ/.
2 Point out to students that /tʃ/ and /dʒ/ are complex sounds, made up of consonants that do exist in French.

Problem   /θ/ and /ð/ as in 'think' and 'this'

European French speakers will often substitute /s/ and /z/ for /θ/ and /ð/, whereas Canadian French speakers will substitute /t/ and /d/, respectively.

Tips
See 'Common problems': '/θ/ and /ð/', page 104.

Problem   English /r/

Some French speakers will substitute a uvular /r/ for the English /r/ whereas others will substitute a trilled /r/.

Tips
See 'Common problems': 'English /r/', page 105.

Problem   /h/

While the letter /h/ exists in the French spelling system, it is not pronounced. In English words beginning with /h/, French learners tend to substitute a glottal stop for the /h/. Native English speakers will hear such words as beginning with vowels. On the other hand, in English words that begin with a silent *h* (as in 'honor', 'hour', and 'honest'), French speakers tend to insert an /h/ sound.

Tips
1 Have the students produce the /h/ as a breath of air before vowels.

2 Work on pairs of words such as the following:

eat	heat
ate	hate
all	hall
owed	hoed
ad	had
Ed	head

3 In order to eliminate the addition of /h/ in words that begin with a vowel, do linking exercises, linking consonants to vowels and vowels to vowels. See 'Connected speech': 'Linking' (page 84) and 'Common problems': 'Linking', page 108.

Vowels

Problem   Tense vs. lax vowels: /iy/ vs. /ɪ/, /ey/ vs. /ɛ/, /uw/ vs. /ʊ/

The distinction between tense and lax vowels does not exist in French. French speakers produce vowel sounds that are between the tense and lax vowels of English.

Tips

See 'Common problems': 'Tense vs. lax vowels', page 96.

Problem　/ɛ/ vs. /æ/ vs. /ʌ/ vs. /a/

French speakers may have difficulty with all four of these vowels sounds, particularly with the distinction between /ʌ/ and /a/.

Tips

See 'Common problems': '/ɛ/ vs. /æ/ vs. /ʌ/ vs. /a/', page 98.

Stress, rhythm, and intonation

Problem　Word stress

Stress in French is quite different from stress in English. Stress generally falls on the final syllable of a polysyllabic word or of a phrase and is accompanied by a rise in pitch. French learners often have a great deal of difficulty mastering English word stress.

Tips

See 'Common problems': 'Stress' and 'Word stress', page 106.

Problem　Rhythm

As French is a syllable-timed language (see Chapter 6, 'Connected Speech'), French speakers' pronunciation of English words and sentences may lack the vowel reduction necessary for English rhythm, even though French does have a schwa-like vowel.

Tips

See 'Common problems': 'Rhythm' (page 107), and also Chapters 11, 12, and 13 in Part Three for exercises in vowel reduction and English rhythm.

German

German and English are both Germanic languages and share many features of pronunciation. For example, both are stress-timed languages and have similar stress systems, meaning that German learners do not have much difficulty with English stress and rhythm. Furthermore, German intonation patterns are very similar to those of English.

Consonants

Problem   Word-final voiced consonants: /b/, /d/, /g/, /v/, /ð/ as in 'breathe', /z/, /ʒ/ as in 'beige', and /dʒ/ as in 'judge'

German speakers usually produce voiceless versions of stops, fricatives and affricates at the ends of words. They can, however, voice these sounds in other positions in words.

Tips
See 'Common problems': 'Voicing of fricatives' (page 101), and 'Common problems': 'Voicing of final stop consonants', page 102.

Problem   /θ/ and /ð/ as in 'think' and 'this'

German does not have the interdental fricatives /θ/ and /ð/. German speakers generally substitute /s/ for /θ/ and /z/ for /ð/.

Tips
See 'Common problems': '/θ/ and /ð/', page 104.

Problem   /dʒ/ as in 'judge'

As the /dʒ/ sound does not exist in German, German speakers often substitute /tʃ/ for /dʒ/. When the English /dʒ/ sound is represented in spelling by *j* as in 'jug', German speakers may substitute /y/. This is because the German letter *j* is pronounced as /y/.

Tips
1   Point out to the students that they are substituting a voiceless sound for its voiced counterpart. Since voiced stops and fricatives occur in German (initially and medially), German learners should be able to produce the voiced affricate when made aware of their substitution.
2   Tell students that /dʒ/ is a combination of the familiar voiced sounds /d/ and /ʒ/, and that it can be pronounced as a consonant cluster.

Problem   /w/ vs. /v/ as in 'west' and 'vest'

German speakers may substitute /v/ for /w/, producing 'vine' instead of 'wine'.

Tips
Point out the different articulations of /w/ and /v/. The lower teeth and upper lip should not come together for the pronunciation of the /w/ sound.

Problem   English /r/

Speakers of northern German dialects will often substitute a uvular /r/ for the English /r/, while speakers of southern German dialects will substitute a trilled /r/ for the English /r/.

Tips
See 'Common problems': 'English /r/', page 105.

Vowels

Problem   Tense vowels /iy/, /ey/, /uw/, and /ow/

German speakers tend to produce the tense vowels of English as long vowels without the characteristic semi-vowels of the English tense vowels.

Tips
See 'Common problems': 'Tips for teaching tense vowels', page 96.

Problem   /ɛ/ vs. /æ/ vs. /a/ vs. /ʌ/

German speakers tend to substitute /ɛ/ for /æ/ and /a/ for /ʌ/.

Tips
See 'Common problems': '/ɛ/ vs. /æ/ vs. /a/ vs, /ʌ/', page 98.

Greek

Greek displays a great deal of dialectal variation. In the northern dialects, there is more vowel reduction than in southern dialects. This means that the northern dialect speakers adjust more easily to the vowel reduction so important to the rhythm of English. Speakers of southern dialects sound much like Spanish speakers with respect to the overall rhythm of their speech.

Consonants

Problem   Aspiration: /p/, /t/, and /k/

Greek speakers will fail to aspirate the voiceless stops, /p/, /t/, and /k/ in initial position.

Tips
See 'Common problems': 'Aspiration', page 101.

Problem   Word-final consonants

Greek speakers may produce voiceless versions of stops, fricatives, and affricates at the ends of words, or add a vowel to the end of English words that end in voiced consonants.

Tips
1 Attempt to eliminate these 'finishing' sounds through work on linking. For example, you could begin by having students link consonants to vowels and then identical consonants in short phrases such as 'big game'

or 'bad day'. Finally, practise linking different consonants, being sure that the students do not release the final consonant of the first word: 'big day', 'bad game'.

2 See 'Common problems': 'Voicing of fricatives' (page 101), and 'Common Problems': 'Voicing of final stop consonants', page 102.

Problem   /s/ vs. /ʃ/ as in 'ship', /z/ vs. /ʒ/ as in 'beige', /ts/ vs. /tʃ/ as in 'church', /dz/ vs. /dʒ/ as in 'judge'

Greek speakers will often substitute the tooth ridge fricatives, /s/ and /z/, for the palatal fricatives /ʃ/ and /ʒ/. Thus, 'ship' may be pronounced as 'sip', and 'beige' as 'bays'. The English affricates /tʃ/ and /dʒ/ will be pronounced as the non-English affricates, /ts/ and /dz/. Thus, 'church' will sound like 'tsurts' and 'judge' will sound like 'dzudz'.

It is interesting to note that a sound very much like /ʃ/ does occur instead of /s/ in some dialects of Greek. This sound has a rustic quality and is socially unacceptable for some speakers.

Tips
1 Greek has the sound combinations /sy/ and /zy/, which are closer to the English /ʃ/ and /ʒ/ than /s/ and /z/. It may be a good idea at first to relate these sounds to the English /ʃ/ and /ʒ/.

2 Point out that in making the appropriate hard palate sounds, the blade of the tongue must be raised so that it approaches the hard palate. In addition, the lips are rounded. See 'Individual sounds': 'Sounds made with the blade of the tongue', page 15.

Problem   Insertion of nasals

Greek speakers may pronounce the voiced stops /b/, /d/, /g/ as /mb/, /nd/, and /ŋg/. This may result in 'bubble' sounding like 'bumble'; 'fodder' sounding like 'fonder'; and 'juggle' sounding like 'jungle'.

Tips
Make the students aware of the inserted nasal sound preceding these stops by giving them word pairs involving the difference.

fad	fanned
figure	finger
cobble	combo
bubble	bumble

Problem   /p/, /t/, /k/ following nasals

Voiceless stops /p/, /t/, and /k/, when preceded by nasals, are voiced. This may result in 'hamper' being pronounced with a /b/; 'center' being pronounced with a /d/; and 'banker' being pronounced with a /g/. Furthermore, the nasal may be deleted resulting in 'habber', 'sedder' and 'bagger'.

Tips

Have students practise word pairs such as those below.

centre	sender	sander	sadder
symbol	simple	limber	libber
crumble	crumple	longer	logger
angle	ankle	hunger	hugger
amble	ample	rumble	rubble

Problem   /s/ vs. /z/

When /s/ precedes /m/, /n/, or /l/ at the beginning of a word as in 'smile', 'snow' and 'sleep', Greek speakers may pronounce it as /z/, producing 'zmile', 'znow', and 'zleep'.

Tips

1 Greek students will be able to produce /s/ at the end of a word. Thus, have students practise saying phrases like 'kiss lips' → 'ss lips' → 'slips', gradually eliminating the first part of the first word.

2 You could also have students lengthen the /s/: 'sssssslip'.

Problem   English /r/

The English /r/ is generally pronounced as a trill.

Tips

See 'Common Problems': 'English /r/', page 105.

Problem   /h/

English /h/ may be pronounced very strongly by Greek learners. This will sound like the velar fricative in the German pronunciation of 'Bach'. See 'Individual Sounds': 'Fricatives', page 19.

Tips

Have the students produce the /h/ as a breath of air before vowels. Tell them that there is no friction in the mouth in the pronunciation of the English /h/.

Problem   Final consonant clusters

Greek has no final consonant clusters and very few single consonants at the ends of words. Thus, Greek students will have difficulty pronouncing final clusters and some single consonants in final position. Often vowels will be inserted after single consonants.

Tips

Do exercises that involve linking word final consonants to following vowels. See 'Common problems': 'Linking' (page 108), and 'Common problems': 'Final consonant clusters', page 104.

Vowels

Problem   Tense vs. lax vowels: /iy/ vs. /ɪ/, /ey/ vs. /ɛ/, /uw/ vs. /ʊ/

Greek speakers will not distinguish between the tense and lax vowels of English. They usually produce a vowel that is between the tense and lax vowels.

Tips
See 'Common problems': 'Tense vs. lax vowels', page 96.

Problem   /æ/ vs. /ʌ/ vs. /a/

Greek speakers will need practice in the production of the low vowels of English. They may confuse /æ/, /ʌ/ and /a/, producing a single vowel for all three.

Tips
See 'Common Problems': '/ɛ/ vs. /æ/ vs. /ʌ/ vs. /a/', page 98.

Stress, rhythm, and intonation

Problem   Rhythm

Many Greek dialects do not have a short, reduced vowel equivalent to the English schwa. This affects the rhythm of English words and sentences as Greek speakers may give equal weight to each syllable.

Tips
See 'Common Problems': 'Rhythm' (page 106), and also Chapters 11, 12, and 13 in Part Three for exercises involving vowel reduction and rhythm.

Hindi and Punjabi

As Hindi and Punjabi are related languages, many of the pronunciation problems of Hindi and Punjabi speakers may be similar. The characteristic accent of Hindi and Punjabi speakers, in fact of most speakers of the languages of the Indian subcontinent (e.g. Urdu, Bengali, Tamil, Malayalam, etc.), is partly a result of the use of retroflex consonants. In English, the /r/ sound is considered to be a retroflex because the tongue is curled back slightly when /r/ is produced. In Hindi and Punjabi, there are many more retroflexed consonants than in English. For example, the /t/ and /d/ sounds in Hindi and Punjabi may be retroflexed. In producing these sounds the tongue is slightly curled. Thus, the underside of the tongue tip touches the tooth ridge in the production of /t/ and /d/. It is generally very difficult to change the articulation of these retroflexed consonants.

Consonants

Problem   Aspiration: /p/, /t/, and /k/

Hindi and Punjabi speakers may appear to be substituting the voiced stops /b/, /d/, and /g/ for the voiceless aspirated stops /p/, /t/, and /k/. For example, English speakers may hear 'bit' for the word 'pit'. Interestingly, Hindi and Punjabi have aspirated voiceless stops, unaspirated voiceless stops, and voiced stops. The problem arises because the aspiration of the voiceless stops in Hindi and Punjabi is much stronger than in English. Hindi and Punjabi speakers, thus, do not hear the aspiration of the initial stops /p/, /t/, and /k/ in English. Instead, they hear voiceless unaspirated stops and produce them as such. English speakers hear the Hindi and Punjabi speakers' voiceless unaspirated stops as voiced stops, just to add to the confusion.

Tips
See 'Common problems': 'Aspiration', page 101.

Problem   /f/ vs. /p/ and /v/ vs. /b/

The sounds /f/ and /v/ in Hindi and Punjabi are quite different from their English counterparts. Hindi and Punjabi speakers produce an /f/ that sounds like a /p/ to English speakers, leading to confusion between pairs of words such as 'pair' and 'fair'. Similarly, /v/ will often sound like /b/, leading to confusion between words such as 'berry' and 'very'.

Tips
1 Exaggerate the differences in articulation between the stops /p/ and /b/ and the fricatives /f/ and /v/. Show the closure of the lips for /p/ and /b/ and the upper teeth on the lower lip for /f/ and /v/.
2 Use minimal pairs contrasting /p/ and /f/ and /b/ and /v/.

/p/	/f/	/b/	/v/
pan	fan	boat	vote
pry	fry	buy	vie
lap	laugh	rebel	revel
supper	suffer	robe	rove

Problem   /w/ vs. /v/ as in 'wine' and 'vine'

Hindi and Punjabi speakers tend to substitute a sound similar to /v/ for /w/. To the English ear, 'wine' sounds more like 'vine'.

Tips
Point out the different articulations of /w/ and /v/. The lower teeth and upper lip should not come together for the pronunciation of the /w/ sound.

Problem   /θ/ and /ð/ as in 'think' and 'this'

Hindi and Punjabi speakers tend to substitute a heavily aspirated /t/ for /θ/ in words like 'think' and a /d/ for /ð/ in words like 'this'.

Tips

See 'Common problems': '/θ/ and /ð/', page 104.

Problem   Initial consonant clusters

Hindi and Punjabi speakers tend to insert a vowel in initial consonant clusters, producing 'sitreet' or 'istreet' instead of 'street' or 'silow' instead of 'slow'.

Tips

See 'Common problems': 'Initial consonant clusters', page 103.

Problem   Final consonant clusters

Hindi and Punjabi speakers tend to delete a consonant from a difficult final consonant cluster, producing 'tax' [tæks] instead of 'taxed' [tækst], or 'laugh' [læf] instead of 'laughed' [læft]. Alternatively, vowels may be inserted to break up these clusters.

Tips

See 'Common problems': 'Final consonant clusters', page 104.

Vowels

Problem   /ε/ vs. /æ/ as in 'bet' and 'bat'

Hindi and Punjabi speakers tend to substitute the vowel /ε/ as in 'bed' for the vowel /æ/ as in 'bad'.

Tips

See 'Common problems': '/ε/ vs. /æ/ vs. /ʌ/ vs. /a/', page 98.

Problem   Tense versus lax vowels: /ey/ vs. /ε/

Hindi and Punjabi speakers may have difficulty with the distinction between /ey/ and /ε/.

Tips

See 'Common probems': 'Tense vs. lax vowels', page 96.

Stress, rhythm, and intonation

Problem   Word stress

Stress in Hindi and Punjabi is fairly regular, with stress normally falling on the first syllable of a word. Hindi and Punjabi speakers may incorrectly stress the first syllable of words in English that have stress on the second syllable. Thus, the words given below may be incorrectly stressed.

Correct stress	Incorrect stress
. ●	● .
above	above
below	below

Tips
Practise stressing different syllables in English words. See 'Common problems': 'Word stress', page 106.

Problem   Rhythm

Hindi and Punjabi are syllable-timed languages (see Chapter 6, 'Connected speech') and thus Hindi and Punjabi speakers' pronunciation of English words and sentences may lack the vowel reduction necessary for English rhythm. Hindi and Punjabi do not have a short, reduced vowel equivalent to the English schwa.

Tips
See 'Common problems': 'Rhythm' (page 107), and also Chapters 11, 12, and 13 in Part Three for exercises in vowel reduction and English rhythm.

Problem   Stress

Hindi and Punjabi use pitch as the primary indicator of accent (stress). Recall that stressed syllables in English are marked primarily by length and loudness. Because English and Punjabi mark stress in different ways, Punjabi speakers may have difficulty both producing and perceiving the characteristic stress patterns of English.

Tips
Focus on the length associated with stressed vowels in English. When stressed vowels are lengthened, unstressed vowels will more likely be reduced, leading to a more characteristic English rhythm. See 'Common problems': 'Stress', page 106.

Problem   Intonation

Hindi and Punjabi speakers may have difficulty with the characteristic intonation patterns of English. The rising intonation pattern used in English 'yes-no' questions may be replaced by a rising-falling pattern, causing Hindi and Punjabi speakers to appear abrupt or even rude to the English ear.

Tips
Practise all of the common intonation patterns of English. See 'Connected speech', page 76 for a description of intonation in English. See also Chapters 11 and 12 in Part Three for activities.

Italian

Italian is a Romance language, as are French, Spanish, and Portuguese. There is a great deal of dialectal variation and, as a result, speakers of different dialects may have different pronunciation problems. The problems outlined below are common to most dialects of Italian.

Consonants

Problem   Aspiration: /p/, /t/, and /k/

Italian speakers may not aspirate the voiceless stops /p/, /t/, and /k/ in word-initial position.

Tips
See 'Common problems': 'Aspiration', page 101.

Problem   /θ/ and /ð/ as in 'think' and 'this'

Italian speakers tend to substitute /t/ for /θ/ in words such as 'think' and /d/ for /ð/ in words such as 'this'.

Tips
See 'Common problems': '/θ/ and /ð/', page 104.

Problem   /h/

Italian speakers may fail to produce word-initial /h/. Thus, a word such as 'heart' may be pronounced as 'art'.

Tips
1 Have the students produce the /h/ as a breath of air before vowels.

2 Work on pairs of words such as the following:

eat	heat
ate	hate
all	hall
owed	hoed
ad	had
Ed	head

Problem   English /r/

The English /r/ may be pronounced as a trill.

Tips
See 'Common problems': 'English /r/', page 105.

Problem   /ʒ/ as in 'measure' vs. /ʃ/ as in 'wish' or /dʒ/ as in 'judge'

Italian speakers tend to substitute a /ʃ/ or a /dʒ/ for /ʒ/ in words such as 'measure'.

Tips

1 Point out that the /ʒ/ sound is voiced and that the tongue does not touch the roof of the mouth.

2 Use word pairs such as those below to contrast these sounds.

/ʃ/	/ʒ/	/dʒ/
wish		wedge
masher	measure	
bash		badge
shoot		jute
Aleutian	allusion	

Problem   /s/ vs. /z/ in initial consonant clusters

Italian speakers tend to pronounce /s/ as /z/ before /m/, /l/, and /n/ in initial consonant clusters. Thus, they may pronounce [zmowk] for 'smoke', [zlow] for 'slow', and [znab] for 'snob'.

Tips

1 Italian students will be able to produce /s/ at the end of a word. Thus, have students practise saying phrases, gradually eliminating the beginning of the first word. For example:

kiss lips → ss lips → slips.

2 You could also have students lengthen the /s/: 'ssssssslip'.

Problem   Word-final consonants

Italian does not permit any word-final consonants. Italian speakers will often add a final vowel to English words that end with consonants. Therefore, 'big' and 'bad' may be pronounced as [bɪgə] and [bædə].

Tips

1 Attempt to eliminate these 'finishing' sounds through work on linking. For example, you could begin by having students link consonants to vowels and then identical consonants in short phrases such as 'big game' or 'bad day'. Finally, practise linking different consonants, being sure that the students do not release the final consonant of the first word: 'big day', 'bad game'.

2 See 'Common problems': 'Linking', page 108.

Vowels

Problem   Tense vs. lax vowels: /iy/ vs. /ɪ/, /ey/ vs. /ɛ/, /uw/ vs. /ʊ/

The distinction between tense and lax vowels does not exist in Italian. Italian speakers produce vowel sounds that are between the tense and lax vowels of English.

Tips
See 'Common problems': 'Tense vs. lax vowels', page 96.

Problem   /æ/ vs. /ʌ/ vs. /a/

Italian speakers may have difficulty with these three relatively low vowels, producing a single vowel sound rather than the three sounds found in English. Therefore, it will be difficult for them to distinguish between 'hat', 'hut', and 'hot'.

Tips
See 'Common problems': '/ɛ/ vs. /æ/ vs. /ʌ/ vs. /a/', page 98.

Stress, rhythm, and intonation

Problem   Rhythm

Italian does not have a reduced, short vowel equivalent to the English schwa. This affects the rhythm of the Italian speaker's English as function words and unstressed syllables may not be reduced.

Tips
See 'Common problems': 'Rhythm' (page 107), and also Chapters 11, 12, and 13 in Part Three for activities that provide practice in vowel reduction and rhythm.

Japanese

As mentioned in Chapter 4, 'The shape of English words', Japanese has predominantly open syllable types. This means that Japanese speakers may encounter difficulty in pronouncing English words with consonant clusters and/or closed syllables. Japanese is a syllable-timed language, and thus Japanese speakers may have difficulty with the stress-timed rhythm of English. In addition, Japanese has a five-vowel system, meaning that Japanese learners of English must learn to make many new vowel distinctions.

Consonants

Problem   /s/ vs. /ʃ/ as in 'ship' and /t/ vs. /tʃ/ as in 'chip'

When /s/ and /t/ occur before the high front vowels /ɪ/ or /iy/, as in the English words 'sip' and 'sea' or 'tip' and 'tease', Japanese speakers may pronounce them as /ʃ/ and /tʃ/ respectively, producing words that sound like 'ship' and 'she' or 'chip' and 'cheese'.

Tips

Give students practice in making these distinctions using minimal pairs such as those below.

/s/	/ʃ/		/t/	/tʃ/
seen	sheen		teak	cheek
seat	sheet		tick	chick
see	she		tease	cheese
sin	shin		tin	chin
massing	mashing		matting	matching
classing	clashing		patting	patching

Problem   /b/ vs. /v/

While Japanese has a /b/ sound, it has no /v/ and Japanese learners will often substitute /b/ for /v/, producing 'berry' instead of 'very'.

Tip

Exaggerate the differences in articulation between /b/ and /v/. Show the closure of the lips for /b/ and the upper teeth on the lower lip for /v/. Use minimal pairs contrasting /b/ and /v/.

/b/	/v/
boat	vote
buy	vie
rebel	revel
robe	rove

Problem   /l/ and /r/

Japanese has only one liquid sound which is between the English /r/ and /l/. To the English ear, a word such as 'light' may sound like 'right', and 'arrive' may sound like 'alive'. On the other hand, a word such as 'right' may sound like 'light', and 'alive' may sound like 'arrive'. This is because the sound the Japanese learner is substituting is the same in both cases and the English speaker usually hears the opposite of what the Japanese speaker intended. In word-final position, Japanese speakers most often delete /l/ and /r/.

Tips

1   One way of helping Japanese speakers to make the distinction between the English /l/ and /r/ is to point out that the /l/ sound is made with the

tip of the tongue *touching* the tooth ridge while the /r/ sound is made with the tip of the tongue touching *no* part of the roof of the mouth.

2 Give students practice in making this distinction using minimal pairs such as those below.

/l/	/r/
long	wrong
lamb	ram
lip	rip
lime	rhyme
play	pray
fly	fry
filing	firing
feeling	fearing

Problem   Word-initial /w/ and /y/

Japanese speakers may omit word-initial glides before their high vowel counterparts. Thus, a word such as 'year' may be pronounced as /ir/ and a word such as 'would' may be pronounced as /ʊd/.

Tips
As Japanese speakers will have little difficulty in making word-initial glides before other vowel sounds, it may be good to point out the word-initial glides in words such as 'yes' and 'we'.

Problem   Consonant clusters

Japanese has no consonant clusters in initial or final position. Japanese learners will generally break up consonant clusters through the insertion of a vowel, pronouncing words such as 'sky' as 'suky'.

Tips
See Chapter 4, The shape of English words (page 58), for lists of initial and final consonant clusters. See also 'Common problems': 'Initial consonant clusters' (page 103), and 'Common problems': 'Final consonant clusters' (page 104).

Problem   Word-final consonants

The only consonant permitted in word-final position is a nasal sound similar to (but not identical with) English /ŋ/ as in 'sing'. Japanese learners will often insert a vowel after a word-final consonant so that a word such as 'match' is pronounced as 'matchi'.

Tips
1 Draw the students' attention to the inserted vowels following word-final consonants.

2 Do linking exercises in which words ending in consonants are followed by words beginning with vowels, See 'Common problems': 'Linking', page 108.

Vowels

Problem   Tense vs. lax vowels: /iy/ vs. /ɪ/, /ey/ vs. /ɛ/, /uw/ vs. /ʊ/

The distinction between tense and lax vowels does not exist in Japanese. Japanese speakers produce vowel sounds that are between the tense and lax vowels of English.

Tips
See 'Common problems': 'Tense vs. lax vowels', page 96.

Problem   /ɛ/ vs. /æ/ vs. /ʌ/ vs. /a/

Japanese speakers may have difficulty with all four of these vowel sounds, the /æ/ and /ʌ/ sounds being particularly problematic.

Tips
See 'Common problems': '/ɛ/ vs. /æ/ vs. /ʌ/ vs. /a/', page 98.

Stress, rhythm, and intonation

Problem   Rhythm

Japanese is a syllable-timed language (see Chapter 6, 'Connected speech'), and thus Japanese speakers' pronunciation of English words and sentences may lack the vowel reduction necessary for English rhythm. Japanese does not have a short, reduced vowel equivalent to the English schwa.

Tips
See 'Common problems': 'Rhythm' (page 107), and also Chapters 11 and 13 in Part Three for exercises in vowel reduction and English rhythm.

Problem   Stress

Japanese is what is termed a pitch accent language. In pitch accent languages the primary indicator of accent (stress) is pitch. Recall that stressed syllables in English are marked primarily by length and loudness. Because English and Japanese mark stress in different ways, Japanese speakers may have difficulty both producing and perceiving the characteristic stress patterns of English.

Tips
Focus on the length associated with stressed vowels in English. When stressed vowels are lengthened, unstressed vowels will more likely be reduced, leading to a more characteristic English rhythm. See 'Common problems': 'Stress' and 'Word stress' (page 106).

Problem   Intonation

Japanese learners may have difficulty with the characteristic intonation patterns of English because pitch functions differently in Japanese.

Tips
See 'Common problems': 'Intonation', page 108.

Korean

The pronunciation problems of Korean speakers can be quite severe because of the radical differences between the sound systems of Korean and English. Korean has few word-final consonants and lacks both initial and final consonant clusters. Voicing in Korean is quite different from voicing in English and Korean speakers can have difficulty with the voiced/voiceless distinction.

Consonants

Problem   /p/ vs. /f/ and /b/ vs. /v/

Korean does not have the sounds /f/ and /v/, and Korean speakers tend to substitute /p/ and /b/, respectively.

Tips
1 Exaggerate the differences in articulation between the stops /p/ and /b/ and the fricatives /f/ and /v/. Show the closure of the lips for /p/ and /b/ and the upper teeth on the lower lip for /f/ and /v/.

2 Use minimal pairs contrasting /p/ and /f/ and /b/ and /v/.

/p/	/f/	/b/	/v/
pan	fan	boat	vote
pry	fry	buy	vie
lap	laugh	rebel	revel
supper	suffer	robe	rove

Problem   Voicing of fricatives

Korean has no voiced fricatives and Korean learners tend to substitute voiceless stops or affricates for English voiced fricatives. Very often the substituted sounds are quite different from any English sounds and this can result in incomprehensibility. Particularly troublesome is the English /z/ sound in words such as 'zone' and 'zoo'. Korean learners generally pronounce this /z/ sound as /dz/ or /ts/. When accompanied by some distortion of the vowel sound, these words are very difficult to comprehend for an English listener, even with sufficient context.

Tips
See 'Common problems': 'Voicing of fricatives', page 101.

Problem   Voicing of stops

Korean has aspirated voiceless stops and unaspirated voiceless stops but no voiced stops. Thus, Korean learners may have difficulty in perceiving and producing the difference between voiced and voiceless stops in non-initial position. (In initial position the aspiration of English voiceless stops will help Korean learners in making the voiced/voiceless distinction.)

Tips

1 For tips relating to the voicing of stops word-finally, see 'Common problems': 'Voicing of final stop consonants', page 102.

2 In helping students make the distinction medially, use minimal pairs or near-minimal pairs such as those illustrated below:

/p/	/b/	/k/	/g/
ripping	ribbing	lacking	lagging
staple	stable	slacking	slagging
maple	Mabel	sacking	sagging

Notice that in most dialects of North American English, there are no minimal pairs contrasting /t/ and /d/ in medial position (if the following syllable is unstressed) as both /t/ and /d/ become flaps. See 'Positional variation': 'Flapping', page 41.

Problem   /s/ vs. /ʃ/ vs. aspirated /s/

In Korean, /s/ is pronounced as either /ʃ/ (before high and mid front vowels) or as aspirated /s/ in most other positions. Thus, words such as 'seat' and 'sheet' may sound the same (like 'sheet'). Furthermore, words in which learners substitute their aspirated /s/ will sound quite odd to the English ear.

Tips

1 Give students practice in making the /s/ vs. /ʃ/ distinction using minimal pairs such as those below.

/s/	/ʃ/
seen	sheen
seat	sheet
see	she
sin	shin
massing	mashing
classing	clashing

2 Students must first be made aware that they are aspirating /s/ at the beginning of words. Work on having students lengthen the /s/ sound.

When the /s/ is lengthened the aspiration should disappear. Point out that the vowel should begin as soon as the /s/ is finished. Compare the learners' pronunciation of 'Seoul' with yours. Learners should have an aspirated /s/ in this word while yours should be the normal English /s/. Have them work on the English pronunciation of /s/ in this word.

Problem   /l/ vs. /r/

Korean students tend to substitute /l/ for /r/ in initial position, producing 'light' instead of 'right'. Alternatively, they may substitute what sounds like an /r/ or a flap /D/ for /l/ between vowels, producing 'firing' or 'fighting' for 'filing'.

Tips

1 One way of helping Korean speakers to make the distinction between the English /l/ and /r/ is to point out that the /l/ sound is made with the tip of the tongue *touching* the tooth ridge while the /r/ sound is made with the tip of the tongue touching *no* part of the roof of the mouth.

2 Give students practice in making this distinction using minimal pairs such as those below.

/l/	/r/
long	wrong
lamb	ram
lip	rip
lime	rhyme
play	pray
fly	fry

3 For medial position, first check to ensure that the students are indeed having a problem. If they are, use words such as those below. (Only use the middle column if you have a flap in your pronunciation.)

/l/	/D/	/r/
filing	fighting	firing
ceiling	seating	searing
bowling	boating	boring
failing	fading	faring

Problem   /θ/ and /ð/ as in 'think' and 'this'

Korean spakers will usually substitute aspirated /t/ for /θ/ and unaspirated /t/ for /ð/.

Tips

See 'Common problems': '/θ/ and /ð/', page 104.

Problem Affricates

In words ending with affricates, such as 'match', Korean speakers tend to insert a short vowel sound, /i/, producing 'matchi'. The voiced affricate /dʒ/, as in 'judge', is especially problematic. Korean learners may pronounce 'judge' with what sounds like a final /g/ or /d/ (errors which are perhaps based on the English spelling), or may insert a vowel sound at the end of the word. This sound may also be difficult in initial position and requires extensive work.

Tips
1 Try to make students aware of the additional vowel sound in words such as 'match'. They may be able to eliminate the sound if they can become aware that they are making it. This should be followed up with linking exercises.

2 For the /dʒ/ sound the teacher should teach the students the articulation of the sound, followed by practice in initial, medial, and final positions:

jug	budget	huge
jail	rigid	rage
juice	midget	strange
George	raging	judge

This should also be followed by work on linking.

Problem Consonant clusters

Korean students have difficulty with both initial and final consonant clusters. They tend to insert a short /u/ sound between consonants in order to break up the clusters.

Tips
See 'Common problems': 'Initial consonant clusters' (page 103), and 'Common problems': 'Final consonant clusters' (page 104).

Vowels

Problem Tense vs. lax vowels: /iy/ vs. /ɪ/, /ey/ vs /ɛ/, /uw/ vs. /ʊ/

The distinction between tense and lax vowels does not exist in Korean. Korean speakers usually produce a long vowel sound for the tense vowels and a short vowel sound for the lax vowels.

Tips
See 'Common problems': 'Tense vs. lax vowels', page 96.

Problem   /ε/ vs. /æ/ vs. /ʌ/ vs. /a/

Korean speakers may have difficulty with these four vowel sounds. In particular, they will have difficulty in distinguishing between /ʌ/ and /a/ as in 'putt' and 'pot'.

Tips
See 'Common problems': '/ε/ vs. /æ/ vs. /ʌ/ vs. /a/', page 98.

Stress, rhythm, and intonation

Problem   Stress

Korean stress is quite different from English stress, being mainly realized as a higher pitch on the initial syllable of a word or phrase. Thus, Korean speakers must be taught the acoustic correlates of English stress (i.e. length and loudness).

Tips
See Chapter 5, 'Word stress and vowel reduction', and also 'Common problems': 'Stress' and 'Word stress' (page 106).

Problem   Rhythm

Korean is a syllable-timed language (see Chapter 6, 'Connected speech'), and thus Korean speakers' pronunciation of English words and sentences may lack the vowel reduction necessary for English rhythm.

Tips
See 'Common problems': 'Rhythm' (page 107), and Chapters 11, 12, and 13 in Part Three for exercises in vowel reduction and English rhythm.

Problem   Intonation

Korean learners may have difficulty with the characteristic intonation patterns of English because pitch functions differently in Korean.

Tips
See 'Common problems': 'Intonation', page 108.

Polish

Polish is a Slavic language closely related to other Slavic languages such as Czech, Slovak, Ukrainian, and Russian. The pronunciation problems of speakers of other Slavic languages may be similar.

Consonants

Problem   Aspiration: /p/, /t/, and /k/

Polish speakers often fail to aspirate the voiceless stops /p/, /t/, and /k/ in initial position.

Tips
See 'Common problems': 'Aspiration', page 101.

Problem   Word-final voiced consonants: /b/, /d/, /g/, /v/, /ð/ as in 'breathe', /z/, /ʒ/ as in 'beige', and /dʒ/ as in 'judge'

Polish speakers produce voiceless versions of stops, fricatives and affricates at the ends of words. They can, however, voice these sounds in other positions in words.

Tips
See 'Common problems': 'Voicing of fricatives' (page 101), and 'Voicing of final stop consonants' (page 102).

Problem   /w/ vs. /v/ as in 'west' and 'vest'

Polish speakers may substitute /v/ for /w/, pronouncing 'vine' instead of 'wine'.

Tips
Point out the different articulations of /w/ and /v/. The upper teeth and lower lip should not come together for the pronunciation of the /w/ sound.

Problem   /θ/ and /ð/ as in 'think' and 'this'

Polish speakers will substitute /t/ for /θ/ and /d/ for /ð/.

Tips
See 'Common problems': '/θ/ and /ð/', page 104.

Problem   Final /ŋ/ as in 'thing'

Polish learners tend to insert a final /k/ after the /ŋ/ sound. They produce a word that sounds like 'sank' rather than 'sang'. They may alternatively produce an /n/ instead of an /ŋ/ in final position, producing 'thin' rather than 'thing'.

Tips
1 The addition of a /k/ after words that end with the consonant /ŋ/ is not a critical error. Many native English speakers, especially those with an Eastern European background, do this and no confusion results. If you do attempt to correct this problem, one of the main difficulties is in making the Polish speaker aware of the inserted final /k/ sound. This can be accomplished best through the use of a tape recorder.

2 If an /n/ is substituted for an /ŋ/, the problem is more critical. In this case, it is necessary to go over the articulation of /n/ and /ŋ/. Point out that /n/ is made with the tip of the tongue and that /ŋ/ is made with the back of the tongue as are /k/ and /g/. Use minimal pairs involving /n/ and /ŋ/ at the end of a word, e.g.:

/n/	/ŋ/
sin	sing
fan	fang
ran	rang
pan	pang

Problem   /l/ vs. /w/ as in 'mole' and 'mow'

Polish speakers will produce a sound more like a /w/ than a dark /l/ after a vowel. Thus 'mole' will be pronounced as 'mow', 'goal' as 'go', and 'old' as 'ode'.

Tips
Have students produce the vowel /ow/. During the pronunciation of this vowel, they should raise their tongue until it touches the tooth ridge. At the same time the lips should be unrounded. This should result in the production of dark /l/. Then practise distinguishing between words such as 'mole' and 'mow', 'goal', and 'go', and 'cold' and 'code'.

Problem   English /r/

Polish speakers pronounce English /r/ as a trill.

Tips
See 'Common problems': 'English /r/', page 105.

Vowels

Problem   Tense vs. lax vowels: /iy/ vs. /ɪ/, /ey/ vs. /ɛ/, /uw/ vs. /ʊ/

Polish speakers will not distinguish between the tense and lax vowels of English. They usually produce a vowel that is between the tense and lax vowels of English.

Tips
See 'Common problems': 'Tense vs. lax vowels', page 96.

Problem   /æ/ vs. /ʌ/ vs. /ɛ/

Polish speakers will usually have difficulty with these three vowel sounds. They may substitute /ɛ/ for both /æ/ and /ʌ/.

Tips
See 'Common problems': '/ɛ/ vs. /æ/ vs. /ʌ/ vs. /a/', page 98.

Stress, rhythm, and intonation

Problem   Word stress

Polish is what is termed a fixed-stress language. In such languages, stress always falls on the same syllable—in Polish this is the second-last syllable. This regularity is in contrast to the seeming irregularity of the English stress system.

Tips

Polish students must learn to place stress on different syllables of English words. This can be done through exercises that involve stress shift on related words. See 'Common problems': 'Stress' and 'Word stress' (page 106).

Problem   Rhythm

Polish is a syllable-timed language and lacks the reduction of vowels so important to English rhythm.

Tips

Polish learners should be given activities that practise reduction of unstressed syllables and lengthening of stressed ones. See 'Common problems': 'Rhythm' (page 107), and for more activities see Chapters 11, 12, and 13.

Portuguese

Portuguese is a Romance language closely related to Spanish and there are similarities between the pronunciation problems of Portuguese and Spanish speakers. There are two main dialects of Portuguese, Brazilian Portuguese and European Portuguese. An important difference between Brazilian Portuguese and European Portuguese concerns rhythm: Brazilian Portuguese is a syllable-timed language, whereas European Portuguese is stress-timed and has vowel reduction.

The characteristic accent of a European Portuguese speaker is caused in part by the widespread substitution of /ʃ/ for /s/ at the end of English words. On the other hand, the accent of a Brazilian Portuguese speaker is in part marked by the replacement of /l/ with /w/ at the end of a word.

Teachers with a large number of Portuguese students would be wise to familiarize themselves with the sound-spelling correspondences of Portuguese. Many of the mispronunciations of Portuguese speakers can be traced to the influence of the Portuguese spelling system rather than to an inability to produce particular sounds.

Consonants

Problem   /ʃ/ vs. /tʃ/ as in 'share' and 'chair'; /ʒ/ vs. /dʒ/ as in 'version' and 'virgin'

As European Portuguese does not have the sounds /tʃ/ and /dʒ/, Portuguese speakers may substitute /ʃ/ for /tʃ/ and /ʒ/ for /dʒ/. Thus, pairs of words such as 'share' and 'chair', and 'version' and 'virgin', may be pronounced alike. In Brazilian Portuguese, /tʃ/ and /dʒ/ are positional variants of /t/ and /d/, occurring before high front vowels.

Tips
1 Have students place the tip of the tongue at the tooth ridge as if they were about to make a /t/ or a /d/ and then release the sound as a /ʃ/ or /ʒ/.

2 Point out to students that /tʃ/ and /dʒ/ are complex sounds, made up of consonants that do exist in Portuguese.

Problem   /θ/ and /ð/ as in 'think' and 'this'

Portuguese speakers tend to substitute /t/ for /θ/ in words such as 'think' and /d/ for /ð/ in words such as 'this'.

Tips
1 See 'Common problems': '/θ/ and /ð/', page 104.

2 A sound very similar to English /ð/ exists in some dialects of Portuguese as a positional variant of /d/. Thus, if your students are having difficulty producing /ð/ in English, try to make them aware that they may pronounce the /d/ in *amado* as /ð/.

Problem   /s/ vs. /ʃ/

Portuguese students may pronounce /s/ as /ʃ/ at the end of a word or before a consonant. This can result in words such as 'mass' and 'lease' being pronounced as 'mash' and 'leash'. Similarly, 'mast' and 'messed' may be pronounced as 'mashed' and 'meshed'.

Tips
Use minimal pairs such as those below for comprehension and production.

/s/	/ʃ/
last	lashed
mess	mesh
mass	mash
lease	leash
crass	crash

Problem   /l/ vs. /w/ as in 'mole' and 'mow'

Brazilian Portuguese speakers will produce a sound more like a /w/ than a dark /l/ after a vowel. Thus 'mole' will be pronounced as 'mow', 'goal' as 'go', and 'old' as 'ode'.

Tips
Have students produce the vowel /ow/. During the pronunciation of this vowel, they should raise their tongue until it touches the tooth ridge. At the same time the lips should be unrounded. This should result in the production of dark /l/. Then practise distinguishing between words such as 'mole' and 'mow', 'goal' and 'go', and 'cold' and 'code'.

Problem   Consonants in word-final position

Single consonants (except /ʃ/) may be dropped or weakened (difficult to hear) at the end of a word, or a vowel may be inserted after the consonant.

Tips
Do exercises that involve linking word-final consonants to following vowels. See 'Common problems': 'Linking', page 108.

Problem   Word-final /m/, /n/, and /ŋ/ as in 'ram', 'ran', and 'rang'

Portuguese speakers often omit word-final nasals. Preceding vowels often take on the nasal quality of the omitted nasal, and thus the distinction between /m/, /n/, and /ŋ/ is lost word-finally. Words such as 'some', 'sun', and 'sung' may all be pronounced in the same way, with a nasal vowel but without a nasal consonant.

Tips
Practice nasal consonants in word-final position in minimal pairs and triplets such as those below.

/m/	/n/	/ŋ/
seem	seen	sing
came	cane	
ram	ran	rang
some	sun	sung

Problem   Consonant clusters

Consonant clusters may be difficult for Portuguese students to pronounce in any position (word-initial or word-final) and may be simplified by the insertion of a vowel or by the deletion of a consonant in word-final position. Therefore, /s/ + consonant clusters at the beginning of a word will probably be pronounced as /eʃ/ + consonant, as in [eʃkuwl] for 'school'.

Tips
See 'Common problems': 'Initial consonant clusters' (page 103), and 'Final consonant clusters', page 104.

Vowels

Problem   Tense vs. lax vowels: /iy/ vs. /ɪ/, /ey/ vs /ɛ/, /uw/ vs. /ʊ/

The distinction between tense and lax vowels does not exist in Portuguese. Portuguese speakers usually produce vowel sounds that are between the tense and lax vowels of English.

Tips
See 'Common problems': 'Tense vs. lax vowels', page 96.

Problem   /ɛ/ vs. /æ/ vs. /ʌ/ vs. /a/

Portuguese speakers may have difficulty with these four vowel sounds. In particular, they will have difficulty in distinguishing between /ɛ/ and /æ/ as in 'bed' and 'bad'.

Tips
See 'Common problems': '/ɛ/ vs. /æ/ vs. /ʌ/ vs. /a/, page 98.

Stress, rhythm, and intonation

Problem   Word stress

Portuguese word stress is quite regular, with most words being stressed on the second-last syllable. This means that the rather unpredictable stress patterns of English may prove difficult for the Portuguese learner.

Tips
See 'Common problems': 'Stress' and 'Word stress' (page 106).

Problem   Rhythm

Brazilian Portuguese does not have a reduced, short vowel equivalent to the English schwa. This affects the rhythm of the Brazilian Portuguese speaker's English, as function words and unstressed syllables may not be reduced. As European Portuguese is a stress-timed language, European Portuguese speakers will have less difficulty with the characteristic rhythm of English.

Tips
See 'Common problems': 'Rhythm' (page 107), and also Chapters 11, 12, and 13 in Part Three for activities that provide practice in vowel reduction and rhythm.

Spanish

Spanish has considerable dialectal variation and, as a result, speakers of different dialects may have different pronunciation problems. Most of the problems outlined below are common to all dialects of Spanish.

Consonants

Problem   /b/ vs. /v/

Although the letter 'v' is used in Spanish spelling, the sound /v/ does not exist. In initial position, Spanish speakers may pronounce the English /v/ sound as /b/. In other positions, they may pronounce it as a bilabial fricative, a sound that does not exist in English. To the English ear, this bilabial fricative may sound like a /w/.

Tips

Exaggerate the difference in articulation between /b/ and /v/. Show the closure of the lips for /b/ and the upper teeth on the lower lip for /v/. Use minimal pairs contrasting /b/ and /v/.

/b/	/v/
boat	vote
buy	vie
rebel	revel
robe	rove

Problem   Aspiration: /p/, /t/, and /k/

Spanish speakers may not aspirate the voiceless stops /p/, /t/, and /k/ in word-initial position.

Tips

See 'Common problems': 'Aspiration', page 101.

Problem   /ʃ/ vs. /tʃ/ as in 'ship' and 'chip'

Most Spanish speakers will pronounce 'ship' as 'chip', or 'wash' as 'watch', substituting /tʃ/ for /ʃ/. Argentinian Spanish speakers may do the opposite, substituting /ʃ/ for /tʃ/ and pronouncing 'chip' and 'watch' as 'ship' and 'wash'.

Tips

Have students produce a prolonged 'ssshhh'. Be sure that their lips are rounded in producing this sound. Then, have them transfer this sound to the appropriate words: 'sssshhh ip', 'wasssshhh'. For the Argentinian speakers go over the difference between fricatives and affricates, pointing out that the affricates are complex sounds made up of the familiar sounds /t/ + /ʃ/.

Problem   /y/ vs. /dʒ/ as in 'use' and 'juice'

Speakers of many Spanish dialects will substitute /dʒ/ for /y/, producing 'juice' rather than 'use'. Speakers of other dialects may substitute /ʒ/ as in 'beige' for /y/ in the same position.

Tips

Have students begin words such as 'yet' or 'yes' with the vowel /iy/: 'iiiyy-yet', 'iiiiyyyes'. Tell the students that the tongue should not touch the hard palate in the pronunciation of /y/.

Problem   /s/ vs. /z/

In Spanish, the /z/ sound is a positional variant of /s/, occurring only before voiced consonants. In English words such as 'zoo' and 'amazing', /z/ may be pronounced as /s/.

Tips

See 'Common problems': 'Voicing of fricatives', page 101.

Problem   Word-final /m/, /n/, and /ŋ/ as in 'ram', 'ran', and 'rang'

In some dialects of Spanish, /m/, /n/ and /ŋ/ can be freely substituted for each other at the end of a word. Therefore, Spanish-speaking students may substitute one of these nasals for another at the end of a word. For example, they may pronounce 'sing' as 'sin' or 'sim'.

Tips

Tell students that they are not consistently producing the appropriate nasal sounds at the ends of words. Use minimal pairs or triplets in comprehension and production exercises.

/m/	/n/	/ŋ/
Pam	pan	pang
ram	ran	rang
hem	hen	
ham		hang
	sin	sing

Problem   English /r/

Spanish students often substitute a trilled /r/ for the English /r/.

Tips

See 'Common problems': 'English /r/', page 105.

Problem   /s/ + Consonant in word-initial position: 'spit', 'stay', and 'sky'

When /s/ is followed by another consonant in word-initial position,

Spanish speakers usually insert a vowel at the beginning of the word. For example, 'I speak Spanish' is pronounced 'I espeak espanish'.

Tips

1 Tell the students to lengthen the /s/ sound when it occurs before another consonant: 'ssssssspeak'.

2 Have students practise /s/ + consonant combinations in words such as 'mistake' or 'misspell'. They should gradually eliminate the initial 'mi' to arrive at 'stake' or 'spell'. You can also use phrases such as 'sauce pan'. The students should gradually eliminate the beginning of the word '(sau)ce' to arrive at the word 'span'.

3 See 'Common problems': 'Initial consonant clusters', page 103.

Problem   Final consonant clusters

Spanish speakers will have difficulty with most final consonant clusters in English. Thus, words such as 'tired' may be pronounced as 'tire', 'hold' as 'hole', 'lasts' as 'las', etc.

Tips

See 'Common problems': 'Final consonant clusters', page 104.

Problem   /d/ vs. /ð/ as in 'mother'

Because /d/ and /ð/ are positional variants in Spanish, Spanish speakers may substitute /ð/ for /d/ between vowels and at the end of a word, producing 'heather' for 'header' and 'lathe' for 'laid'.

Tips

As /d/ and /ð/ are positional variants in Spanish, it is quite difficult to make students aware that they are substituting /ð/ for /d/. In Spanish, the sounds equivalent to English /t/ and /d/ are pronounced with the tip of the tongue touching the teeth rather than the tooth ridge. Point out that /d/ is a tooth ridge sound and should not be produced with the tongue touching the teeth. Changing the place of articulation of the /d/ sound may help students to realize that they are substituting the fricative /ð/ for the stop /d/.

Problem   /θ/ and /ð/ as in 'think' and 'this'

Spanish students will often substitute /t/ for /θ/ in 'think' and /d/ for /ð/ in 'this'. As was pointed out above (/d/ vs. /ð/), a sound very similar to English /ð/ exists in Spanish as a positional variant of /d/, occuring between vowels and at the end of a word. This means that Spanish speakers will be able to produce /ð/, while not necessarily realizing it (see Chapter 3, 'English sounds in context', page 45).

Tips

If your students are having difficulty producing /ð/ in English, try to make them aware that /d/ in Spanish words such as *abogado* ('lawyer') or *dedo* ('finger') is produced as /ð/. Then, try to have them transfer this sound to the appropriate words in English, such as 'this', 'the', 'then', etc. For more tips see 'Common problems': /θ/ and /ð/, page 104.

European Spanish also has a /θ/ sound, as in the *c* and *z* of *cerveza* (beer). It may be worth pointing this out to students, and making sure that they do not lisp on English *c* and *z*.

Problem   Past tense: -ed

Spanish speakers inevitably pronounce all variants of the regular past tense as a separate syllable. This may be the result of the English spelling of the regular past tense, but is more likely the result of Spanish learners' more general problem in producing final consonant clusters.

Tips
See 'Common problems': 'Final consonant clusters' (page 104), and also 'English sounds in context': 'Grammatical Endings', page 47.

Vowels

Problem   Tense vs. lax vowels: /iy/ vs. /ɪ/, /ey/ vs. /ɛ/, /uw/ vs. /ʊ/

The distinction between tense and lax vowels does not exist in Spanish. Spanish speakers produce vowel sounds that are between the tense and lax vowels of English.

Tips
See 'Common problems': 'Tense vs. lax vowels', page 96.

Problem   /ɛ/ vs. /æ/ vs. /ʌ/ vs. /a/

Spanish speakers may have difficulty with all four of these vowel sounds. They may have particular difficulty distinguishing between /ɛ/ and /æ/ as in 'bed' and 'bad'.

Tips
See 'Common problems': '/ɛ/ vs. /æ/ vs. /ʌ/ vs. /a/', page 98.

Stress, rhythm, and intonation

Problem   Word stress

Spanish word stress is quite regular, with most words being stressed on the second-last syllable. However, Spanish does use variation in stress position to differentiate words of different meanings. When stress is not on the second-last syllable, the Spanish orthography employs an accent mark to indicate the irregular stress.

Tips

1 When a word is stressed on a syllable other than the second-last one, use an accent mark to indicate where the stress is:

    Cánada   abóve   América   diséase   machíne

2 See 'Common problems': 'Stress' and 'Word stress' (page 106).

Problem   Rhythm

Spanish is a syllable-timed language (see Chapter 6, 'Connected speech'), and thus Spanish speakers' pronunciation of English words and sentences may lack the vowel reduction necessary for English rhythm. Spanish does not have a short, reduced vowel equivalent to the English schwa.

Tips

See 'Common problems': 'Rhythm' (page 107), and Chapters 11, 12, and 13 in Part Three.

Vietnamese

As the sound systems of English and Vietnamese differ greatly, Vietnamese speakers can have quite severe pronunciation problems. Vietnamese is a tone language; that is, pitch changes distinguish word meaning. Most words in Vietnamese consist of only one syllable; there are fewer consonants than in English and there are no consonant clusters. On the other hand, the Vietnamese vowel system makes a large number of distinctions and, therefore, speakers of Vietnamese do not experience too much difficulty with the English vowels. Vietnamese uses a modified Roman alphabet but many of the letters have quite different sound values from those of English.

Consonants

Problem   Word-final voiceless stop consonants: /p/, /t/, and /k/

In Vietnamese, the voiceless stop consonants /p/, /t/, and /k/ occur at the end of a word, but these consonants are never released in final position and are much shorter than their English equivalents. This means that even when Vietnamese speakers pronounce these consonants in final position, English speakers may have difficulty hearing them. Thus, a word such as 'beat' may sound like 'bee'.

Tips

1 Have students release the final voiceless stop consonants in words such as 'top', 'taught', and 'back'. A small puff of air, similar to aspiration, should

accompany the release of the consonants. Practise these words in sentence-final position where they receive major sentence stress. This may involve some exaggeration of your own speech because these consonants are not always released in English in this position.

> Put it up on *top*.
> I didn't know that you *taught*.
> Do you mind sitting near the *back?*

2 Do linking exercises in which words ending in voiceless stops are followed by words beginning with vowels. See 'Common problems': 'Linking', page 108.

Problem   Voiced vs. voiceless stops in word-final position: /b/, /d/, /g/ vs. /p/, /t/, /k/

As Vietnamese has no voiced stops at the ends of words, Vietnamese speakers need practice in distinguishing between voiced and voiceless stops in this position. For example, words such as 'cap' and 'cab' may sound identical, with a short unreleased /p/ at the end of both words.

Tips

Once Vietnamese speakers have practised releasing voiceless stops at the ends of words (as outlined above), begin exercises that have them distinguish between voiced and voiceless stops. See 'Common problems': 'Voicing of final stop consonants', page 102.

Problem   Word-final fricative consonants: /f/, /v/, /θ/ as in 'truth', /ð/ as in 'bathe', /s/, /z/, /ʃ/ as in 'wash', and /ʒ/ as in 'beige'

As fricatives do not occur in word-final position in Vietnamese, Vietnamese speakers may omit fricatives at the ends of words. A sentence such as:

> The boys always pass the garage on their way home.

may sound like:

> The boy alway pa the gara on their way home.

Tips

1 Since Vietnamese speakers can produce some of these fricatives at the beginning of English words—/f/, /v/, /s/, and /z/—point out the similarity between these initial and final sounds.

2 Do linking exercises in which words ending in these fricatives are followed by words beginning with vowels.

> Don't give‿up your seat.
> Don't play with‿it.
> Breathe‿in and then breathe‿out.
> Pass‿out the books.
> Your wish‿is my command.

3 Practise the pronunciation of the /s/ and /z/ in words that have grammatical endings—the plural, the possessive, and the third person singular present tense.

Problem   Consonant clusters

As Vietnamese has no consonant clusters in initial or final position, Vietnamese speakers must learn to produce a large variety of new syllable types that contain consonant clusters. Generally, Vietnamese speakers tend to delete one or more consonants from a difficult cluster.

Tips
See Chapter 4, 'The shape of English words' (pages 55–8) for lists of initial and final consonant clusters. See also 'Common problems': 'Initial consonant clusters' (page 103), and 'Final consonant clusters' (page 104), for tips.

Problem   /θ/ and /ð/ as in 'think' and 'this'

Vietnamese speakers will often produce a heavily aspirated stop /t/ instead of /θ/ in words like 'think'. This is probably based on the orthographic system of Vietnamese, where the letter combination *th* represents a heavily aspirated /t/. They will usually substitute a /d/ for /ð/ in words like 'this'.

Tips
See 'Common problems': '/θ/ and /ð/', page 104.

Problem   Word-final /tʃ/ as in 'march'

Once Vietnamese speakers have learned to produce the fricative /ʃ/ in word-final position, they may substitute /ʃ/ for /tʃ/, saying 'marsh' instead of 'march'.

Tips
Vietnamese does have a sound similar to the English /tʃ/ in word-initial position. This occurs in the Vietnamese word *chua* [tʃuə], 'not yet'. Have students pronounce this word, pointing out the similarity between its initial sound and the final sound in a word such as 'march'.

Problem   /p/ vs. /f/ and /b/

As /p/ does not occur in initial position in Vietnamese, Vietnamese speakers may substitute a /b/ or an /f/ for /p/. Thus, 'put' may sound like 'foot', and 'Peter' may sound like 'beater'.

Tips
1 For substitution of /f/ for /p/, point out that the lips come together for the English /p/ sound, whereas the bottom lip touches the top teeth for /f/.

2 For substitution of /b/ for /p/, work on the aspiration of the /p/ may be helpful. See 'Common problems': 'Aspiration', page 101.

Vowels

Problem   Tense vs. lax vowels: /iy/ vs. /ɪ/, /ey/ vs. /ɛ/, /uw/ vs. /ʊ/

While Vietnamese makes many vowel distinctions, the English tense/lax vowel pairs can still pose difficulties for Vietnamese learners.

Tips
See 'Common problems': 'Tense vs. lax vowels', page 96.

Problem   /ɛ/ vs. /æ/

Vietnamese speakers may have difficulty distinguishing between /ɛ/ and /æ/ as in 'bed' and 'bad'.

Tips
See 'Common problems': '/ɛ/ vs. /æ/ vs. /ʌ/ vs. /a/', page 98.

Stress, rhythm, and intonation

Problem   Word stress

As Vietnamese words generally consist of only one syllable, Vietnamese speakers may have difficulty in producing the longer words of English with appropriate stress patterns. Furthermore, each syllable of an utterance will receive equal weight, giving Vietnamese learners' English a staccato-like rhythm.

Tips
Always include some practice in the production of longer words in the pronunciation class. See Chapters 11 and 12 in Part Three . See also 'Common problems': 'Stress' and 'Word stress' (page 106), and 'Rhythm' (page 107) for activities.

Problem   Linking

As we have stated above, Vietnamese students often omit consonants at the ends of English words. Consequently, words will not be linked in connected speech.

Tips
See 'Common problems': 'Linking' (page 108). For more linking activities, see Chapter 11, page 185. See Chapter 6, 'Connected speech' (page 73), for a description of linking.

Problem   Contractions

Vietnamese students often have difficulty with contractions because of the difficult consonant clusters that are created.

Tips
See 'Common problems': 'Contractions', page 108.

Problem   Intonation

Vietnamese speakers may have difficulty with the characteristic intonation patterns of English because pitch functions differently in Vietnamese (Vietnamese is a tone language).

Tips
See Chapters 11 and 12 in Part Three for activities that provide intonation practice. See also 'Connected speech': 'Intonation' (page 176), and 'Common problems': 'Intonation', page 108.

PART THREE

Classroom activities

INTRODUCTION

Parts One and Two of this book provide technical information essential to effective pronunciation teaching but do not relate this information to methodology or the development of a pronunciation curriculum. The following chapters cover a range of themes from the description of teaching techniques to the design of a pronunciation syllabus to the more global issue of unintelligibility among ESL learners.

In Chapter 15, Elson reminds us that miscommunication among interlocutors, whether native speakers or non-native speakers, is a natural part of the communication process. These communication problems, of course, may be exacerbated by the pronunciation problems experienced by ESL learners. Just as native speakers have strategies for repairing communication breakdowns, so, Elson argues, ESL learners should be encouraged to employ such strategies while also developing their pronunciation skills. Firth in Chapter 14 addresses the issue of 'carry-over'. While learners may achieve target or near-target pronunciation during the pronunciation class, too often there is little or no 'carry-over' into 'real life' with its other pressures. Firth, like Elson, is concerned with the development of strategies that facilitate communication outside of the pronunciation class. Clearly, the development of such strategies is an important consideration for ESL teachers and one not often discussed in the context of pronunciation skills.

Equally important, however, is situating pronunciation teaching squarely among other language skills taught in the ESL classroom. In order that pronunciation skills can be developed in a systematic manner, attention should be given to the creation of a syllabus. In Chapter 10, Firth outlines the steps involved in the designing of such a syllabus—from the collection of speech samples to the diagnosis of learners' speech to the design of a syllabus. While time constraints may not always permit teachers to carry out a detailed analysis of learners' problems, information on common pronunciation difficulties experienced by speakers from a wide variety of language groups (such as that provided in Chapter 7 of Part Two) can provide a useful short-cut in the design stage.

Once a pronunciation syllabus has been designed, teachers can refer to Chapters 9, 11, 12, and 13 for practical techniques in the teaching of pronunciation. These articles provide the teacher with numerous ideas for creating pronunciation lessons, ranging from traditional techniques to more communicative ones, and from production-oriented exercises to reception-oriented ones. The articles also reflect current thinking on the importance of suprasegmentals in the pronunciation classroom.

In Chapter 15, Archibald introduces acting techniques into the pronunciation class. Particularly innovative is Archibald's emphasis on warm-up activities and activities designed to develop 'confident' speech.

Taken together, these chapters should help teachers situate pronunciation teaching within the broader ESL curriculum and facilitate the creation of varied and enjoyable pronunciation lessons.

9 A COMMUNICATIVE APPROACH TO PRONUNCIATION TEACHING

Neil Naiman

Introduction

The trend towards 'communicative' language teaching has continued to grow over the past five years to encompass most aspects of ESL teaching. As ESL teachers, we attempt to develop communicative competence in our students by providing them with creative opportunities for meaning-ful exchange of language. In a communicative, student-centred classroom students should be provided with authentic language materials and should be engaged in a meaningful interchange of language beyond the word and sentence level. However, it appears that such conditions do not seem to apply generally to the teaching of pronunciation. Pronunciation teaching has lagged far behind the remainder of ESL teaching in its communicative focus. In the next few pages I will attempt to show how the communicative approach can be applied successfully to the teaching of pronunciation.

Historically, much of the teaching of pronunciation has involved the prac-tice of isolated sounds or stress and intonation patterns without regard for the wider context in which these sounds and patterns occur. Slowly, however, changes are beginning to occur in the teaching of pronunciation. The clearest evidence of this change has been the shift in emphasis from the teaching of segmentals (individual vowel and consonant sounds) to the teaching of suprasegmentals (stress, rhythm, and intonation). This shift in emphasis reflects the realization on the part of practitioners and theoreticians that pronunciation practice must take place beyond the indi-vidual sound and word level. English pronunciation is inextricably linked to meaning at the discourse level and must be presented to students in that way and practised accordingly.

This trend towards greater emphasis on suprasegmentals began with the publication of Joan Morley's book, *Improving Spoken English* (1979), and has continued with the publication of Judy Gilbert's book *Clear Speech*

(1984) and the TESOL publication *Current Perspectives on Pronunciation* (Morley 1987). There is still a long way to go, however, in providing pronunciation practice which is truly communicative. Before presenting some ideas about communicative pronunciation teaching it is important to address a few issues related to the teaching of pronunciation.

Should a separate class be devoted to pronunciation teaching?

My comments are based on the practical experience I gained during eight years of teaching at the community college level. It was my impression that if pronunciation was not given a separate class it often did not get taught at all. Many teachers felt that they did not have enough training or expertise to teach pronunciation, so they felt it was safer not to do it. Other teachers believed they really didn't have an 'ear' for pronunciation so they felt they really wouldn't be helping their students if they taught pronunciation. Many colleagues were conscious of their poor understanding of the technical aspects of the sound system of English and therefore felt extremely uncomfortable teaching pronunciation. As a result, it was often left to the end or totally neglected.

Consequently, with pronunciation being so erratically taught, students often didn't comprehend the importance of pronunciation to their language learning. However, once pronunciation is given its own class and teachers begin to feel more comfortable teaching it, students immediately see the importance of pronunciation. When taught communicatively, pronunciation can be both interesting and fun for students. More importantly, as students begin to realize how much more they understand and are understood, they see the importance of pronunciation teaching and actually cry out for more. Pronunciation can and should always be integrated into all aspects of language teaching and reinforced in all classes, but it is my feeling that setting aside a separate class or part of a class for pronunciation ensures that it is taught. Moreover, doing so guarantees that students attach the importance to pronunciation that it deserves.

Do you need a language laboratory to teach pronunciation?

You do not need an expensive language laboratory to teach pronunciation. It does help if you and some of your students have access to tape recorders, both for recording and monitoring in-class production and for taping outside-of-class natural conversations. None of the activities described in this chapter requires the use of a language laboratory.

Do you need to be an expert in phonetics to teach pronunciation?

It is true that one needs an understanding of the sound system of English in order to teach pronunciation effectively, but one does not need to be an expert phonetician. With good resources, effective and committed ESL teachers can rapidly become effective pronunciation teachers as well.

Communicative pronunciation teaching should include emphasis on the following areas, which are crucial to all forms of communicative language teaching:

1 meaningful practice beyond the word level
2 task orientation of classroom activities
3 development of strategies for learning beyond the classroom
4 peer correction and group work
5 student-centred classroom

The following pages describe some of the major aspects of such a communicative pronunciation course, designed at Seneca College in Toronto. Examples are provided of sample communicative activities, along with approaches and techniques that can be adapted for use in a variety of different language teaching situations. Examples are presented of communicative activities related to three aspects of the pronunciation curriculum: consonants and vowels, connected speech, and suprasegmentals.

Consonants and vowels

In the teaching of consonants and vowels, it is important to introduce characteristic aspects of their articulation (e.g. voiced vs. voiceless, stops vs. fricatives, aspiration, etc.). The realization of these articulatory features can be practised through a variety of communicative activities such as those presented below.

Information-gap activities

One of the easiest techniques for practising consonants and consonant contrasts in a communicative way is to use 'information-gap' activities.

For example, if students are confusing /b/ and /v/, the following activity can be used. Choose a topic such as food and have students brainstorm and think of as many food words as possible which contain the /b/ and /v/ sounds. It is best for the students to work in groups so that they have more opportunity to generate these words in a communicative fashion. If students are beginners, clues or pictures can be provided to help them with the generation of words. Students might come up with 'berry', 'veal', 'liver', 'brown bread', 'vegetables', 'vitamins', 'vanilla', 'beans', 'bacon', etc. Students may also be asked to generate examples of names containing these two sounds. In this case, students might come up with Bill, Bob, Vickie, Barbara, Steve, Virginia. It may be necessary to provide students, especially beginners, with some of these names.

When enough words have been generated, the teacher can number the names and foods on slips of paper and hand out even-numbered foods and odd-numbered names to one group and odd-numbered foods and even-numbered names to the other group. Blank grids can be handed out and students can work in pairs or in groups questioning each other about 'Who bought what' at the store. Once the grids are filled out, the result of the activity can be presented to the class. In so doing, the students gain further communicative practice with these sounds. Role plays which incorporate some of the food words and names identified above can be used as a follow-up to this activity.

Variations on these activities can be carried out with many pronunciation and vowel contrasts around a variety of themes. Ideas for such activities can be found in Celce-Murcia (1987).

Matching exercises

Another way of practising a sound contrast such as /b/ and /v/ involves the use of matching exercises. Divide the class into two groups. Group A has a written description of several people. Group B has a picture containing all of the people for which there are descriptions. The object of this activity is to match the written descriptions with the appropriate people. Some sample descriptors might be:

> Becky has big boots.
> Vicky has a velvet vest.
> Barbara is carrying a big bag.
> Virginia is wearing gloves.
> Bill has a shiny belt-buckle.

In attempting to match the descriptor with the appropriate person, the students gain practice producing the relevant sounds. A variation on this activity has these descriptors generated by the students themselves. Creating such descriptors, especially in groups, provides additional communicative practice of these consonant and vowel sounds.

Chain stories

Each student receives a phrase containing the sound contrasts being practised. The first student must embed that phrase in a short story (or string of related sentences) of no longer than four sentences. The task of the other students is to guess the embedded phrase based on the correct pronunciation of the relevant sound or sound contrasts. The next student continues the story using the phrase that he or she has received.

Sample phrases might include:

big beautiful baby	oven gloves
very bad brakes	broken bracelet
lovely building	seventy vehicles

'Fluency square' activities

A less communicative technique, requiring less preparation for the teachers can be found in the book *Story Squares* (Knowles and Sasaki 1980).

In this book, there are usually four illustrated squares used to contrast at least two sounds. A large square is divided into four squares with each of the smaller squares depicting an activity differing from a contrasting square in terms of one variable. For example:

> Square 1: Cassie took a bus this morning.
> Square 2: Cassie took a bath this morning.
> Square 3: Cathy took a bath this morning.
> Square 4: Cathy took a bus this morning.

Squares 1 and 4 differ in the contrast between /s/ and /θ/ in 'Cassie' and 'Cathy'. Squares 1 and 2 and squares 3 and 4 differ in the contrast between /æ/ and /ʌ/ and /θ/ and /s/ in 'bath' and 'bus', etc. Students must describe the activities in each square so that another student is able to identify the correct square. For students to be able to gain the correct information about the activities, they have to be able to both hear and produce the differences between these vowel and consonant contrasts.

Dialogues, role-plays, and games

Many of the vowel and consonant contrasts are clustered around a variety of interesting themes in the book *Survival Pronunciation* (Hecht and Ryan 1984). In illustrating the difference between /ɪ/ and /iy/, words containing these sounds are presented through a realistic dialogue in a doctor's office. For example, words such as 'hip', 'injection', 'needle', 'injury', 'hit', and 'feel' are included in the dialogue. Students can be asked to practise the original dialogue and then create role plays of the same situation without using the original dialogue. Many of the highlighted words will no doubt enter into the role play that the students generate.

Survival Pronunciation also provides models for language games such as Bingo and Tic-Tac-Toe. These can be used for practising individual vowel and consonant contrasts. The bingo sheet, rather than having numbers, contains pictures of words which display a minimal contrast. For example, the contrast between /ɪ/ and /iy/ is practised by having pictures of the following items: 'peel' and 'pill', 'sheep' and 'ship', and 'meat' and 'mitt'. The teacher calls out a list of words and the students put markers on the words that they hear. Of course, the students can only win when they have recognized the vowel contrasts and have, therefore, identified the words correctly.

Connected speech

One of the results of the characteristic rhythm of English is the use of contractions, linking, and common reduced expressions such as 'gonna', 'hafta', and 'wanna'. At first, many students have to be convinced that it is 'correct' to use these expressions. However, as they begin to practise them, they notice their use in spoken language and realize their importance for comprehensibility. The following activities provide communicative practice in these important aspects of English pronunciation.

Questionnaires and surveys

Many common contractions occur with questions in English such as:

> How long've you been looking for an apartment?
> Where'd'you live now?
> Wheredja live before?
> Whyd'ya want to move?

Students can make up questions commonly found in surveys and opinion polls and then follow through by actually conducting a survey either inside or outside the classroom. These questionnaires will undoubtedly contain many common question contractions. Be sure to practise these expressions in class before students conduct their own research.

Rhymalogues

In *Improving Spoken English*, Joan Morley uses 'rhymalogues' as a way of practising contractions and reduced expressions in a semi-communicative fashion. For example, students can work in pairs or in groups with one member of the pair asking a question and the other providing a response.

> **Q** What did you do, Lou?   (Whaddja do, Lou?)
> **A** I lost my pen, Ben.
> **Q** When's the play, Ray?
> **A** It's at eight, Kate.
> **Q** Where did you go, Joe?   (Wheredja go, Joe?)
> **A** To the play, May.

Dialogues and role plays

Common reduced expressions such as 'gonna', 'wanna', 'hafta', 'shoulda', and 'coulda' can be practiced in dialogues and role plays. It is often necessary to provide students with models of such dialogues. When possible, these should be done with the students attempting to generate the dialogues and the teacher serving primarily as a resource person. For example, words can be provided or generated to practise linking of final stop consonants (/p/, /t/, /k/, /b/, /d/, /g/) with following vowels. Students can construct dialogues which contain these words. In addition, they should be instructed to use examples of 'and', 'or', 'on', 'in', 'under', 'over', 'of', and 'about' in their dialogues so that the final stop consonants have to be linked to the vowels that follow. Thus, sentences such as the following could be constructed:

I saw Bob in the bookstore.
Did he buy that book about Atomic Energy?
No, I think he bought a book about an energetic athlete.

Games

Palatalization (d + y = /dʒ/, as in 'didja') can be practised effectively in games such as 'Find Your Twin', in which a set of cards is passed out to students containing a list of activities they were said to have performed on the weekend. Each card has one perfect match but the activities displayed on all the cards should be similar. Each student is asked to find his or her 'twin' (i.e. the perfect matching card) by asking yes/no questions beginning 'didja . . .?', all practised with the appropriate palatalization. Variations on such games can be practised incorporating other question words (e.g. 'wheredja . . .?' 'whendja . . .?').

The reduction of initial /h/ in the personal pronoun 'he' can also be practised by making twenty questions-type game about a famous male no longer living ('Did'e . . .?'). To avoid discussing only famous males, linking can be practised by making the game about famous living females ('Is she . . .?').

Suprasegmentals

Students should practise the suprasegmentals aspects of English pronunciation from the earliest stages (e.g. the schwa, major sentence stress, intonation, and information focus). After practising suprasegmentals in a variety of more controlled exercises (see Chapters 11, 12, and 13 in this section), students should be given an opportunity to practise suprasegmentals in longer stretches of discourse. It is through these longer samples of real language that the relationship between suprasegmentals and meaning becomes so evident. These practice activities can initially take the form of simple teacher-student modelling and imitation, as well as oral reading. The language used for this practice should be taken from realistic dialogues, transcripts of news reports, natural conversations (as long as the language is truly spoken language and not written language).

Shadowing

After the oral reading activities above have been practised extensively, the students can attempt 'shadowing'. This technique requires that students follow the rhythm and intonation contours of natural language samples by producing the language at the same time as the teacher models it. (See Ricard 1986 for a detailed description.) I have found this technique to be both useful and fun for students.

Focused activities

Other more focussed communicative activities involving suprasegmentals can be developed as well. For example, students can attempt to practise the difference between content and function words and the stress patterns associated with them by completing tasks where they have to send a telegram (see Chapter 12 in this section).

Students might also practise the relationship of intonation to persuasive techniques with the help of tag questions. Role plays could be developed in which a salesperson is trying to convince a customer to buy an item. For example, 'That dress is a beautiful colour, isn't it?' 'It really brings out the colour of your eyes, doesn't it?' 'It's not a lot of money for such a wonderful dress, is it?' etc.

As with other aspects of the pronunciation curriculum, teachers should attempt to identify appropriate situations for the practice of suprasegmentals.

Monitoring

It is crucial that students begin to monitor and correct each other's pronunciation. When students are monitoring rhythm, stress, and the production of segments, they must comment on it. This means that they are communicating about pronunciation. They are beginning to develop a metalanguage which allows them not only to talk about pronunciation but also to become more aware of their own pronunciation. For monitoring to succeed, students must have the tools and the concepts necessary to discuss individual sounds as well as rhythm and stress in English.

In my experience, the ability to monitor pronunciation is invaluable. It provides students with the opportunities and the strategies to continue their learning beyond the classroom. They begin to listen to language differently because they have been sensitized to English sound and rhythm and have acquired the tools for analysis. They begin to mimic the speech of native speakers whom they hear on the radio, on the television, on the bus, or at work. It is as if learning about pronunciation has opened up a part of English to them that they had previously missed or had been unable to understand.

Students can be told to practise at home in front of the mirror or with native speakers. They will often bring to class examples of speech they have heard but now understand—meanings which were previously mysteries to them.

This ability will extend their learning beyond the classroom. It also serves to improve their aural comprehension and to build confidence in the language they are producing. For more information on self-monitoring, see Chapter 14.

Conclusion

In this short space, I hope to have provided a few ideas as to how the teaching of pronunciation can be approached communicatively. The more the teaching of pronunciation is given the same focus as the teaching of English as a second language in general, the more effective pronunciation teaching and learning will become.

10 PRONUNCIATION SYLLABUS DESIGN: A QUESTION OF FOCUS

Suzanne Firth

Introduction

The design of a pronunciation course should consist of several distinct stages: a general assessment of learner variables; the collection and diagnosis of speech samples; the design of a syllabus; and, finally, careful teaching and appropriate feedback. The degree of success achieved in a pronunciation course can be greatly increased if syllabus design and teaching are carried out according to the 'zoom principle'.

The zoom principle

The 'zoom principle' relies on an ability to adjust one's field of vision. Older pronunciation texts urged a close-up approach: test a student's ability to discriminate between sound contrasts in words such as 'bit' and 'bet' and then practise producing these contrasts. More recently, the angle of vision has been widening: texts such as Judy Gilbert's *Clear Speech* (1984) emphasize the importance of stress, rhythm, and intonation, putting work on these aspects of pronunciation ahead of work on individual sounds. In fact, the angle can be widened even further to include the kinds of general speaking habits addressed in 'effective presentation' or 'public speaking' seminars for native speakers. A pronunciation syllabus should begin with the widest possible focus and move gradually in on specific problems. Just as a photographer may rearrange some element in the composition of a photograph and then move back to survey the overall effect, so too does work on pronunciation rely on a constantly shifting focus—from overall effectiveness of communication, to a specific problem, to overall effectiveness of communication, and so on.

Assessing learner variables

Learner variables have not always been considered important in the teaching of pronunciation. Logically, however, the 'what' and 'how' of a pronunciation syllabus should depend in large part on 'who' the students are. More specifically, a consideration of the attitudes and motivation of students should determine to some extent how much emphasis an instructor will place on accurate pronunciation. Not all adults will have the same attitudes towards losing or modifying their accents. A number of factors may influence their view of pronunciation and, consequently, their commitment to improvement. Among the most significant factors affecting attitude are age, education, occupation, length of time in host country, feelings about the host culture and willingness to part with one's original 'cultural identity'.

Personality, too, can influence the motivation of students. A gregarious student who joins an adult class in order to socialize may be more concerned with sharing ideas than with accuracy of pronunciation. On the other hand, an individual anxious to speak 'correctly' may prefer to be accurate rather than fluent.

Attitude towards pronunciation may be affected by a student's level of proficiency. Given the complexity of communicating in a new language and the apparent importance of vocabulary and grammar, students may believe that pronunciation practice is an unnecessary frill.

The accumulation of information related to learner variables can help an instructor gauge the relative importance of accurate pronunciation to particular students.

Collection of speech samples

A diagnosis of a student's oral English should be related, in part, to learner variables. A student who is an actor, for example, may require a highly detailed analysis of every aspect of pronunciation because her goal may be the attainment of native-like accuracy. A student whose use of English is restricted to the communication of basic needs does not require as detailed an analysis. In this case, the diagnosis should focus on aspects of English pronunciation which affect comprehensibility. Stress, rhythm, and intonation, for example, appear to be far more critical to successful communication than individual sounds.

There are several techniques for gathering information about students' pronunciation:

Contrastive studies   Comparing the sound system of English to that of the learner's native language can provide information about potential pronunciation difficulties. See Chapter 8, 'The problems of specific language groups' (page 111) and Swan and Smith (1987) for examples of contrastive studies.

In-class surveys   A teacher can create a situation which requires students to use particular stress and intonation patterns or particular sounds. For example, students' ability to produce falling intonation in '*wh*-questions' (e.g. 'who', 'where', etc.) could be checked by having students ask questions about a picture. During the activity, the accuracy of each student's production of the pattern could be noted on a master sheet.

Oral reading   A teacher tapes a student reading a passage and then uses a checklist to record items which need remedial work. The textbook *A Manual of American Pronunciation* (Prator and Robinett 1985) uses a reading passage carefully designed to diagnose a wide range of possible student problems.

Spontaneous speech   Using a tape recorder, samples of spontaneous speech can be gathered during a regular class. For example, students can interview each other with questions keyed to their proficiency level. Classroom activities which yield spontaneous speech can be taped and analyzed for diagnostic purposes.

Each sampling technique has advantages and disadvantages. Contrastive studies cannot accurately predict all problems for all speakers of a language. In some instances, students do not have the predicted problems; in others, their problems are different from the predicted ones. In-class surveys can be inefficient, as they only permit a teacher to deal with one problem at a time. The oral reading task requires the student to be able to interpret a text at the moment of reading. Normally, only actors and broadcasters are called on to carry out such an activity. However, the student's task can be made easier by allowing some time for practice before the actual taping. Collecting spontaneous speech allows for samples of more natural language but may not reveal all of a student's pronunciation problems. If the questions in an interview are carefully selected, however, students will have to answer in such a way that they produce the sounds and/or stress, rhythm and intonation patterns desired. Presumably, teachers will choose to gather data according to the time available, the objectives of the pronunciation component and the recording equipment available.

Diagnosis of speech samples

Keeping in mind the 'zoom' principle, the teacher can begin to analyze the diagnostic information in order to design a syllabus. A diagnostic profile sheet is advisable for each student as it provides a permanent record of strengths and weaknesses, permits the recording of progress within specific areas and allows the instructor to develop priorities for a particular class. Using a diagnostic profile such as the one provided in the Appendix to this chapter allows teachers to organize specific information regarding the pronunciation of their students. A comparison of the profiles of a group of students can allow the teacher to select items for class work which reflect the needs of the majority of students. In the remainder of this section, the categories of the diagnostic profile sheet will be expanded upon.

General Speaking Habits

Clarity   Is the student's speech muffled because she/he speaks with a hand covering the mouth? Because the head is held down? Because posture is bad?

Speed   Does the student speak too quickly? Does inaccurate articulation become incomprehensible because the student speaks too quickly?

Loudness   Does the student speak too softly? Does a lack of volume combined with non-standard pronunciation diminish comprehensibility?

Breath groups   Does the student speak with appropriate pauses, breaking up a sentence into thought groups?

Eye gaze   Does the student face the other speaker in a conversation and attempt to use eye gaze behaviour appropriate for the context?

Fluency   Does the student speak with either long silences between words or with too many 'filled pauses' (i.e. expressions such as 'uhm' or 'ah')?

Voice   Is the student's voice unnaturally high or nasal? Too breathy or monotonous because of too little variation in pitch?

Other   (gestures, expressiveness) Does the student over-use gestures? Do facial expressions correspond to attitude?

For more information on general speaking habits, see Grasham and Goodner (1960) and Fisher (1975).

Intonation

Is the student using appropriate intonation patterns? Are yes/no questions signalled through the use of rising intonation? Is falling intonation used with *wh*-questions? Is the student changing pitch at the major stressed word in the sentence? Examples of the intonation patterns to be evaluated are found in the diagnostic profile in the Appendix. (For a description of English intonation, see Chapter 6, 'Connected speech', page 76.)

Stress and rhythm

Word level stress   Can the student use loudness and length to differentiate between stressed and unstressed syllables? Can the student produce the schwa sound in unstressed syllables? Can the student use a dictionary to check stress patterns? Can the student predict stress patterns based on suffixes? (See Chapter 5, 'Word stress and vowel reduction', for details on word stress.)

Sentence level stress   Is the student incorrectly stressing every word of a sentence equally? Is he/she able to produce appropriate strong and weak stresses? Are content words stressed and function words unstressed? Is the student placing major sentence stress on the appropriate words?

Linking   Is the student linking words appropriately within sentences? For example, are identical consonants linked to identical consonants (as in 'grab Bill')? Are consonants linked to vowels (as in 'grab it')? Is the student producing contractions where appropriate? (See Chapter 6, 'Connected speech', page 84, for a description of linking in English.)

Consonants

Substitution   Is the student substituting a different consonant for the appropriate one (e.g. substituting /t/ for /θ/ so that 'thought' sounds like 'taught')?

Omission   Is the student omitting consonants (e.g. omitting final consonants so that 'pace' sounds like 'pay')?

Articulation   Is the consonant being articulated properly (e.g. is /p/ aspirated word initially)?

Clusters   Is the consonant properly articulated in clusters (e.g. /r/ in 'pray')? Are consonants being omitted from clusters (e.g. 'except' is pronounced as 'eset')? Are vowels being inserted to break up clusters (e.g. 'speak' is pronounced as 'sipeak'?)

Linking   Is the consonant being linked properly in connected speech? Are alternations typical of relaxed speech being made (e.g. are flaps produced in the appropriate places)?

Vowels

Substitution   Is the student substituting one vowel sound for another (e.g. substituting /ɛ/ for /æ/ so that 'tan' sounds like 'ten')?

Articulation   Is the student articulating vowel sounds properly (e.g. are the lips rounded for /uw/)?

Length   Does the vowel have the appropriate length (e.g. is /iy/ longer than /ɪ/)? Are stressed vowels longer than unstressed ones?

Reduction   Are vowels reduced in unstressed syllables (is the second vowel in a word such as 'campus' pronounced as schwa)?

Linking   Are vowels being properly linked to other vowels across word boundaries (e.g. two oranges)?

From diagnosis to syllabus design

Having completed a diagnostic profile for each student, the teacher is in a position to make choices for the group and for individuals within the group. Prior to the actual selection of items, however, the teacher may wish to discuss the syllabus with students. (See Richard 1986 for a description of such an approach.)

Decisions as to the selection and ordering of items within each category of the student diagnostic profile can be made after several questions have been considered. In general, these questions relate to the time available for pronunciation work; the importance of pronunciation accuracy to a particular class; students' overall English proficiency; the effect of pronunciation items on students' comprehensibility; the relative difficulty of items and their frequency of use. (Catford 1985 discussed a pronunciation syllabus based, in part, on frequency of pronunciation items.) For example, less advanced students appear to benefit more from work on suprasegmentals as such work greatly increases their comprehensibility even when individual segments are mispronounced.

A syllabus should be designed in accordance with the 'zoom principle.' General speaking habits can be worked on in every class. Then, one by one, intonation patterns can be practised. As a student moves from more controlled practice of a pattern to more communicative work, the focus can be shifted to include a very specific problem such as an individual sound. Below, each of the categories from the diagnostic profile sheet is considered with respect to the 'how' of the syllabus.

General speaking habits

All students must be sensitized as to the effect of poor speaking habits on communication. An instructor can quite easily demonstrate the adverse effects of such habits by using humorous exaggerations. However, this must be done with tact and sensitivity to avoid embarrassing students and destroying confidence. It is suggested that teachers use examples from outside the class (e.g. video or audio tapes), without linking particular poor speaking habits to particular students.

More proficient students may also be interested in discussing how good speaking habits help compensate for pronunciation difficulties. In addition, cross-cultural norms for oral communication can be discussed. In keeping with the 'zoom principle,' all pronunciation teaching should first focus on general speaking habits and, if necessary, should continue to return to them.

Intonation

Intonation practice should be included in the pronunciation syllabus whether students are beginners or advanced. With more basic classes, the focus should be on the use of appropriate intonation patterns and the appropriate pitch range of English. (For some excellent intonation practice see Esarey 1977 and Morley 1979.)

In introducing intonation patterns to more advanced classes, it is useful to discuss accompanying nonverbal cues. Often, for example, speakers may open their eyes wider than normal and tilt their heads when asking a question. Cross-cultural comparisons of nonverbal cues may be discussed. Work can be also be done on the interpretation and production of intonation patterns which express attitudes towards what is said (e.g. answering 'yes' to a question but using an intonation pattern which suggests uncertainty by rising at the end).

Stress and rhythm

Stress and rhythm practice should be included in every pronunciation syllabus. Different points can be emphasized as students become increasingly proficient.

In general, a syllabus for basic students should allow for the practice of stress and rhythm with key vocabulary items and simple sentence patterns. Names, addresses, telephone numbers, and other 'survival' words and phrases can be practised using both visual clues (capital letters or underlining for stressed syllables, diagonal slashes through letters for indicating the use of the schwa) or kinesic clues (clapping hands or beating time for stress, wave-like motions with hands for showing pitch levels). Poems, limericks, skipping rhymes, and songs with accompanying hand or body movements can reinforce stress, rhythm, and intonation patterns. Simple rules can be taught (e.g. stress the first word of compound nouns; stress the syllable preceding '-ion' endings).

With more advanced students teachers can pay attention to the consonant system and features of it which facilitate the production of rhythm patterns, particularly in more relaxed speech (e.g. pronouncing words such as 'butter' and phrases like 'What a book' with a 'd-like' flap sound /D/ rather than a /t/ sound; combining identical sounds across word boundaries instead of pronouncing them twice as in 'Did Donna bake a cake?').

Similarly, students can be taught to shift consonant sounds from the end of a word to the beginning of the next word (e.g. an orange, with a, watch it). This *linking* of words minimizes jerkiness and maintains rhythm. It also helps students with listening comprehension. (For excellent stress and rhythm activities see Bowen 1975 and Gilbert 1984.)

Consonants

Using the diagnostic profile in the Appendix, an instructor can record the nature of each consonant problem and then develop priorities for these. In general, consonant sounds are easier for students to modify than vowel sounds are. This is because consonant production can be more easily illustrated and felt by the speaker; furthermore, production can often be observed using mirrors. When selecting the order of work on consonants, several points are helpful to remember. Consonants made in the front of the mouth (e.g. /m/, /f/) are generally easier to correct than are consonants made in the middle or back of the mouth (e.g. /ʃ/, /ŋ/). Another consideration is the fact that certain consonants do not occur as frequently as others. For example, /ʃ/ and /ʒ/ are less frequent than /s/ and /z/ (Gimson 1980). Students may have difficulty with consonants in specific positions in words or in specific combinations with other consonants (e.g. /θ/ in final position, 'with', but not in initial position, 'thick'; /l/ in 'wealth', but not in 'lake').

In designing a syllabus, teachers can sometimes boost morale by ensuring that the first consonants taught are ones which students perceive to be important for good pronunciation. For example, the incorrect pronunciation of /θ/ and /ð/ may not seriously interfere with comprehensibility, but may be of concern to students. In addition, the /θ/ and /ð/ sounds are relatively easy to teach as they are visible and can be felt; this gives students the confidence to tackle more difficult sounds.

Work on consonants should include sound/spelling correspondences to allow students to predict pronunciation accurately. In addition, variations in the pronunciation of grammatical endings should also be introduced.

Vowels

In selecting vowel sounds to focus on, it is wise to begin with those which contribute most to the production of correct stress and rhythm patterns. As mentioned before, the schwa is the most frequently heard vowel sound in English. (See Woods 1979b for a summary of the frequency of English vowel sounds.) Students must be able to produce the schwa sound in unstressed syllables.

Following work on the schwa, students can be encouraged to practise the off-glide sounds in the tense vowels /iy/, /ey/, /ow/, and /uw/. In many languages these are pure sounds, but in English they consist of two parts: the tongue begins in the position for the pure vowel and moves toward the position associated with /y/ or /w/. The tense vowels are found more frequently in stressed syllables than are the lax or 'short' vowels /ɪ/, /ɛ/, /æ/, or /ʊ/. Helping students produce the tense vowels with an appropriate off-glide will help them to hold the sound longer. This will in turn contribute to the student's production of accurate stress and rhythm patterns.

The most difficult vowel sounds to correct are the lax vowels. Substitution of /iy/ for /ɪ/, for example, will persist long after other problems have disappeared. Because of this, concentration on these sounds can be kept for advanced classes.

All work on vowels should be reinforced by referring to sound/spelling relationships. (See Morley 1979 for a summary of the frequency of spelling patterns for each English vowel sound.)

Monitoring progress

Part of a syllabus should be devoted to developing strategies in students for self-monitoring and self-correcting in order that students gradually become independent of the pronunciation teacher. (See Chapters 14 (page 215) and 9 (page 163) in this section, for more detailed comments on self-monitoring.) Students must be able to focus on areas of weakness, listen for errors, and correct those errors. To develop this ability, students require adequate feedback during class time from their instructor and their peers. With adequate feedback they can learn to evaluate their own performance and measure their progress in pronunciation.

Both the teacher and the student must remember that pronunciation change is gradual in nature. Pronunciation inaccuracies do not miraculously disappear; instead, production becomes more accurate by stages. A realistic set of expectations and positive, constructive feedback from peers and the instructor will help keep motivation among students high.

Conclusion

The design of a pronunciation sylllabus will be most effective if steps are first taken to identify student needs through an analysis of learner variables. This should be followed by a careful diagnosis of students' pronunciation problems. The choice and ordering of items in a syllabus will then be influenced by the results of this diagnosis as well as learner variables. When teaching a pronunciation course, it is important that the teacher keep in mind the 'zoom principle'. Remember that the goal of pronunciation teaching is to make the students more effective in their attempts at communication in English. In general, a pronunciation syllabus should begin with wide angle approach and narrow the focus as students master the elements which contribute most to comprehensibility. In other words, more 'global' aspects of pronunciation such as general speaking habits and suprasegmentals should take priority over more 'local' aspects such as segmentals.

Appendix

Table 10.1: Student diagnostic profile

LEARNER VARIABLES

Background

Name: _____ Age: _____ Length of residence: _____

Native language: _____ Other languages spoken: _____

Education: _____

Occupation: _____

Is English used in the workplace? _____

Frequency of use of English: _____

English proficiency level: Basic ☐   Intermediate ☐   Advanced ☐

Standardized test scores: _____

General speaking habits

a Clarity: very intelligible _ _ _ _ _ _ unintelligible

b Speed: very fast _ _ _ _ _ _ very slow

c Loudness: easily heard _ _ _ _ _ _ difficult to hear

d Breath groups: too many pauses _ _ _ _ _ _ not enough pauses

e Eye gaze: appropriate _ _ _ _ _ _ inappropriate

f Fluency: fluent _ _ _ _ _ _ halting

g Voice: pitch range too narrow?   voice too nasal?

h Other:

Intonation

a Statement (final rising-falling)

b Yes-No question (final rising)

c Wh-question (final rising-falling)

d Tag questions (final rising and final rising-falling)

e Series (non-final rising)

Stress and rhythm

a Word level stress

b Phrase / sentance level stress

c Linking

Consonants

Consonant	Key Word	Substitution	Omission	Articulation	Clusters	Linking	Rank
/p/	Poland						
/b/	Bolivia						
/m/	Mexico						
/f/	Finland						
/v/	Vietnam						
/θ/	Lithuania						
/ð/	The U.S.						
/t/	Tanzania						
/d/	Denmark						
/s/	Singapore						
/z/	Zambia						
/n/	Norway						
/l/	Libya						
/r/	Romania						
/ʃ/	Bangladesh						
/ʒ/	Malaysia						
/tʃ/	China						
/dʒ/	Japan						
/k/	Canada						
/g/	Guyana						
/ŋ/	Hong Kong						
/w/	Wales						
/y/	Yemen						
/h/	Hungary						

Vowels (Key Words adapted from Finger 1985)

Vowel	Key Word	Substitution	Articulation	Length	Reduction	Linking	Rank
/iy/	green						
/ɪ/	pink						
/ey/	grey						
/ɛ/	red						
/æ/	black						
/ay/	sky blue						
/aw/	brown						
/oy/	turquoise						
/ər/	purple						
/ʌ/	mustard						
/ə/	tomato						
/uw/	blue						
/ʊ/	wood						
/ow/	yellow						
/ɔ/	auburn						
/a/	olive						

11 SUPRASEGMENTALS IN THE PRONUNCIATION CLASS: SETTING PRIORITIES

Maureen McNerney and David Mendelsohn

Introduction

When asked to teach pronunciation courses, ESL teachers are invariably faced with a situation in which they have limited time. Discussion with such teachers and an examination of some traditional pronunciation texts quickly reveal that the norm has been to devote the majority of time and effort to segmentals (individual sounds), and usually vowels. This is because in a multilingual group of ESL learners, vowels usually pose more of a problem than consonants. Teachers and texts usually begin with the high front vowels, and then work around the vowel chart systematically, followed by some work on diphthongs and selected consonantal problems. This segmental work, which takes up the majority of the time available, is occasionally followed by some brief superficial attention to stress and intonation.

We believe that the traditional approach to teaching pronunciation gives priority to the wrong aspects of pronunciation. This stems from a failure to grasp the importance of suprasegmentals—'those features of speech which extend over more than one segment, such as intonation [and stress]' (Crystal 1980:314). Suprasegmentals are extremely important in the communication of meaning in spoken language. It is the suprasegmentals that control the structure of information. This will be discussed in detail below. What is more, being able to comprehend or to convey the intended attitude in English hinges on mastery of suprasegmentals. Unfortunately, suprasegmental features such as stress and intonation are often treated by ESL teachers as 'peripheral frills' and not as central to the conveying of meaning. The truth, however, is that they are far *more* important and central to communication than accurate production of the individual sounds, because individual sounds can usually be inferred from the context. For example, if a student says 'I cooked the meat in a pen' (meaning 'pan'), it is very simple to interpret the correct meaning. If, on the other hand, a student, in response to hearing the statement: 'He went on holiday', says the words: 'Where did he go?' with rising intonation, although his/her intention was to find out the location of the holiday (which calls for rising-falling intonation), this will be processed by native speakers as expressing surprise or requiring confirmation that he had indeed gone on holiday. The context will not help to clarify this question. (For further detail, see Benson, Greaves, and Mendelsohn 1988.)

No pronunciation course can teach everything. Therefore, we are arguing that a short-term pronunciation course should focus first and foremost on suprasegmentals, as they have the greatest impact on the comprehensibility of learners' English. We have found that giving priority to the suprasegmental aspects of English not only improves learners' comprehensibility, but is also less frustrating for students because greater change can be effected in a short time.

This chapter provides a set of priorities for a short-term pronunciation course. These include: stress/unstress, major sentence stress, intonation, linking, and pausing. Following a brief description of each of these aspects of English pronunciation, some classroom activities are suggested. Many of the ideas and exercises presented below are drawn from the work of Morley (1979), Gilbert (1984), and Wong (1987).

It should be borne in mind throughout the discussion below that pronunciation work should always be tied to meaning; it should *never* be purely mechanical. As Wong (1987:2) states: 'The goal of pronunciation teaching is to foster communicative effectiveness.'

Stress/unstress

Word level

Research has shown that incorrect stressing of polysyllabic words greatly affects comprehensibility. For example, a graduate student in linguistics once said that he was doing research on 'me*ta*phors', and only when he gave an example did we realize what was intended. The same is true of proper nouns. A guide in Paris announced: 'Now we are going to see the famous 'Mo*na*lisa', which patterned like the word 'an*a*lysis'. It took several minutes for this to be processed as 'Mona Lisa'. These errors in stress can take the form of stressing the wrong syllable within a word or, more commonly, of assigning equal stress to all syllables within a word. For example, pronouncing 'pro*noun*cing' as '*pro-noun-cing*' makes it sound as if it has something to do with 'pronouns'.

Errors in word stress are often a result of transfer from the learner's first language. For example, stress in Punjabi usually falls on the first syllable of a word, so that a Punjabi speaker is likely to pronounce '*a*bove' and 'be*low*' as '*a*bove' and '*be*low'. Or conversely, Hebrew usually places the word stress on the last syllable of a word, so that Hebrew speakers are likely to say 'si*lent*' for '*si*lent'.

When introducing new vocabulary items, teachers should be as concerned about correct stress patterns as they are about correct usage. (See Chapter 5, 'Word stress and vowel reduction' (page 67), for some generalizations about the placement of word stress in English.) Always ensure that students are able to stress new vocabulary items correctly. Do not assume that hearing the word pronounced will necessarily result in correct stress placement. What is more, from the very first introduction of a new vocabulary item, care must be taken not only to stress the word correctly, but also to *unstress* it correctly; that is, the word should not, for reasons of clarity, be produced with stress where unstress is in fact called for. For example, the word '*band*age' should not be given as '*band-age*'. The same rule should be adhered to in all dictation work.

Sentence level

From the outset, students should be made aware that unstress is not a sign of slovenly, careless, or degenerate speech. Rather, it is essential to the appropriate rhythm of English.

Content vs. function words   A very important equation that learners must grasp is that generally, stressed words = content (meaning-carrying) words, and unstressed words = function (grammatical) words. Consider, for example, the following sentences where the content words are stressed and the function words are unstressed:

    •   •   ●   **●**   ●

I want you to take the dog for a walk near the park.

    ●   **●**   •   ●   •

The woman with the gun in her hand is a hospital patient.

The equation of generally stressing content words and generally unstressing grammatical words needs to be tied to the structure of the message: that the stressed words in a sentence minus the grammatical words yields the essence of the message in telegraphic form. This means that attention to the stressed words, which, we will argue, students can learn to identify acoustically, guides them to the essence of the message. This is a very important point for students in their listening, since they can then begin to listen 'selectively', that is, not to give equal attention to every word they hear. This is equally important in their production of English, because competent listeners with whom they interact will be applying precisely the same rule when processing what they hear.

Learners, then, must be able to identify and produce stressed words appropriately, making them louder, clearer, and longer. Unstressed words, on the other hand, are usually reduced, and are thus much shorter than stressed words. The goal is for students to grasp the way the stress/unstress system reflects the way information is structured in English. For more information see Chapter 6, 'Connected speech', page 115.

Activities

Marking stress on nonsense words   Distribute sheets with a set of nonsense sentences modelled on real English sentences. As you read the sentences aloud, students mark the stressed and unstressed words. For example, the teacher could read sentences such as the two below, with the stressed words as indicated with dots. Be careful to reduce the nonsense function words.

●   ●   ● ●

son geefies flugged min hox wazily.

● ●   ● ●

Model: The pilots flew their planes expertly.

● ● ● ●

hy fiss pold deesh tur looty wo um trewy.

● ● ● ●

Model: My dear old friend is busy in the garden.

Working initially with nonsense words rather than English words trains students to listen for the acoustic signals of stress, i.e. the words that are said more loudly, more clearly, and more slowly. Using nonsense words ensures that students give full attention to the words that are stressed.

Marking stressed words in English   Follow the same procedure as with the nonsense words, only this time use real English sentences. For example, students may have a sentence in a text like the following:

It's been raining since she started her vacation.

They would mark the sentence indicating the stressed words:

●   ●   ●

It's been raining since she started her vacation.

A variation on this activity involves having students read the sentences aloud while other students mark the stress.

Telegrams   See Chapter 12 (page 202) for an example of a telegram exercise.

A good variation on this game involves the use of newspaper headlines. The students must construct the full message from the headline.

Stress and rhythm

It is almost a contradiction in terms to ask students to concentrate on unstress, because unstressed vowels tend to be obscured in English. The ultimate goal of stress/unstress work is to teach students to produce utterances whose rhythm will be English-like. This requires that students be made aware of the stress-timed rhythm of English, wherein the amount of time it takes to say a sentence in English depends on the number of syllables receiving stress, not on the number of syllables in the sentence. Students, particularly those who speak syllable-timed languges such as Polish, Cantonese, French, and Spanish, tend to give equal stress to every syllable and to space all the syllables equally. This is only appropriate when, as in the following English sentence, all the syllables are stressed:

● ● ● ●
Please use John's car.

However, problems occur when students produce the following sentence of seven syllables with equal stress on all syllables when it should be produced with only four stressed syllables:

● ● ● ● ●● ●
Linda can use Charlie's car.

When a student does not produce utterances with the appropriate rhythm, the results can range from incomprehension to annoyance on the part of the listener.

Activities

Expanding sentences   Construct sentences in which the number of stressed syllables is the same, but the number of unstressed syllables varies. Have the students read the sentences provided and then have them create their own:

● ● ● ●
Lynn used Tim's car.

● ● ● ●
Linda uses Timothy's car.

● · ● ·
Linda could've driven Manfred's car.

Tapping   To ensure that students have perceived the characteristic rhythm of English, use sentences such as those above and have them tap out the stressed syllables at regular intervals. It is also possible to have the students speak in time to a metronome. Virtually any language sample could be used for this activity.

Major sentence stress

Major sentence stress generally occurs on the content word of a sentence to which the speaker is directing the listener's attention. This is often referred to as the *information focus* of a sentence. Major sentence stress usually falls on the last content word of a sentence. This is not always the case, however, as the last content word does not necessarily coincide with the information focus. Variation in major sentence stress can be illustrated with a series of questions and answers.

Where did he go?

      ●
He went to Ottawa.

If this exchange were followed by:

      ●
How did he get there?

The answer would not be:

      ●
He drove to Ottawa.

but rather:

   ●
He drove to Ottawa.

or, simply:

   ●
He drove.

Here, the place, Ottawa, is no longer the information focus and so does not receive the major sentence stress. The focus is now on the means of transportation.

Similarly, the following two sentences convey very different meanings:

    ●
Harry went to Barbados.

 ●
Harry went to Barbados.

The first sentence is simple statement of fact; the speaker is merely reporting that Harry went to Barbados. The second sentence, with the major sentence stress on Harry, has a rather different interpretation. The fact that someone went to Barbados is already shared information. The focussed information is that it was Harry and not anyone else who went to Barbados.

Traditionally, if handled at all, pronunciation work on the placement of major sentence stress has involved mechanical production of such strings as the following, with the major stress being shifted to different positions in the same sentence:

       ●
My uncle from Calgary's a dentist.

     ●
My uncle from Calgary's a dentist.

  ●
My uncle from Calgary's a dentist.

 ●
My uncle from Calgary's a dentist.

The ability to produce these mechanically is, in our opinion, inadequate, if not futile. Contextualization and the linking of sentence stress to meaning are essential.

Activities

It should be noted that shifts in major sentence stress occur in dialogues where information is being exchanged. Consequently, we recommend that dialogues be used extensively in the practice of this pronunciation feature.

Dialogues   Gilbert (1984) provides some excellent contextualized practice in manipulating major sentence stress. Her dialogues show the relation of major stress to the information structure of a longer stretch of speech.

Dialogue 1

A Where are you going?

B Europe.

A Where in Europe? to the north or to the south?

B Neither. I've already been north and south. I'm going east.

Dialogue 2

X What've you been doing?

Y I've been studying.

X Studying what? Math or English?

Y Neither. I'm sick of math and English. I'm studying nutrition, because

I'm always hungry.

(Gilbert 1984: 28–9)

Paraphrasing   In this activity, the teacher reads sentences with the major sentence stress located in different positions. The students are required to paraphrase each sentence, indicating an understanding of the focussed information.

Teacher The chair in the garden is broken.
Student It's the chair in the garden, not the one elsewhere, that's broken.

Teacher Well, I liked the movie.
Student Someone else may have disliked the movie, but I liked it.

Multiple choice   The above exercise can also be done as a multiple choice. Prepare a set of sentences like the one in the following example:

The man wearing the baseball cap is the murderer.

The teacher reads this sentence aloud, placing the major sentence stress in a position that makes one of the following choices appropriate:

a A simple statement of fact that the man in the baseball cap is the murderer.
b It's the man, not the woman, in the baseball cap that is the murderer.
c It's the man in the baseball cap, not any other man, that is the murderer.

The student must decide which paraphrase is equivalent in meaning to what the teacher said.

Questions   Another useful exercise in the mastery of major sentence stress involves asking the students questions that require them to place the major sentence stress on the appropriate word in their answers. In each case, the student repeats the same sentence but assigns major sentence stress to a different word. (A variation of this activity would be to prepare a set of pictures and ask questions about them.)

My doctor is great.

Teacher Who is great?

Student My doctor is great.

Teacher Whose doctor is great?

Student My doctor is great.

Intonation

Intonation is not only central to conveying meaning in spoken English but is also important in conveying the attitude of the speaker towards what is being said. A simple word such as 'oh' spoken with different intonation contours can express meanings which range from complicity to shock and disbelief, from surprise to disappointment, from 'I didn't know that' to frustration. Students must grasp the function of intonation in conveying attitude and be able to recognize the difference between different intonation contours.

Final falling intonation is the most common pattern used in the production of English sentences. It is used in most statements, commands, and *wh*-questions. Final rising intonation is used primarily in 'yes-no' questions. The rising pitch indicates to the listener that the speaker genuinely does not know whether the answer is yes or no.

Tag questions can be produced with either rising or falling intonation. When a tag question is spoken with falling intonation, it is referred to as a rhetorical question as no answer is sought; simple agreement is expected: (e.g. 'It's hot today, isn't it?'—no answer sought). With rising intonation, the tag question requires a yes or no answer (e.g. 'It's payday, isn't it?'—possible answer: 'No, payday is tomorrow').

Special kinds of questions can be produced by using rising intonation on a declarative sentence (e.g. 'She's going to Japan?'), in echo questions (e.g. 'She's going where?') or even on a partial repetition of an utterance (e.g. '... an accident?'). These are usually expressions of surprise or disbelief, or requests for confirmation, and are seldom taught in ESL classrooms. This is probably because they do not fit the regular grammatical rules we all learned. We believe that they should be taught, as students should be made aware of the flexibility of spoken English.

Activities

Eliciting information   Any activity focusing on the function of asking for/giving directions, suggestions, instructions, etc. gives a great deal of contextualized communicative practice in both *wh*-question intonation and yes-no question intonation. Construct information gap activities to be done in pairs where one student must elicit certain information from the other member of the pair. Possible questions that could be formed in eliciting information about the post office are provided below:

> Where is the post office?
> How do I get there?
> Are you sure?
> When is it open?
> Till six?
> How much is an overseas letter?

Using persuasion   Tag questions with both rising and falling intonation can easily be practised through activities requiring information-getting and persuasion. Taped commercials can be used for this purpose and then students can make up their own advertisements using the same technique.

> A You're looking for a new apartment, aren't you?
> B Yes, I am.
> A You're a student, aren't you?
> B Yes.
> A You don't have a lot of money to spend on housing, do you?
> B No, I don't.
> A Then you'd like our new Metropolitan Apartments that are only $400.00 a month, wouldn't you?

The listener in all cases is required to determine the 'meaning' behind the speaker's questions and should respond appropriately. This not only assesses the listener's awareness of what is being asked, but also the speaker's ability to produce the appropriate intonation pattern (based on the speaker's desired outcome of the interaction).

Analyzing tapes   Bring a tape of native speaker conversation into class and have the students listen to the intonation patterns. Bring to their attention the attitudes conveyed through the use of intonation.

Linking and pausing

Differences in linking and pausing can convey different sentence structures. Consider the following two sentences (after Gilbert 1984):

> 'John', said the professor, 'is disorganized'.
> John said, 'The professor is disorganized'.

The difference in structure and meaning of these two sentences is clearly indicated by the different location of pauses.

When no pauses occur between words, we say that the words are linked. In sentences where linking is required students must not pronounce words as separate entities, but make the words flow smoothly together. Linking should be introduced to students, not only as a natural aspect of connected speech, but also as a necessary one for comprehensibility. There are times when a potentially ambiguous sentence can only be disambiguated when the appropriate linking (combined with the appropriate stress and intonation pattern) is used. Consider the example below, where the meaning changes depending on whether the pronoun 'him' is linked to the preceding verb 'hit'.

> John hit Bill and then Tom hit him.
> **a** John hit Bill and then Tom hit *him*. [paraphrased as John hit Bill and then Tom hit John.]
> **b** John hit Bill and then Tom hit 'im. [paraphrased as John hit Bill and then Tom hit Bill.]

Incorrect linking and pausing can cause misunderstanding not only in examples such as the one above, but also in our world of numbers and codes (phone numbers, postal or zip codes, etc.). The inability to pause and link appropriately can have serious consequences, particularly when relevant information is given orally. For example, an address consisting of a number and then a numbered street name (e.g. 3021 211th Street) produced with incorrect pausing could lead to an undelivered package! Exercises to help students with linking and pausing are provided below.

Activities

Identify the sentence   Prepare pairs of sentences, such as those below, and have the students identify which member of the pair you are reading. Then have the students try them on each other.

> 'Alfred', said the Boss, 'is stupid'.
> Alfred said, 'The Boss is stupid'.

> He sold his house, boat, and trailer.
> He sold his houseboat and trailer.

> She likes pie and apples.
> She likes pineapples.
> > (Gilbert 1984: 48–9)

> She wants a coconut burger.
> She wants a coke and a burger.
> > (Acton 1984)

Information sharing   Have the students exchange phone numbers, postal codes, addresses, birthdays, and other number groupings relevant to their lives. You could also have them spell their own names or street names aloud. All of these activities require that the students pause and link properly. When someone gives a phone number incorrectly, this can cause confusion. For example, someone who gives a phone number as 534 pause 734 pause 8 would not necessarily be understood by a native North American English speaker.

Analyzing tapes   Bring a tape of native speaker conversation into class and have the students listen to the patterns of pausing and linking. It may be helpful to provide a transcript of the conversation. Note where the speakers pause and discuss the possible reasons for their pauses.

Palatalization

In casual conversation, we pronounce sequences of words such as 'would you' and 'could you' as /wʊdʒə/ and /kʊdʒə/ (see Chapter 6, 'Connected speech', page 87, for a description of palatalization). These pronunciations indicate a less formal atmosphere and, therefore, a closer relationship between speakers. Students need to be able to recognize and comprehend such patterns and the relationship intended. What is more, the ability to switch to these forms of speech allows the ESL student to shift from a formal to an informal style of speech in a natural way.

It is extremely important that students are assured that these forms in English are neither sloppy nor incorrect; they are, on the contrary, natural and appropriate in many situations.

Activities

Invitation and persuasion   Present a situation such as the following to students:

> You have arranged to have a surprise birthday party for your friend at her/his house. Your job is to get her/him out of the house so that things can be set up. Your friend refuses your invitation to go out.

It then becomes necessary for a form of persuasion to take place using such phrases as:

> Why can't you go out with me?
> Couldn't you change your plans?
> Won't you change your plans?
> Won't you try to get a babysitter?
> Did you have something special to do?
> Would you like to do something else?

Advertising campaign   Have students set up an advertising campaign. They must persuade the rest of the class to buy a service or product, to visit their home country, etc.

'Would you', 'could you', 'did you', 'can't you', 'won't you', etc. are all phrases which could be used in this context and they all contain sound combinations which would be palatalized.

> Wouldn't you like to spend a month by the sea?
> Can't you imagine yourself driving this magnificent car?
> Don't you think you need a holiday?
> Did you ever dream of paradise? Well, that's what my country's like.

Conclusion

In this chapter, we have argued that the pronunciation teacher must give priority to suprasegmental features. Although this may require a shift in focus, the adoption of new material, or the adaptation of existing material, we feel that it is through focussing on the suprasegmental features that the short-term pronunciation course can be of greatest benefit to students.

12 PRONUNCIATION-BASED LISTENING EXERCISES

Ilsa Mendelson Burns

Introduction

In *A Manual of American English Pronunciation* (Prator and Robinett 1985:xvi), it is stated that the first step in learning to pronounce is 'learning to hear and identify a sound or sound contrast when a native speaker produces it'. By contrast, Penny Ur (1984:12), in *Teaching Listening Comprehension*, maintains that 'it is certainly true that if the learner learns to pronounce . . . sounds accurately . . ., it will be much easier . . . to hear them correctly when said by someone else'.

Experience tells us that neither of these statements is completely true. If our students had to be capable of hearing a sound distinction before producing it, we would certainly encounter frustration and boredom when faced with the monotony of the time-consuming drill-type exercises that become necessary in order to achieve our somewhat unrealistic goal. We would have to require students to perform perfectly on sound recognition tasks before moving on to sound production tasks. This would amount to having students recognize the difference between 'seat' and 'sit' (and other minimal pairs of this type) all of the time, and only then moving on to the production of the distinction. If the particular sound distinction were not meaningful in the student's native language, or if one or both segments did not exist in the student's native language, the effort required to perform accurately on a sound discrimination task might discourage students from ever achieving comprehensible speech.

On the other hand, if accurate pronunciation were to be a prerequisite for comprehension tasks, as Ur seems to maintain, we would conclude that only those learners who had mastered the pronunciation of a particular sound would ever be able to distinguish that sound from a phonetically similar one. Yet we have all seen advanced, fluent students who are perfectly able to make fine discriminations aurally while still being unable to make them orally.

In this chapter, I do not claim that students have to succeed in comprehension before production, or in production before comprehension. I do claim, however, that exposure to listening exercises of the type provided in this article will help students to realize what has to be accomplished in the production of English sounds. We can help our students most by concentrating on how native speakers actually pronounce the sounds that we expect them to produce. The focus in this chapter is on teaching pronunciation through listening activities.

The activities presented below not only improve students' listening comprehension, but also heighten their awareness of certain aspects of English pronunciation. These activities involve the recognition of specific sounds, stress patterns, sound modifications, and intonation contours. They should be an integral part of the pronunciation class and can be viewed as complementing the students' production activities. They can reinforce grammatical points or language functions that have been covered at another time. They allow the pressure to be taken off students who feel uncomfortable or embarrassed when speaking in front of a group. They encourage co-operation among classmates, thus enhancing the enjoyable aspects of classroom learning for everyone. In addition, the students receive immediate feedback, so frustration, which is frequently present in the traditional pronunciation class, is minimized.

The multi-level class

Classes which are composed of students of various proficiency levels often present a challenge to the teacher of pronunciation. Indeed, many traditional techniques that are suitable for advanced students cannot be used with beginners. Similarly, material that is appropriate for beginners is soon rejected by more proficient students. The activities in this chapter help to minimize these problems. They provide reticent learners with the opportunity to remain out of the limelight, while still being able to gain confidence, as they master new skills. And better students, who might be more willing to take risks, are able to try out new-found skills in an active and challenging manner.

The multi-lingual class

Mixed classes, with students from a variety of language backgrounds, are also often a source of anxiety to the teacher of pronunciation. The various pronunciation problems often seem too numerous to tackle in a short time. The activities given here can accommodate many students with very different types of pronunciation problems. The variety of activities will enable the teacher to select features that present difficulties to all students (see Chapter 7, 'Common problems').

Procedure

Although handouts are mentioned in the description of the activities below, the chalkboard can also be used. With all of the exercises, students can provide their answers in writing. With some of the activities, students could indicate their responses by raising their hands, pointing to the correct answer or saying a word or number. Before the teacher supplies the correct answers, students can work in pairs or groups so that they have the opportunity to compare their responses. This provides additional practice in speaking and adds variety to otherwise test-like activities. Ensure that you go over your students' mistakes, contrasting the incorrect with the correct responses. Too many errors usually indicates that the students haven't grasped the point, and that you will have to present it again. These tasks become futile when the students' responses are based on chance and not on the ability to listen effectively.

One of the more common complaints among ESL students concerns the difference between the language heard in the ESL classroom and the language heard in the 'real' world. Students may be able to understand their teachers but are not necessarily able to transfer this ability to the world outside the classroom. It is, therefore, incumbent upon the teacher to provide students with natural speech. In using the activities below, it is important that the teacher speak at a natural pace and with as little distortion in the articulation of sounds as possible. This differs from work on the production of sounds or sound contrasts, where it is often essential to exaggerate one's pronunciation. Some of the activities presented below will aid students in understanding the sound modifications and reductions which are so prevalent in natural speech, while others simply focus on the recognition of sound contrasts. None of the activities should be presented until the particular aspect of pronunciation under consideration has been demonstrated and explained in class.

Minimal pairs

Minimal pairs can make students aware of troublesome sounds. In selecting pairs, try to use words with which your students are familiar so that they will appreciate the importance of performing well. For further details on minimal pairs, see page 207.

Identification task

Give the students two columns of words which are minimal pairs, such as those listed under 'Vowels' below. Read one member of a pair and have the students indicate whether you are reading from Column 1 or Column 2.

	Vowels		Consonants	
	1	2	1	2
Contrast	pan	pen	thank	sank
	sand	send	thick	sick
	land	lend	thumb	some
	laughed	left	tenth	tense
	ham	hem	mouth	mouse

Discrimination task

Prepare a list of word pairs such as those under 'Vowels' below. Some of these pairs should repeat the same word and some should be minimal pairs. Read each pair aloud to the students, having them indicate on a piece of paper whether the words are the same (S) or different (D). This exercise serves as a good diagnostic test, as you can determine the particular sound contrasts which present difficulties for your students.

Vowels			Consonants			
1 beet	bit	D	1 chair	share	D	
2 green	green	S	2 sheet	sheet	S	
3 sin	scene	D	3 sherry	cherry	D	
4 slip	slip	S	4 watch	watch	S	

Isolation task

Read aloud a list of four words, three of which are the same. Have the students identify the one which is different.

Vowels

1 bit	beat	beat	beat
2 pool	pool	pool	pull
3 tan	tan	ten	tan
4 bet	bait	bet	bet

Consonants

1 play	pray	pray	pray
2 save	save	save	safe
3 raced	raised	raced	raced
4 tank	thank	tank	tank

Sorting task

Give the students one word as a representative of each vowel sound you have introduced. Read aloud a number of common one-syllable words which contain these sounds. Have the students place the words in the appropriate column (i.e. under the word with the same vowel sound).

1	2	3	4	5
beat	bit	bait	bet	bat

Example words: 'mitt', 'plate', 'feet', 'tan', 'mad', 'desk', 'me', 'lake', 'egg', 'ran', 'head', 'scene', 'fit', 'trip', 'raise', etc.

Minimal pair sentence task

Give students pairs of sentences which differ in terms of a single sound. Read one of the sentences aloud. Have the students indicate which one you are reading.

Notice that the students must make this choice solely on the basis of a single sound contrast because each sentence is meaningful. Be careful! It is difficult to create meaningful sentences which contain minimal pairs. For some good examples, see Gilbert (1984) and Prator and Robinett (1985).

1 a John bit the dog.
   b John beat the dog.

2 a Show me your bag.
   b Show me your back.

3 a He wants to sell his boat.
   b He wants to sail his boat.

4 a He loves sweet yams.
   b He loves sweet jams.

Picture task

Draw or cut out pictures of objects which contain difficult sound contrasts (e.g. 'pen' vs. 'pan', 'sheep' vs. 'ship', 'lake' vs. 'rake', etc.). Read aloud sentences such as the ones below, having students follow the instructions. Later, have them work in pairs or small groups.

Circle the *pen.*
Put a square around the *sheep.*
Put an X through the *rake.*

Stress assignment

Schwa identification task

Prepare a list of two-syllable words, all of which are related to your daily classroom work. Read them aloud and have your students cross out the reduced vowel.

student   forget   lettuce   open   connect

Stress identification task

Prepare a list of polysyllabic words. Read them aloud in random order and have your students indicate which syllable is stressed.

Stressed syllable:	**first**	**second**	**third**
	music	musician	sympathetic
	photograph	photography	photographic
	fortune	forgive	admiration

Discrimination task

Give your students a list of various pairs of polysyllabic words. Have them indicate whether the stress falls on the same syllable in each pair of words.

a purpose—prevent   D
b possible—vegetable   S
c economy—economic   D
d before—maybe   D
e morning—table   S

Function words

Telegrams

Before introducing the following exercise, it is important to make students aware of the distinction between content and function words. This can best be done by bringing up the topic of telegrams, which should be familiar to most students. Begin by explaining that you must send a telegram, then give details of the message, which should be adapted to the level and interests of your students. For example:

TO: YOUR FRIEND IN SAN FRANCISCO

MESSAGE: MY AUNT WILL ARRIVE ON SUNDAY AT 4:00 FROM TOKYO. PLEASE MEET HER AT THE AIRPORT IN CUSTOMS AND TRANSLATE FOR HER.

The students, in pairs, attempt to create the shortest (and cheapest!) telegram, while still preserving the meaning of the message. The attempts can be written on the board, with a discussion of the relative merits of each pair's response. The students should come up with:

AUNT ARRIVE SUNDAY 4:00 TOKYO. MEET AIRPORT CUSTOMS TRANSLATE.

Once a consensus has been reached, have the students listen attentively while you read the entire (original) message aloud. Ask them to focus on the difference betweeen the words that they omitted from the message and the words that they left in the telegram. The message should sound like this:

MY **AUNT** WILL **ARRIVE** ON **SUNDAY** AT **4:00** FROM **TOKYO**. PLEASE **MEET** HER AT THE **AIRPORT** IN **CUSTOMS** AND **TRANSLATE** FOR HER.

Note that the words in bold type receive prominence, while the words that are omitted from the telegram are spoken much more quickly and less clearly. It is also worth pointing out that by eliminating 13 words from a 22-word message, little meaning has been lost. This should encourage elementary students to refrain from attempting to understand *every* word that they hear. At the same time, intermediate and advanced students will be encouraged to interpret the sound changes that they hear.

This opportunity to heighten students' awareness of the vowel reductions and deletions in function words will aid the students in their attempts to produce fluent English and to comprehend the speech of native English speakers outside the classroom.

See Ur (1989) for a discussion of the advantages of competition between students in maintaining a high level of interest and motivation in the classroom.

Focussing on reduction

Prepare a list of sentences. Read the sentences aloud and ask your students to supply the function words.

Prepositions
1 Come (for) tea (at) four.
2 Fly (to) Toronto (in) July.

Articles
1 (The) bus was late.
2 Give me (an) apple.
3 He wants (a) meal.

Modals/auxiliary verbs
1 John (can) talk to you now.
2 They (have) (been) running.
3 What (do) you do?

Conjunctions
1 Give John bread (and) jam.
2 He seems tired (but) happy.

Pronouns
1 Give (him) the boot.
2 Give (her) a break.
3 That's (our) car.

Sentence stress task

Read a list of sentences aloud and have the students indicate which words are stressed and which are unstressed. As with the telegram exercise, this develops students' ability to distinguish between stressed and unstressed words, helping them to become aware of which words in a sentence should be reduced (i.e. the unstressed ones).

    ●   ●   ●   ● ●
The teacher has decided to give us some homework.

Inference task

This exercise requires students to recognize and understand function words in order to make an inference. Prepare sentences like the ones below. The students are provided with two possible responses and must decide which is appropriate based on the form of the function word they hear.

1 **Teacher** John should've studied more.
  Students a Why? Did he fail his exam?
            b Why? Did he pass his exam?

2 **Teacher** Mary can speak French well.
  Students a Where did she learn French?
            b She should take a French course.

Word counting task

Prepare a list of sentences containing instances of modified function words. Read the sentences and have the students indicate how many words there would be in each sentence if the sentence were written. You can easily adapt this exercise to your students' level of English by choosing from a number of possible styles of speech, which are presented here in descending order of difficulty. You might decide to choose some styles as only being suitable for comprehension and not for production.

1 When did you come?
  a Whenja come?
  b When didja come?
  c When didya come?

2 When do you want to go?
  a When dye wanna go?
  b When de ye wanna go?
  c When de ye want te go?

3 Do you know what you are going to do?
  a Ja know whatcha gonna do?
  b De ye know whatcha gonna do?
  c De ye know whatcher gonna do?
  d De ye know what yor going te do?

Intonation

The following exercises focus on a variety of English intonation contours. See Chapter 6, 'Connected speech': 'Intonation' (page 76) for a description of English intonation contours.

Recognizing final rising intonation

Prepare a series of sentences with *declarative* word order. Read them aloud, varying the intonation so that some must be interpreted as yes-no questions and others must be interpreted as statements. Have the students indicate which are questions and which are statements. Alternatively, if the students hear the sentence as a question, instruct them to answer the question.

1 You're coming.
2 He's leaving.
3 The class is over?

Recognizing non-final rising intonation

Prepare a number of 'shopping lists'. Read each one aloud to your students. At times, stop reading *before* the list is over, so that your voice rises on the item that is not final on the list. At other times, read the list to the end. Have the students tell you when the list is finished and when they expect to hear more items. In this way, the students must recognize the difference between non-final rising intonation and final rising-falling intonation.

1 I need apples (and oranges) (and bananas) (and cheese).
2 She ordered a hamburger (and french fries) (and a coke).

Tag questions

Read aloud a number of tag questions, varying the intonation contour of the tag. Have the students indicate whether you are stating a fact (i.e. expecting an affirmative response, and thus engaging in social 'small talk') or genuinely requesting information.

1 It's a beautiful day, isn't it? (falling intonation)
2 You're not hungry, are you? (rising intonation)

Conclusion

Do not expect all students to benefit equally from these exercises. Vary the vocabulary level and the grammatical complexity of your sentences according to the proficiency of your students.

Taped versions of authentic conversations between native English speakers are sure to have fine examples of connected speech that can be used in the listening-pronunciation class. Your students can listen to these recordings in order to focus their attention on spoken English. With beginners, you might not be able to use the tape recorder. However, you can still focus on sound modifications in your own speech.

In general, you should be raising your students' awareness of how English is actually spoken. The listening activities presented above will benefit your students both inside and outside the classroom. They will find it easier to comprehend the speech of native English speakers. At the same time, their increased awareness of English pronunciation may aid them in their own production.

13 TEACHING PRONUNCIATION: AN INVENTORY OF TECHNIQUES

Douglas Jull

Introduction

This article provides an inventory of techniques used in the teaching of pronunciation. Most of these are production-oriented; their purpose is to improve students' production of spoken English. For techniques which emphasize the receptive aspect of pronunciation instruction, see Chapter 12.

Individual sounds

Minimal pairs

Techniques designed for demonstrating the production of individual sounds generally make extensive use of minimal pairs. This term refers to pairs of words which have different meanings and which differ in pronunciation on the basis of one sound only. For example, 'sheep' and 'ship' are a miniminal pair. Both consist of three sounds—a consonant, a vowel, and a consonant—the initial and final consonants are the same (/ʃ/ and /p/) but the vowels are different (/iy/ in 'sheep' and /ɪ/ in 'ship'). Similarly, the words 'ship' and 'sip' constitute a minimal pair because the initial consonants in each words are different (/ʃ/ in 'ship' and /s/ in 'sip'), while the vowel (/ɪ/) and final consonant (/p/) in each are the same.

Let us imagine, for example, that your students fail to distinguish between an initial /b/ and /v/, so that words like 'boat' and 'vote' are pronounced the same (i.e. like 'boat', [bowt]). Minimal pairs can first be used to help students develop an awareness of the distinction between the two sounds. Subsequently, the minimal pairs can be used to improve students' production of this distinction.

To begin to explain the difference between /b/ and /v/, you could put two or three minimal pairs with the /b/–/v/ contrast on the board:

/b/	/v/
boat	vote
berry	very
bat	vat

Tell your students to look at your mouth as you pronounce the pairs of words, and have them pay careful attention to the position of your lips as you make the first sound in each of the words.

Once you are certain that the students are beginning to hear the distinction between /b/ and /v/, put the numbers one and two above the minimal pairs on the blackboard. Pronounce one member of the miminal pair and have the students indicate which word you have said by referring to the appropriate number. Then, say both words of the minimal pair in different orders. This time, the students must indicate the order in which the two words have been pronounced.

After you have demonstrated the production of the contrasting sounds and are certain the students have begun to hear the difference between them, have the students pronounce the minimal pair. They can first repeat the minimal pair after you. Then, you can produce one member of the pair, after which they produce the other. Finally, a student produces one member of a minimal pair and other students identify it.

Once your students have produced the relevant contrasts correctly in minimal pairs of words, you should move to larger units of language, such as minimal pair sentences. Minimal pair sentences are sentences which are identical with the exception of a single sound. An example is provided below:

I like boating.   I like voting.

As with minimal pairs, minimal pair sentences can be used in developing students' ability to recognize sound contrasts and their ability to produce these contrasts.

Do not over-use minimal pairs. The goal of teaching individual sounds is to have students produce the sound contrasts of English in their normal speech. Minimal pairs are isolated examples, and the ability to produce the appropriate distinctions in isolation is not necessarily extended to the students' connected speech. Furthermore, the over-use of minimal pairs can lead to a very boring pronunciation class. Therefore, make sure that you eventually contextualize the sounds which you are working on. For communicative exercises involving individual sounds of English, see Chapter 9, page 163.

A final word of caution regarding minimal pairs concerns the way in which you say them in class. Very often, a teacher will say the two members of a minimal pair, such as 'main' and 'men', and ask the students to say whether or not they notice a difference in pronunciation between the two. The students may say they detect a difference, but that difference may not in fact be between the vowels /ey/ and /ɛ/, but between the intonation of the two words. That is, when we say pairs of words in isolation, we have a tendency to say the two words with different intonation contours: the first word is said with a non-final intonation contour and the second is said with a final intonation contour. In order to avoid this problem, imagine the minimal pair as the first two words in a set of three words. For instance, if you were to say a list of three words (e.g. 'apples', 'oranges', and 'pears'), the first two would be spoken with the same non-final intonation contour (see Chapter 6, 'Connected speech', pages 77–9), for a discussion of final vs. non-final intonation). Therefore, if you want to say 'main' and 'men' with the same intonation, begin as if you were going to say 'main', 'men', and 'man', and simply stop speaking after you have said the first two words.

Visual aids

Exaggerating articulation

There are characteristics about the place and manner of articulation of certain sounds which can be demonstrated visually. Sounds which are easily demonstrated involve the lips (/p/, /b/, and /m/), teeth (/f/ and /v/), and tip of the tongue (/t/, /d/, /n/, /θ/ as in 'think', and /ð/ as in 'this'). For some sounds, a secondary articulation such as lip rounding (/ʒ/ as in 'beige' and /r/) or aspiration (/p/, /t/, /k/) can also be demonstrated visually. All of these sounds are easily 'seen', as well as being easily 'felt'.

For example, to help your students notice the difference in the place of articulation between /b/ and /v/, prepare to pronounce a minimal pair contrasting the two sounds in initial position, e.g., 'boat' vs. 'vote'. Hesitate for a moment or two before each word, keeping the lips together before you say 'boat' and keeping your upper teeth on your lower lip before you say 'vote'. Furthermore, by sustaining the /v/ at the beginning of 'vote', as in

vvvvvvvvote

you can demonstrate that the /v/ is continuous in nature. Then, explain that this cannot be done with a /b/ because it is an unvoiced stop consonant.

For the vowels, you can visually demonstrate that some vowels are produced with the lips spread, e.g. /iy/, while others involve various degrees of lip-rounding, e.g., /uw/.

'Sammy diagrams'

Diagrams of the different places of articulation are also useful in demonstrating sounds. For example, if you want to show the difference in tongue position between /θ/ and /f/, as in 'thin' and 'fin', you can both demonstrate the sounds visually and show the students 'Sammy diagrams', such as those in Figures 13.1 and 13.2, below.

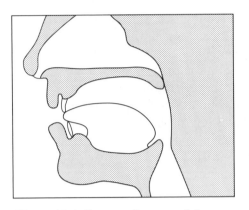

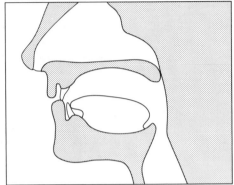

Figure 13.1: Sammy diagram of the sound /θ/

Figure 13.2: Sammy diagram of the sound /f/

'Sammy diagrams' are particularly useful in demonstrating the place of articulation of sounds which cannot be seen by looking at the mouth, such as the final /ŋ/ in 'sing'. In this case, the diagram can illustrate that the back of the tongue is involved in the articulation of the sound.

Mirrors

Mirrors are also useful in increasing students' awareness of the production of sounds. Students can make sounds while looking at their mouths in a mirror, noting the position of their lips and tongue. Encourage your students to bring small pocket mirrors to class for this purpose.

Stress, rhythm, and intonation

Conducting

Conducting refers to moving the arms and hands in concert with the rhythm, stress, and intonation of a word, phrase, or sentence. For example, you can show which syllable of a polysyllabic word receives the major stress by a rapid downward motion of the arm. Indicate the stressed words of phrases and sentences in a similar way. In illustrating intonation patterns, you can demonstrate the rising and falling contours by raising and lowering your arm as you say the sentences.

After having performed for your students, you can have them do the conducting. Encouraging your students to imitate your movements can help them to produce natural English rhythm and stress patterns.

Tapping

A less strenuous way of encouraging correct stress and rhythm is to demonstrate the patterns of stressed and unstressed syllables of words, phrases or sentences by tapping on a desk or table with the tips of your fingers, or with a pencil. You can tap only on the stressed syllables or you can tap on both the stressed and the unstressed ones. You can find, in the second case, that you automatically tap much harder on a stressed syllable than on an unstressed one.

Nonsense syllables

The characteristic rhythm of English can be illustrated with nonsense syllables. That is, you can substitute a simple syllable such as 'da' for the syllables of a word or sentence. Let us suppose that your students are having difficulty with the stress and/or intonation pattern of a sentence such as:

What did you do with it?

First of all, repeat the sentence several times for your students (try 'conducting' as you say it). Then replace the six syllables of the sentence with 'da' and try it again being careful to preserve the rhythm and intonation of the original sentence:

Da da da DA da da?

Nonsense syllables can also be used to demonstrate and practise differences in word stress (e.g. *in*sult vs. in*sult*), words families (e.g. e*lec*trical vs. elec*tri*city vs. e*lec*trify) and contrastive sentences-stress (e.g. I *flew* to Paris vs. I flew to *Paris*).

Exercises involving nonsense syllables can also function as warm-up exercises at the beginning of a pronunciation lesson (for more on warm-up exercises, see Chapter 15, page 221).

Exaggeration

For the most part, you will want to pronounce words and sentences in a natural manner. Sometimes, however, it pays to exaggerate, especially with the suprasegemental features of English: stress, rhythm, and intonation. Learners of English often have difficulty hearing the difference between stressed and unstressed syllables. You can exaggerate this difference by putting more stress on stressed syllables than would seem normal (i.e. by making stressed vowels longer and louder than normal). Learners of English also tend to underdifferentiate between stressed and unstressed syllables in their own speech. If you encourage them to exaggerate, what seems like an exaggeration to them may, in fact, be quite normal to an English ear.

Developing fluency

There are several common characteristics of non-native speech that fluency exercises are designed to alter. For example, some students are hesitant in their speech. These students may pause inappropriately in the middle of sentences or stumble over certain combinations of sounds, resulting in incorrect rhythm. Other students may be less hesitant, but they may fail to link words, giving the impression of 'staccato' speech. Finally, other students may give the impression of speaking too slowly or too quickly.

The techniques described below (as well as some of those above) are designed to help students develop fluency.

Slow speech

Like a music teacher trying to assist a piano student in mastering a difficult passage, pronunciation teachers should at times encourage their students to say a sentence with a difficult combination of sounds slowly and accurately before working up to a more natural tempo. Take, for example, the following sentence:

The pronunciation class lasts three hours.

Students will generally have difficulty with the sound combinations underlined above. This difficulty often results in very hesitant, non-fluent speech. Say the sentences to your students as slowly as you can without pauses, maintaining the correct rhythm, and slightly exaggerating the intonation. Once again, 'conducting' is a useful aid here. Then ask your students to imitate the way you said it, and have them pay careful attention to how their articulators are involved in the production of the various sounds. It is much better for a student to slow down when producing difficult sound combinations than to produce fast but incomprehensible speech.

Acceleration

From the slow speech technique described above, you can then turn to the acceleration or 'train' technique. It sometimes helps to mimic a train accelerating—a few slow-to-rapid 'choo-choo's' will help clarify the increase in speed you would like from your class. Then demonstrate with a sentence. Start the sentence very slowly and increase your speed gradually as you complete it. With each repetition of the sentence, increase your speed even more. Usually, you will have said the sentence four or fives times by the time you hit a normal conversational speed.

This technique illustrates the vowel reduction and contraction that accompany fast speech. Your first pronunciation of a sentence such as:

Do you think he will have arrived?

will probably not contain any examples of contraction or vowel reduction. By the time you have reached normal conversational speed, the sentence will sound more like:

D'ya think 'e'll've arrived?

Backward buildup

An effective technique for developing fluency over longer utterances and for improving linking and intonation is called *backward buildup*. As the name suggests, this technique involves starting with the final word of a sentence and adding to it the preceding words, one at a time. For example,

I can't remember what I did with my keys.

would be built up as follows:

keys
my keys
with my keys
did with my keys
I did with my keys
what I did with my keys
remember what I did with my keys
can't remember what I did with my keys
I can't remember what I did with my keys

It is best to build sentences up from the end rather than from the beginning because that way the intonation contour of the original sentence is preserved. If you build a sentence up from the beginning, the intonation contour may become distorted.

Limericks

Another helpful and entertaining way of developing fluency involves the use of limericks. Generally speaking, limericks are used in pronunciation class as examples of the stress-timed nature of English. To begin, prepare one or two limericks on a hand-out, or write one on the board:

There was an old lady from Crewe,
Who found a large mouse in her stew,
Said the waiter, 'Don't shout,
And wave it about,
Or the rest will be wanting one, too!'

Recite the limerick once or twice for your students. Because the important feature of limericks is the regular, rhythmical way in which they are spoken, many of the techniques described above can be used with them. For example, you can tap out the strong beats on a desk while you simultaneously indicate the rhythm with nonsense syllables. Thus, the first line of the above limerick would be:

> tap   tap   tap   tap
> la LA la la LA la la LA (pause)

Note that there is a 'silent' beat at the end of the first line. Similar 'silent' beats occur at the end of the second and fifth lines, thus giving a total of sixteen beats.

After you have demonstrated the rhythm with tapping and nonsense syllables, have your students try the same thing. Then, have them substitute the actual words of the limerick for the nonsense syllables, again while tapping out the sixteen beats. Since the regularity of the beats is so important, start out by having them recite the limerick very slowly. Developing fluency in this case means ensuring that the students maintain the rhythm of the limerick throughout; thus, you want to develop the rhythm first and the speed later. As an alternative to tapping their desks with their fingertips, the students can tap their feet, clap their hands, or indicate the beats with a downward 'conducting' motion of their arm.

Conclusion

As with all techniques, those described above should be used in accordance with your students' learning styles and strategies. Having a wide variety of techniques at your disposal allows you to appeal to the varying needs of different students.

14 DEVELOPING SELF-CORRECTING AND SELF-MONITORING STRATEGIES

Suzanne Firth

Introduction

One of the most serious problems facing all ESL/EFL instructors who deal with pronunciation is that of 'carry-over'. Too frequently, students achieve near-standard versions of segmental articulation, stress patterns, or intonation contours during class time, only to revert to their former non-standard patterns as soon as they leave the classroom. Clearly, the question of carry-over is related in part to individual student variables—degree of motivation, sensitivity to accuracy, age, education—many of which appear to be beyond an instructor's control. Fortunately, however, successful carry-over is also influenced by an instructor's attention to the development of self-correction techniques and self-monitoring strategies.

Self-correction is the ability to correct oneself when a pronunciation error has been pointed out. At this stage, a student is dependent on instructor or peer feedback. Self-monitoring, on the other hand, is the ability to listen for and recognize errors. In working with students who have pronunciation problems, it is critical that the instructor help to develop strategies which will allow the student to self-correct and self-monitor. This can be achieved by focussing on the following areas:

Motivation　Students should understand why accuracy of oral production is important.

Explanations　Students should receive a balance of description and demonstration appropriate to their proficiency levels, so that they may produce and remember specific points being taught.

Practice　Students should be given appropriate, varied and adequate opportunities to practise new points so that they are able to approximate target pronunciations before moving on to more communicative practice.

Feedback　Students should receive supportive, accurate feedback from the instructor and students in a class.

Self-correction

Developing students' ability to self-correct results from clear, concise teaching and appropriate feedback. Both teaching and feedback should aim at making the students more and more independent of the pronunciation instructor. The teaching phase should include discussion of reference books which can aid students in their self-correction. For example, after placement of word stress has been introduced, students can be shown how to use a dictionary to check stress patterns. Similarly, students can be encouraged to decipher a dictionary's pronouncing keys. This task can be simplified if an instructor provides key words to illustrate dictionary codes. For easy reference, students can make a bookmark that contains the stress marking system and the key words for consonants and vowels.

When teaching the production of sounds or stress and intonation patterns, the teacher should involve as many senses as possible (Ling 1976). For example, with individual sounds, draw the students' attention to the feel of the parts of the mouth involved in articulation, the sound of the new sound as compared to the student's incorrect version, and the sight of their own visible articulators (using a mirror or a diagram of the parts of the mouth).

In the process of teaching a new sound, students should be left with a simple mnemonic 'peg' which they can use to recall its proper articulation. These 'pegs' should be simple, but reliable, as the following examples illustrate:

1 For individual sounds, refer specifically to the cause of the problem. For example, if a student confuses /l/ and /r/, the peg could be /l/ = touch (the tooth ridge), /r/ = don't touch.

2 Students can be encouraged to 'walk' through sounds in the way one walks through a new dance step. For example, with /f/, lower the upper teeth against the lower lip, tense the lip slightly, and blow out. This allows the student to retrace the steps in producing a sound and to check whether all steps were passed through correctly.

3 After teaching a new sound, have the student contrast it with his/her non-standard version in order to note the differences in feel, sound and sight between the two. For example, if /v/, had been incorrectly substituted for /w/ in a word such as 'we', have the student say 'we' and 've' alternately.

4 For difficult consonants such as /tʃ/ and /ʃ/, check whether the student uses the former to make a sneezing sound as 'ah-choo' or the latter to quiet an infant as in 'shhhhh'.

5 Use code words to recall vowel or consonant sounds. For example, colour words can be associated with vowel sounds or geographical locations can be associated with consonant sounds. (See student diagnostic profile sheet in Table 10.1 (page 182) for a list of consonant and vowel key words.)

6 Associate some aspect of a written letter with a detail of articulation. For example, the sound /w/ uses two lips as represented by the two rounded shapes in the letter *w*, while /v/ uses one lip held against the teeth as represented by the single point of the letter *v*.

7 For consonant sounds, check whether naming the alphabet letter associated with the sound will produce the correct articulation. For example, a Chinese-speaking student was able to recall the pronunciation of certain sounds by recalling the pronunciation of the corresponding letters of the alphabet. The student found that by saying *l*, his tongue automatically assumed the correct position for /l/. This worked for /r/, /s/, and /t/, among other sounds.

8 Use analogies to help students remember tongue positions for individual sounds. For example, tell the student to shape the tongue like a spoon held just under the upper front teeth for the *th* sounds.

Students may hit upon their own ingenious ways of recalling correction techniques. Encourage them to do so and share these with their peers. Similar tips or 'pegs' can be found in Robinett (1978), Sanderson (1965) and Prator and Robinett (1985).

Feedback techniques

While still mastering a point, the student will often require modelling of the target behaviour by the instructor in order to be able to produce the correct form. Once the student is capable of producing the correct form, the teacher must encourage self-correction. This means that rather than modelling a correct version of a mispronounced sound, the teacher should simply 'remind' the student that a nonstandard form has been used. This will shift the responsibility for actually correcting the problem from the teacher to the student. 'Reminding' may be done in one of the following ways:

1 Repeat the incorrect sound using stress and intonation to suggest a questioning attitude. For example, if a student has substituted /f/ for /θ/, producing 'wiff' instead of 'with', the teacher could say 'wiff a friend?' using heavy stress on the word 'wiff' and a rising, questioning intonation.

2 Alternatively, the teacher could query the word containing the incorrect sound. In this case, the teacher would say, 'he went *what* a friend?', replacing the incorrect word with the question word 'what'.

3 The teacher could also repeat the student's error, exaggerating the incorrect pronunciation in order to draw the student's attention to it. For example, the incorrect /f/ could be made more audible by saying 'wifffff'.

If students cannot identify and/or correct an error after several attempts at 'reminding', tell them the source of the difficulty.

Self-monitoring

The ability to self-monitor has several facets. These are related to the stages involved in mastering a new pronunciation point. At first, a student attempts to produce a new form, listening to determine how closely it approximates the target. This ability to listen critically is a pre-requisite to successful self-monitoring. Having learned to produce forms in isolation, students can move to contextualized pronunciation practice. Here, self-monitoring can involve listening to a taped sample of speech and identifying appropriate and inappropriate forms. In less controlled, more communicative practice, monitoring one's speech can involve anticipating problem areas and determining whether production has been accurate.

Self-monitoring may also vary according to a student's overall language proficiency. Because of the many linguistic demands placed on basic students, they should be encouraged to monitor general aspects of pronunciation such as intonation, phrasing, or rhythm, as these appear to have the greatest effect on students' comprehensibility. Assuming mastery of the suprasegmentals, an instructor can encourage more proficient students to monitor specific segments.

Self-monitoring is more difficult for students who have been making the same pronunciation errors over an extended period of time. With all pronunciation students, but with this group in particular, it is imperative that each individual believe, first, that accurate pronunciation is important, and second, that producing accurate forms is, in part, his or her own responsibility. Allen and Waugh (1986) describe an activity in which francophone students discuss their attitudes towards the inaccurate pronunciation of French. As they become aware that their own reactions are generally negatives, they realize the importance of accurate English pronunciation.

An instructor can actually exaggerate typical pronunciation inaccuracies or poor speaking habits such as speaking too softly, too quickly, or with minimal attention to articulation. By contrasting good with bad habits, the instructor allows students to experience the difficulties which listeners may have in conversation with them. Peer feedback can also convince students that certain areas of their speech need practice. For example, a student could dictate a passage to a class. The class then checks their versions of the text with the original.

Techniques for developing self-monitoring

Students' ability to self-monitor can be enhanced through the use of the following techniques:

1 Have students determine the accuracy of their own pronunciation by using a 'peg'. For example, in producing a /w/, the student should ask 'Have I used both lips? Does it sound like a /v/ or a /w/?'

2 After choral and individual practice of a form, have students tape their own speech, reading from a written text. Prior to taping, have them mark the text for breath groups, stressed and unstressed words, intonation patterns, linking, etc., much in the same way as an actor would in preparing a script. During the listening phase, have students replay the tape several times, focussing on one aspect of pronunciation only during each replay. The teacher can then check the students' monitoring by listening to the tape and commenting on the accuracy of the evaluation.

3 During more communicative activities, have students select one area of pronunciation to focus on (e.g. speed of delivery). Have them judge their own performance and also have a partner or class member judge their pronunciation accuracy. Compare the two opinions.

4 In order to self-monitor outside the class, students must know which areas of pronunciation to focus on. They should establish priorities and work on one problem at a time, paying particular attention to this whenever they speak. Peers in the workplace can be asked to help them monitor specific problems.

Conclusion

The development of self-correcting and self-monitoring abilities should be included in a pronunciation syllabus from the earliest stages. While the individual instructor plays a critical role in the initial stages of pronunciation improvement, it is the individual student who must ultimately take responsibility for ongoing improvement. If students view accurate pronunciation as a goal which is within their control, the 'carry-over' problem which plagues pronunciation instructors can be greatly diminished. Self-correcting and self-monitoring minimize dependence and maximize self-reliance, allowing students to continue pronunciation improvement outside the classroom.

15 DEVELOPING NATURAL AND CONFIDENT SPEECH: DRAMA TECHNIQUES IN THE PRONUNCIATION CLASS

John Archibald

Introduction

The use of drama techniques in the ESL classroom has generally been restricted to the conversation class and, specifically, to the development of talking skills through communicative activities. In teaching students to communicate in a second language, drama can act as a bridge between the classroom and the real world. Drama techniques also have a place in the pronunciation class.

I began to experiment with drama in the pronunciation classroom a few years ago when I noticed an interesting connection: in many ways a drama student and an ESL student make the same kinds of mistakes. Perhaps you have had the misfortune to witness a bad amateur theatrical production where hardly a word spoken on stage was either understandable or believable. The words that might have been believable were not understandable and vice versa. ESL students can suffer from this same problem.

Let us draw a diagram of a continuum of speech types. At one end of the scale we have speech that is fully concerned with the meaning of the words but is not understandable. I call this Egocentric Speech. At the other end of the scale is speech that pays considerable attention to the sounds but no attention to meaning. I call this Hypercorrect Speech (familiar from old-fashioned elocution class).

Egocentric Speech	Natural Speech	Hypercorrect Speech
believable	understandable	

With ESL students (and actors, of course), we are interested in finding a middle ground that is both believable and understandable, which I call Natural Speech.

Natural Speech results, in large part, from looking and sounding (and feeling) confident. People make judgements about us as a result of how we look and how we sound. Thus, if students look and sound extremely tense, people will be uncomfortable listening to them. On the other hand, if students look and sound too lethargic, people will not be interested in what they are saying. It may sound insincere to say it but, if you look and sound confident, people will pay attention to what you say.

Looking confident is a subject that deserves its own article. I will not go into it here but keep in mind such things as posture, stride length, gesture, etc. In this article I will focus on *sounding* confident. In order to develop natural and confident speech we must pay attention to the building blocks of speech: articulation, and variety in pitch, volume, and rate. In this article, I will outline exercises designed to give students more control over each of these aspects of speech. The exercises are taken mostly from the theatre. They are the types of exercises that actors perform to warm up for a performance or just to keep in shape. If ESL students wish to develop skill in pronouncing their second language, they too must gain some measure of control over the way in which they speak.

Articulation

When teaching pronunciation, we must be concerned with much more than simply working through a list of sounds. Even if students have learned to produce sounds, they are often so self-conscious about their pronunciation that they are too nervous to use these sounds in front of a group of people (even a pronunciation class!). Human muscles do not respond well to nervousness. When we get nervous, our hands shake; our knees shake; just think what happens to all the little muscles used in articulation. It's no wonder that students' pronunciation suffers. Relaxed muscles respond better. Thus, we find a kind of self-fulfilling prophecy:

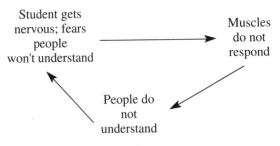

Figure 15.1: Nerves cycle

How can we help learners improve their performance? Just as runners stretch their legs before a race, we must warm up our articulatory muscles before making demands on them. Actors regularly practise a series of exercises designed to improve their articulation. They are constructed to isolate and exercise the muscles used to make particular sounds. (I would like to acknowledge the work of Edith Skinner & Timothy Monich (1980) in the development of these exercises.)

Teachers should not be afraid of using these exercises. I have found that even inhibited students quickly become accustomed to the practice. Please note that in performing these exercises, speed is not important; speed will come with practice.

These articulation exercises serve as a good warm up at the beginning of a class. They are designed to move the muscles of the mouth through the extreme positions found in English articulation. The emphasis is not on form but on loosening up the articulators. Therefore, remember that in doing the exercises, it is not essential that the students produce the sounds with absolute accuracy.

The lips
   iy   uw   iy   uw   iy   uw   iy   uw   etc.

Make sure the lips are as spread as they can be for [iy] and as rounded as they can be for [uw].

Lips and jaw
   iy   a   uw   iy   a   uw   iy   a   uw   etc.

On the /a/ sound, make sure the jaw is open wide with no lip rounding.

Tongue, lips, and jaw
This is a good exercise to concentrate on the tense vowels /ey/ and /ow/.

Figure 15.2

The jaw and middle of tongue
Make the sound [yʌ] as in 'yuppie'

   1 by opening and closing the jaw like a puppet.
   2 by moving only the tongue.

For the first part, do not move the tongue; see how far you can open the jaw. The second part can be quite difficult. Open the jaw and make sure that it does not move. You can do this by resting the hand lightly on the chin. Move only the middle of the tongue.

The back of the tongue and velum

a g a g a g a g a   etc.

Feel the back of the tongue touch the velum with the /g/.

Consonants

pɪ pɪ pɪ pɪ pɪ pɪ pɪ pɪ pa
tɪ tɪ tɪ tɪ tɪ tɪ tɪ tɪ ta
kɪ kɪ kɪ kɪ kɪ kɪ kɪ kɪ ka
bɪ bɪ bɪ bɪ bɪ bɪ bɪ bɪ ba
dɪ dɪ dɪ dɪ dɪ dɪ dɪ dɪ da
gɪ gɪ gɪ gɪ gɪ gɪ gɪ gɪ ga
mɪ mɪ mɪ mɪ mɪ mɪ mɪ mɪ ma
nɪ nɪ nɪ nɪ nɪ nɪ nɪ nɪ na

This exercise works on consonants made with the lips, the tip and back of the tongue, as well as the raising and lowering of the velum.

For /v/ and /ð/ (as in 'this')

vvvɪmmm   vvvɪnnn   vvvɪŋŋŋ
ðððɪmmm   ðððɪnnn   ðððɪŋŋŋ

Concentrate on keeping these consonants fully voiced.

In any type of speech training, we want to develop a mechanism that will respond to the demands we place on it. If the articulators become accustomed to the rigours of the exercises, then chances are they will respond better under pressure.

Pitch, volume, and rate

For our speech to be interesting to listen to, we must vary our pitch, volume, and rate. It is the job of the speaker to tell the listener what is important. He or she does this by emphasizing the appropriate words, and words are emphasized by changing one of the above variables.

Pitch

If a student speaks a language that uses comparatively little pitch variation, the pitch variation of English (two to three octaves) will sound bizarre. These changes are slow to come; students have to trust the teacher enough to know that they will not be allowed to embarrass themselves.

A good exercise to work on expanding the pitch range is the following:

Starting at a comfortable pitch, the student simply counts from 1 to 5 with each number being on a higher pitch than the last one. Then, the pitch and the numbers descend from 5 to 1. Next, the student counts while lowering the pitch with each number (1 to 5) and then returns to the starting pitch.

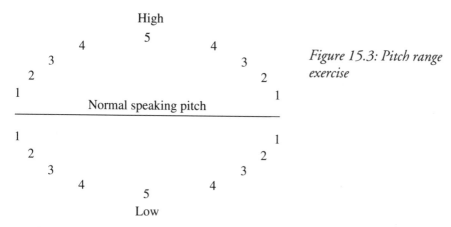

Figure 15.3: Pitch range exercise

In this type of exercise, it is the rising and lowering of the pitch which is important, not the particular notes used. An exercise of this type has two benefits:

1 The students get used to hearing greater pitch variation in their voices;
2 The muscles used for pitch control are exercised.

Volume

Variety in volume is a problem insofar as someone with a quiet voice will be thought of as shy and, perhaps, lacking in confidence. Convincing this type of student to increase the volume is, again, a slow process, but I think a necessary one. Students must become accustomed to hearing their louder voices. Once they realize that other people do not think they are shouting, they will start to feel more comfortable. A good exercise to practise volume control is the following: simply practise making a sound that starts very quietly and gets progressively louder.

ₒₒₒₒₒooooOOOOO

Volume can also be a matter of confidence. As confidence increases, the student will project more. Another way to help things along, though, is to work on dialogues that demand a strong emotional commitment from these students. For example, lines like 'I didn't do it!', 'I didn't say that!', or 'I do not think you're stupid!'

Also, you can help the students learn to recognize the reactions of listeners who are forced to endure a voice that is too loud; they tend to back away or wince. Students can learn to realize that native speakers do not think that they are shouting when they increase their volume.

Rate

There is a maxim in theatre that audiences are stupid. This is not as abusive as it sounds. What it means for the actor is that he or she cannot speak too quickly, or the audience will miss what is being said. There are two advantages to this strategy. The first is that it makes the speaker appear more confident. If we speak too quickly we sound nervous. Slowing down can improve the image of the speaker and increase the receptivity of the audience to the message. (It is, of course, up to the teacher to let the students know if they are slowing down too much and sounding unnatural.) The second advantage is that it gives the speaker more time to make the sounds correctly. Obviously, it is more difficult to keep the sounds clear when we speak quickly. By keeping the speed down, the student has a better chance of being understood. These two factors can lead to a positive cycle:

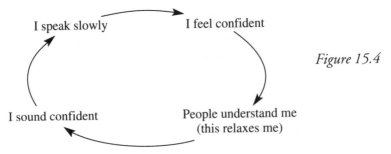

Figure 15.4

Remember, relaxation is not just an affective state, but also a physical state to be sought. The rate of speech must also change to reflect the thoughts behind the words. We tend to speak more quickly when excited and more slowly when relaxed. Have the students practise dialogues like the following:

A (excited and fast) I just heard that the school is on fire and five teachers and about thirty students are trapped inside. Do you want to go down and watch?

B (relaxed and slow) No, I think I'll just go home, have a bath, maybe read for a bit, and go to bed early. Have fun, though.

The students can write their own dialogues, as well.

Variety

An interesting voice must have variety. Obviously, a voice that is a monotone is not interesting to listen to. Ultimately, the students have to be able to achieve variety in spontaneous speech. The exercise below combines variation in pitch, volume, and rate. Students memorize a sentence or poem (a nursery rhyme) and then practice changing the variables. First, work with a single variable:

	Sentence		
quiet	→	loud	For volume

	Sentence		
high	→	low	For pitch

Then, work with two variables:

	Sentence	
quiet		loud
and	$\rightarrow$	and
high		low

For volume and pitch

And finally, work with three variables:

	Sentence	
quiet		loud
and		and
high	$\rightarrow$	low
and		and
fast		slow

For volume, pitch, and rate

This is fun for the class but some of the combinations are definitely more difficult than others. Loud, high, and fast tend to go together, as do quiet, low, and slow. Let the class experiment with these variables.

It is a speaker's job to indicate to the listener what to listen to, that is, what is important. Just as a camera tells us what to look at on TV or film, so the voice must indicate what to attend to. The speaker must decide which words or phrases in an utterance are the most important and make them stand out. This is often achieved by changing the pitch, the volume, or the rate. Thus, working on variety will aid the students in getting their meaning across. Even if they are already conveying the appropriate meaning, communicative power is enhanced by this variation.

Conclusion

The teacher should emphasize that students must *make* their audience:

1 hear them (volume),
2 understand them (articulation), and
3 listen to them (variety).

Please note the word *make* here. Pronunciation is not passive, the students must always be working to achieve these three goals.

Finally, let me offer three Golden Rules of theatre (and pronunciation):

1 Speak loudly.
2 Look like you know what you're doing.
3 Don't bump into things.

And things should be all right.

16 UNINTELLIGIBILITY AND THE ESL LEARNER

Nicholas Elson

Introduction

The painful experience of not being understood is well known to anyone who has actively tried to learn a second language. The familiar scenario is played out when the teacher's remarks confuse the learner, or when one student, in conversation with another, is faced with the realization that he or she does not understand what the speaker is trying to say. Outside the classroom the learner meets similar frustrations, made all the more intense without the support which the classroom offers.

We should remind ourselves, as second language teachers, that there are causes of incomprehension that have little to do with the fact that the people we are speaking with may be learning English as a Second Language. We have only to observe the number of times in a normal day that we ourselves are asked to respond to 'What?', 'Pardon', or 'Sorry, I didn't get that,' from other native speakers to realize that not understanding another person's meaning is a normal aspect of conversation. Contributing elements could be background noise, a too-sudden change of topic, false assumptions about the listener's background knowledge, an ambiguous style of delivery, or simple inattention on the part of the listener. In exchanges with native speakers, these occurrences are usually dealt with smoothly, an elaboration or repetition is inserted and the exchange continues.

Pronunciation is clearly a central factor in students' success in making themselves understood. The ability to employ stress, intonation, and articulation in ways that support comprehension is a skill that for students from many language backgrounds will only come slowly. In the meantime, students need to be encouraged to immerse themselves in the target language, to take chances with the language, to enjoy using it, and to persist in spite of the difficulties that are a natural part of the language-learning process.

In the ESL context the experience of unintelligibility or incomprehension looms larger. Perhaps because of a sensitivity to "correctness," or because of the need to communicate successfully in the target language, the ESL speaker's self-image and sense of accomplishment is closely bound to understanding and being understood. The result can be a high degree of frustration for the speaker or listener who might see each moment of incomprehension as a personal fault and responsibility.

With increased emphasis on learner-centered, communicative language teaching and user-initiated language, instances of incomprehensibility may become more frequent as learners reach beyond their comfortable range of ability. This underlines the need for teachers to help the learners become aware of strategies they need to deal with incomprehensibility, whether in making themselves understood, or in struggling with what another speaker has said.

Regarding incomprehensibility, Joan Klyhn (1986) observes:

> From the first, students in a course should be made aware that every message they utter needs to be understood by their interlocutor. The two parties enter into a negotiation where A gives B the feedback he needs to clean up his message and then the service is reversed. The instructor can be an informant, can suggest avenues of study, can run a workshop on a structure or particular skill that is proving problematic. A German making a presentation to a couple of Spaniards can get a great deal more useful feedback from his/her peers than from an instructor. Many experienced language teachers have developed an unfortunate facility for understanding garbled sentences and poor pronunciation which may make a student quite incomprehensible to his/her peers.

Klyhn's comments point to a value in student-to-student interaction that might ease the teacher's fears about the kind of language models which students present to each other. While activities aimed specifically at practising aspects of speech production (voiced/voiceless contrasts, and so on) would be initiated primarily by the teacher, there is a great deal in the exchanges between students that relates to achieving comprehensibility. As they respond to cues indicating how well the message is getting across and adopt corrective procedures, they absorb elements of the complexity involved in the transmission of meaning. The teacher structures activities and brings in examples of language which will enhance relevant interaction between students, and presents models of 'real language'. This can result in interaction between students where the desire to understand and to be understood on a matter of mutual interest or importance establishes a natural context for developing comprehension skills.

In addition to the factors mentioned above, there are several reasons for incomprehensibility which have particular relevance for the ESL learner.

1 The speaker or listener is struggling with stress, intonation, or sound patterns with which he/she is unfamiliar.

2 There may be words or phrases in the utterance that the listener is unfamiliar with. He/she cannot grasp the message without this specific understanding.

3 There may be a lack of mutual social/cultural background. The speaker makes a reference or assumption for which the listener is unprepared. For instance, a casual assumption on the speaker's part that the listener knows that separatism is a major issue in Canadian society may be behind a comment which leaves the listener lost as to the speaker's intended meaning.

4 Certain grammatical forms used by the speaker may not conform to the listener's experience or expectations, resulting in incomprehension.

If the generation and exchange of relevant language is seen as central to the language development process, and if the emphasis in the class is on encouraging meaningful interaction between the learners as a basis for language development, then incomprehension is a problem in a larger communicative sense. If incomprehensibility slows or detracts from language development, then students can benefit from being able to use devices which will help to keep the language learning process interesting and creative.

The teacher should consider how corrective procedures relate to principles of communication and their importance for language development. Brown and Yule (1983) place the process of dealing with incomprehension squarely in the communicative, student-centred context:

> If it is quite unclear what the student is saying, the person who should be asking for clarification is the interlocutor, the listener, not the teacher. In practice sessions (as opposed to an assessment session), the listener should be permitted, indeed encouraged, to ask questions of clarification, just as native speakers do in normal life. If the listener can make sense of what the speaker is saying, then the speaker is, on this occasion, communicating successfully.

This suggests that strategies for overcoming incomprehension are simply another aspect of the total communication-language learning process. While the classroom is the place for students to immerse themselves in a semi-controlled, communicative environment, they need also to be prepared to deal with the unavoidable times, both inside and outside the classroom, when they do not understand or are not understood themselves. It must therefore be a priority to make learners aware of the strategies we use when faced with incomprehension, either our own or of the person to whom we are speaking, so that meaningful use of language can continue while articulatory and other aspects of the language are developed.

The receiver

The following are some of the strategies the intended receiver can use in a situation where the message is not clear.

Solicit repetition

Chances are that in response to the receiver's 'Would you please say that again?', the student will do exactly that, perhaps resulting in no further understanding on the part of those involved. On the other hand, repetition is useful in that repeated exposure to an initially confusing utterance often results in the mind gradually sorting it out into meaningful components. The student may only repeat the utterance once—continued requests to repeat might drive the level of frustration higher—but the receiver repeats it in his/her mind, relating it to established patterns and information that might trigger recognition of the intended meaning.

The receiver uses phrases which will invite the speaker to repeat the relevant part of the utterance. The forms that this function can take need little elaboration here. It is important though that students be exposed to situations which indicate shifts in register in relation to context. It might be appropriate, for instance, to say 'What?' to someone you know well and are dealing with informally, but the learner should also know that 'What?' could also be considered quite rude in other circumstances. 'Excuse me, I didn't understand what you said' could be equally inappropriate in certain circumstances. Learners need exposure to the kinds of phrases which people use to get information reiterated, with guidance in noting the 'tone' with which they are delivered.

A list of familiar phrases such as:

> 'Sorry, what did you say?'
> 'Pardon, could you say that again?'
> 'Sorry, I don't see what you're getting at.'
> 'Excuse me, what did you say?'

is of little use in itself. While such phrases could be introduced in various ways, they won't have any real meaning until learners have a chance to hear and use them in suitable and realistic contexts. The range of devices used to get speakers to repeat their message is wide and will require the teacher to find extensive samples of relevant language for use in developing this awareness.

Reflect back

The receiver can attempt an exact repetition of the utterance back to the sender. This signals to the initiator that the phrase is being reviewed, that there may be a problem in understanding and says, in effect, 'take another look at what you just said'. The teacher might want to avoid the directness of "I don't understand" although students can be quite blunt in their own exchanges among themselves (Klyhn 1986).

The repetition allows the sender to review the utterance, recognize a problem, and rephrase it in a manner which might better support comprehension. Having students repeat what another student has said as an informal exercise will help them to focus on what they do and do not understand. They will then have to specify to the speaker which part of the utterance, if any, is causing difficulty.

Develop sensitivity as a listener

Learners need to develop a listening attitude as well as listening skills. This is a more nebulous aspect of dealing with incomprehension, but the ability to listen, or even to recognize that there is such a skill to develop, can increase the ability of receivers to appreciate the messages being sent to them. Students need occasions in which they can listen to others in a relaxed and sympathetic manner: traits which one hopes the teacher exhibits as a matter of course and encourages in the learners.

Students might be given a topic to discuss or a problem to work out, but be told not to respond to their partner in the exchange until he/she gives the signal to do so.

Develop skills for outside the classroom

We need to keep in mind that the world for language learners does not begin and end at the classroom door. They will have more language needs outside the classroom than within. Exposure to modes of speech used by native speakers talking among themselves is important in reaching this goal. It has been observed that:

> The learner might well have reached a stage where he can carry on a conversation with a native speaker, understanding virtually everything that is said to him. Should a second native speaker appear on the scene, however, the learner is often unable to understand what the two are saying to each other. This is in most cases not—as some learners assume—because the others are conversing in some kind of 'dialect', but because they have reduced the acoustic-phonetic explicitness of the speech signal to as low a level as possible, consistent with mutual intelligibility. (Dirven and Oakeshott-Taylor 1984)

This reinforces the view that work in the classroom should always have an orientation to the lives students lead outside, and should include good examples of natural language in a range of contexts.

Develop ability to recognize cues

Learners who have difficulty interpreting messages should be helped to become familiar with the many cues which contribute to successful communication. Different activities and exposure to native speaker language models can draw attention to the role of stress, intonation, juncture, and articulation in communicating meaning. At the same time, they can see how meanings can be influenced by varying contexts: physical, linguistic, psychological, or visual. Facial expression, for example, or 'tone of voice' could convey to a listener that 'this message is not to be taken seriously', thus possibly saving the listener some embarrassment.

Predictive skills

Listeners as well as speakers need to be shown how guessing plays a role in understanding. Prediction is as central to spoken contexts as it is in reading. As in reading, incorrect predictions are a normal part of the process of sorting out meaning. Having learners listen to sentences in which certain words are deliberately spoken softly, deleted, or even mispronounced will show learners that it is not necessary to 'hear' every word in order to achieve successful communication. They will benefit from becoming aware that they can often determine meaning even though they may not understand some of the words or phrases used by the speaker.

The sender

As they work their way towards increased fluency in the language, there are a number of strategies ESL learners can employ to make their message understood by the receivers. Such strategies assume that getting the message across is the main priority.

Littlewood (1984) notes several strategies which learners have been known to use in the face of, or in anticipation of, difficulty in communication.

Avoid communicating

This strategy probably has little appeal to the ESL teacher, regardless of the approach to language teaching being used. In an academic context, in particular, and given what we know about the relationship between language and learning, persistent refusal to attempt communication will probably impede language development. This strategy is worth some attention, however, since difficulty in getting a message across or in understanding other people's messages often leads a learner to avoid taking risks with the language. Teachers must also distinguish between a legitimate 'silent' period as a normal part of language learning, and a more extreme avoidance of communicative situations on the part of the learner.

If learners can be encouraged to participate in ways they feel comfortable with, and are able to communicate successfully, the resulting confidence will lead them to be more adventurous in their use of language.

Adjust the message

In this case, the learner, realizing that there is a problem even while the exchange is still taking place, can modify the manner in which the message is being sent. This might result in a scaling down or simplification of the intended message, or breaking it into smaller components, with the eventual result of the intended understanding being achieved.

To develop their awareness of this technique, students can be given a variety of different utterances and be asked to rephrase them. Similarly, a speaker might be stopped from time to time and asked to supply alternative forms of expression for words or phrases which have been used.

Paraphrase

The learner can be shown how alternative words or phrases can be used to help the receiver get a reasonable interpretation. Littlewood (1984) cites examples of 'a learner who did not recall the word for a "car seat belt" [but] avoided the need for it by saying "I'd better tie myself in". A learner who could not recall the word "kettle" spoke of "the thing that you boil water in".'

This technique is familiar to native speakers who, unable to recall a particular word or phrase at the moment will say 'You know, that thing you . . .,' in order to continue the established direction of the exchange without getting side-tracked by details such as exact phrasing. This strategy is not a substitute for working on problematic areas of pronunciation, but can help students extricate themselves from situations of confusion and misunderstanding.

Approximation

Closely related to the above strategy is simply reaching for a word or phrase which best approximates the word the speaker may not be able to pronounce properly or cannot remember.

Creating new words, or even using native language words, are other strategies speakers have used to get the point across. Students can be given cloze passages and asked to supply several possible words or phrases in the blanks.

In addition to these, other strategies serve the learner well:

Rephrasing

Native speakers frequently rephrase their message, perhaps in anticipation of a possible misunderstanding, or in response to a flicker of incomprehension on the face of the receiver. ESL learners should be aware of this strategy, frequently used to present a message in two forms: the first often more complex than the second. Using phrases such as:

> 'In other words . . .'
> 'What I mean is . . .'
> 'That is, . . .'

the speaker offers two versions of the message, the second possibly a more explicit version of the first, thus increasing the chances of understanding on the part of the listener. This is of particular interest to the ESL learner because in common daily discourse, the receiver of the message often responds with his or her own version of the message: 'You're saying that . . .' or 'You mean that . . .'. This response can reinforce the confidence of the sender if it confirms the message has been received, or point out a problem if the interpretation is not what was intended. The listener's response might also present a more accurate target-language version of the message than was originally sent.

Response cues

The ESL learner must be familiar with the feedback cues, those nods, grunts, 'uhuh's', and facial expressions which say to the sender 'I understand what you're saying, please continue.' Likewise, sensitivity to the absence of these cues can help the speaker to see if the message is getting across. Checking feedback with such phrases as 'You see?' or 'Do you see what I'm getting at?' or 'Do you understand what I'm saying?' offers an opportunity for the listener to indicate that he or she is getting lost in the exchange. This is a chance for the speaker to confirm that the intended meaning is being received.

The learner also needs to know that virtually any physical context elements: gestures, facial expressions, drawings, and so on, are legitimate aspects of the effort to get the point across.

Conclusion

In sum, the learner should become comfortable with the notion that incomprehensibility in whatever form or context is a legitimate and expected part of the communication process. Encouragement to understand what lies behind these misunderstandings, and what strategies might be employed to ensure continued communication while specific aspects of articulation are developed, serves the learner well on the long road to fluency.

GLOSSARY

affricate: Complex *consonant* sound composed of a *stop* followed immediately by a *fricative*, e.g. the initial consonant sound of 'chug', made up of /t/ and /ʃ/.

alveolar: Describes sounds where the tongue either touches or approaches the *alveolar ridge* in their production, e.g. /t/, /d/, /l/, /n/.

alveolar ridge: Roof of mouth just behind upper teeth (see Figure 2.1, page 12). Also called *tooth ridge.*

alveopalatal: Describes sounds made with the blade of the tongue approaching the *hard palate* just behind the *alveolar ridge*, e.g. /ʃ/ and /ʒ/.

articulation, manner of: The way in which the airstream is obstructed or altered in the production of speech sounds.

articulation, place of: The location of the obstruction of the airstream, especially in the articulation of *consonants.*

articulators: Movable parts of the mouth used in the production of speech sounds: the bottom lip, the bottom teeth, the tongue, and the jaw.

aspiration: Burst of air which accompanies the voiceless *stop consonants* (/p/, /t/, and /k/) in certain positions in English, e.g. word-initial.

backward buildup: A technique for improving fluency, *intonation, linking*, and *stress.* It involves saying aloud the final words of a sentence and then adding the preceding words, one at a time, until the whole sentence is said.

bilabial: Describes sounds where both lips are involved in production, e.g. /p/, /b/, and /m/.

consonant: Sound which involves a narrowing in the mouth, causing some obstruction of the airstream. See also *vowel.*

consonant cluster: Two or more adjacent *consonants* together, occurring at the beginning (initial consonant clusters) or end (final consonant clusters) of a syllable.

content words: Words which express independent meaning, usually *stressed* in a sentence. See also *function words.*

contractions: Shortened form of auxiliary verbs where the initial *consonant*, and sometimes the *vowel*, are lost, e.g. 'I'll', 'I've'.

contrastive: Describes sounds which create a difference in meaning if substituted for one another. In English, /p/ and /b/ are contrastive, as evidenced by the *minimal pair* 'pit' and 'bit'.

diphthongs: Complex vowel sounds composed of a vowel followed by a semi-vowel, e.g. /aw/, /ay/, and /oy/.

flap: A *positional variant* of /t/ in American pronunciation which occurs between vowels where the first vowel is stressed. The tongue touches the tooth ridge and is quickly pulled back, so that a sound similar to a /d/ is produced, e.g. in 'butter'.

fricative: Consonant sound which involves a partial obstruction of the airstream. The articulator approaches another part of the mouth but does not touch it. Fricatives can therefore be prolonged, e.g. /s/.

function words: Words which have little or no meaning in themselves, but which express grammatical relationships. Usually *unstressed* in a sentence. See also *content words.*

glottal stop: Sound which involves blockage of air at the *glottis,* e.g. the initial and medial sound in American 'uh-oh'.

glottalized: Refers to the pronunciation of a sound with an accompanying glottal stop. In English, some /t/s, particularly word-final /t/s, may be glottalized.

glottis: Opening between the vocal cords. See Figure 2.1, page 12.

hard palate: Part of roof of mouth just behind the *tooth ridge.* See Figure 2.1.

homophones: Words that sound the same but have different meanings, e.g. 'fir' and 'fur'.

information focus: Part of sentence to which the speaker is drawing attention. Usually indicated through the use of stronger *stress.*

interdental: Describes sounds where the tip of the tongue obstructs the airstream by being placed between the teeth, or behind the upper teeth, e.g. /θ/ and /ð/.

intonation pattern or contour: Pattern of rise and fall of the pitch of a sentence.

intonation, rising: Intonation pattern characteristic of yes-no questions in English. The pitch of the voice rises at the *major* sentence *stress,* and continues to rise.

intonation, rising-falling: The most common *intonation pattern* in English, characteristic of simple declarative sentences, commands, and questions that begin with a *wh*-word. The pitch rises towards the end of the sentence, then falls.

labiodental: Describes sounds where the obstruction to the airstream is made by the top teeth touching the lower lip, e.g. /f/ and /v/.

lateral consonants: /l/ sound as made by some English speakers, with air passing out of the mouth over the sides of the tongue.

lax: See *vowels*.

linking: The blending together of words within the same phrase or sentence, so that there is a smooth transition from one word to the next. The final sound of one word may seem to become part of the following word.

liquid: *Consonant* where the air passes through the mouth in a somewhat fluid manner, e.g. /r/ and /l/.

minimal pairs: Pairs of words that differ in only one sound, the sound occuring in the same position in each member of the pair, e.g. 'pit' vs. 'bit'.

nasal: Sounds made with the air passing through the nose, e.g. /m/ and /n/.

non-contrastive: Describes sounds in a given language which do not create a difference in meaning when substituted for one another, and whose pronunciation is predictable depending on position in a word. In English, aspirated and non-aspirated /p/ are non-contrastive, as in 'spit'.

off-glides: *Semi-vowels* where there is movement of the tongue during pronunciation.

palatalization: A sound change such as happens in English when an *alveolar* sound becomes *alveopalatal* under the influence of a following palatal sound such as /y/. For example, in 'did you?' the second /d/ and /y/ become /dʒ/, to produce 'didja?'.

phonetics: The study of speech sounds.

phonology: The study of how sounds pattern in a particular language.

positional variation: Variation in pronunciation dependent on word position. See *non-contrastive*.

/r/-coloring: Way in which the *consonant* /r/ affects the pronunciation of *vowels*.

retroflex consonant: Sound (e.g. English /r/) made with the tip of the tongue slightly curled back in the mouth.

schwa: *Mid central vowel* sound generally used in *unstressed syllables*. Transcribed as /ə/.

segmental: Describes aspects of speech concerned with individual sounds. See also *suprasegmental*.

semi-vowels: Sounds made with a relatively wide opening in the mouth, and little turbulance in the airstream, e.g. /w/ and /y/.

soft palate: See *velum.*

stop consonant: Consonant sound which involves a complete blockage of the airstream, e.g. /p/ and /b/.

stress: Emphasis on a particular *syllable* or word. In English, this involves making *vowels* longer, louder, and higher in pitch.

stress-timed: Describes languages in which rhythm is dependent upon the number of stressed syllables within a spoken unit, e.g. English. See also *syllable-timed.*

stress, major: The strongest level of stress in a word or sentence. See also *stress, minor* and *unstress.*

stress, minor: A level of stress which is not as strong as the *major stress* in a word or sentence. See also *stress, major* and *unstress.*

suprasegmental: Describes aspects of speech above the level of the individual sound: rhythm, *stress,* and *intonation.* See also *segmental.*

syllable: Unit into which a word in divided, usually consisting of a *vowel* with *consonant(s)* before and/or after it.

syllable-timed: Describes languages in which rhythm is dependent upon the number of *syllables* within a spoken unit, e.g. French. See also *stress-timed.*

syllable, closed: A syllable which ends with a *consonant.*

syllable, open: A syllable which ends with a *vowel.*

tense: See *vowels.*

tooth ridge: See *alveolar ridge.*

unstress: Lack of *stress* on a word or *syllable.*

velar: Describes sounds involving the back of the tongue and the *soft palate* or *velum,* e.g. /k/, /g/, and /ŋ/.

velum: Back part of the roof of the mouth. Also called *soft palate.*

voiced: Describes sounds made with the vocal cords vibrating, e.g. /z/.

voiceless: Sounds made without vibration of the vocal cords, e.g. /s/.

vowel: Sound produced by air passing unobstructed through the mouth. See also pages 28–35 for a description of vowel-types.

FURTHER READING

The following is an annotated bibliography of books that may be of interest to pronunciation teachers. Certain books are useful as in-class texts while others are better suited as reference works for the teacher.

In using these pronunciation texts, teachers must be aware that many texts reflect the pronunciation of other dialects of English. Some of the books are based on the pronunciation of British English while others are based on American or Canadian English. The speaker of American or Canadian English must be aware of books that focus on British pronunciation as the vowel system of British English is markedly different. As there is very little variability in the consonants of British and American English, exercises involving consonants do not generally have to be adjusted to accommodate American English pronunciation.

Textbooks

Baker, A. 1981. *Ship or Sheep? An Intermediate Pronunciation Course.* Cambridge: Cambridge University Press.

The book is divided into forty-nine sections, each of which focuses on a different sound or sound contrast of English. Students see a picture of how the sound is made and then practise the sound in selected words, sentences, and dialogues.

– Teacher's and student's books.
– Cassette available.
– British English.

Baker, A. 1982a. *Tree or Three? An Elementary Pronunciation Course.* Cambridge: Cambridge University Press.

This book is organized in the same way as *Ship or Sheep?* but is designed for elementary students rather than intermediate ones.

– Teacher's and student's books.
– Cassette available.
– British English.

Baker, A. 1982b. *Introducing English Pronunciation: A Teacher's Guide to 'Tree or Three?' and 'Ship or Sheep?'.* Cambridge: Cambridge University Press.

This book is the teacher's manual accompanying both of Ann Baker's text-books described above. It contains a useful introduction, covering topics such as the selection of appropriate material and the linking of pronunciation to other course work. Baker also provides teaching suggestions for each lesson of the texts. Of particular interest to the pronunciation teacher is a list of pronunciation difficulties specific to twenty-nine language groups.

Bowen, J.D. 1975. *Patterns of English Pronunciation*. Rowley, Mass.: Newbury House.

This book is difficult for both teachers and students because of the sheer number of pronunciation points covered. Bowen provides comprehensive and imaginative examples of various stress and intonation patterns, as well as standard vowel and consonant contrasts. This book is probably best used as a resource book for teachers rather than as an in-class text.

– American English.

Gilbert, J.B. 1984. *Clear Speech: Pronunciation and Listening Comprehension in American English*. Cambridge: Cambridge University Press.

Clear Speech is a text which combines pronunciation exercises with listening exercises. The book emphasizes suprasegmental aspects of pronunciation such as rhythm, focus, linking, and vowel reduction. There is also a small section on common segmental problems. Gilbert's book is innovative in its focus on suprasegmentals and its inclusion of listening activities in the pronunciation classroom.

– Teacher's and student's books available.
– Cassette available.
– American English.

Morley, J. 1982. *Improving Spoken English: An Intensive Personalized Program in Perception, Pronunciation, Practice in Context*. Ann Arbor, Mich.: University of Michigan Press.

This book is divided into two sections. The first section deals with connected speech: contractions, reduced vowels, linking, etc. The second section provides exercises in the production of English vowels. The appendix to this book contains many interesting teaching techniques including Rhymalogues and Proverbs.

– Cassette available.
– American English.

Mortimer, C. 1985. *Elements of Pronunciation: Intensive Practice for Intermediate and More Advanced Students*. Cambridge: Cambridge University Press.

This book is a collection of five previously published booklets: Weak Forms, Clusters, Link-up, Contractions, and Stress Time. The book emphasizes aspects of English pronunciation relevant to connected speech. These are practised using short dialogues. The teacher may want to alter some of these dialogues as the humor is often specific to British culture.

– Cassette available.
– British English.

Nilsen, D. L. F. and **A. P. Nilsen.** 1971. *Pronunciation Contrasts in English.* New York: Regents.

Essentially, this book is a list of minimal pairs which contrast difficult sound distinctions of English. In addition, a small number of minimal pair sentences are provided for each sound contrast. The format makes the book suited to teachers as a reference from which they can draw exercises for specific problems of students. Teachers find this book useful because the language groups which encounter difficulty with each sound contrast are identified.

– American English.

Ponsonby, M. 1982. *How Now, Brown Cow? A Course in the Pronunciation of English.* Oxford: Pergamon Press.

This book is divided into 58 sections, each of which deals with a particular aspect of English pronunciation. For example, section 1 deals with /p/, section 7 with syllable stress, section 32 with weak forms, etc. Often, the dialogues in which these aspects of pronunciation are practiced are unnatural. However, they can be useful for more mechanical practice.

– Cassette available.
– British English.

Prator, C. H. and **B. W. Robinett.** 1985. *Manual of American English Pronunciation* (Fourth edition). New York: Holt, Rinehart, and Winston.

This book is perhaps the most readily available of all pronunciation texts. It contains exercises which provide practice in articulation of individual segments, stress, intonation, and rhythm. In addition, there is a section on the relationship between spelling and pronunciation. The detailed description of the English sound system contained within this book makes it a useful resource for both teachers and students. The explanations are only appropriate for advanced students; however, the exercises can be used with both intermediate and advanced classes.

– Cassette available.
– American English.

Woods, H. *Contact Canada.* Ottawa: Public Service Commission of Canada.

Contact Canada is an excellent series of booklets designed originally for teaching English to adult francophones. However, most of the exercises contained within these books deal with common pronunciation problems and can thus be used in multilingual classrooms. Titles in the series include:

Sound Production: h. (1976); *Rhythm and Unstress.* (1979); *Sound Production: th.* (1976); *Syllable Stress and Unstress.* (1979); *Intonation.* (1977); *Vowel Dimensions.* (1983).

– Canadian English.

Reference books

Kenworthy, J. 1987. *Teaching English Pronunciation.* London: Longman.

This book is for teachers of pronunciation rather than students. The book is divided into two sections: Part 1 deals with issues related to pronunciation teaching and Part 2 describes the specific pronunciation problems encountered by learners from nine different language groups. The book has many useful suggestions for increasing students' awareness of pronunciation.

Killam, C. E. and **B. Watson.** 1983. *Thirteen Language Groups: Practical Application of Contrastive Analysis for Teachers of English as a Second Language.* Vancouver: Vancouver Community College.

This book provides a comparison between English and thirteen other languages with respect to phonology and grammar. It also provides some interesting cultural comparisons. An excellent resource for teachers. There is a good reference list and glossary of technical terms.

– Canadian English.

Ladefoged, P. 1982. *A Course in Phonetics.* New York: Harcourt Brace Jovanovich.

This book is not a pronunciation textbook but rather a text for an introductory course in phonetics. Teachers may be interested in the detailed description of articulatory phonetics provided in this book. It is a very readable, scholarly introduction to a field of study crucial to pronunciation teachers.

– American English.

MacCarthy, P. 1978. *The Teaching of Pronunciation.* Cambridge: Cambridge University Press.

This is a book designed for teachers of pronunciation rather than students. MacCarthy discusses pedagogical issues relevant to the pronunciation teacher and describes aspects of the English sound system which are of concern in the teaching of pronunciation.

– British English.

Morley, J. (ed.) 1987. *Current Perspectives on Pronunciation.* Washington DC: TESOL.

This is a collection of articles by leading practitioners in the ESL field. Several of the articles provide detailed lesson plans which allow the teacher to integrate pronunciation into a communicative classroom. This book is strongly recommended.

– American English.

Swan, M. and **B. Smith** (eds.) 1987. *Learner English: A Teacher's Guide to Interference and Other Problems.* Cambridge; Cambridge University Press.

This book describes the interlanguages of ESL learners from twenty different language backgrounds. Each chapter includes information on the phonology, orthography, grammar, and vocabulary of the language in question. It is an excellent resource for teachers but assumes some knowledge of linguistics.

– British English.
– Cassette available.

Wong, R. 1987. *Teaching Pronunciation: Focus on English Rhythm and Intonation.* Englewood Cliffs, NJ: Prentice Hall Regents.

This book includes many useful suggestions for the teaching of stress, rhythm, and intonation using a learner-centred approach.

– American English.

BIBLIOGRAPHY

Acton, W. 1984. 'Teaching Intonation.' Paper presented at the 18th Annual TESOL Convention, Houston, Texas.

Allen, W. and **S. Waugh.** 1986. 'Dealing with Accuracy in Communicative Language Teaching.' *TESL Canada Journal*, Special issue 1.

Anderson, V. 1977. *Training the Speaking Voice.* New York: Oxford University Press.

Baker, A. 1981. *Ship or Sheep? An Intermediate Pronunciation Course.* Cambridge: Cambridge University Press.

Baker, A. 1982. *Tree or Three? An Elementary Pronunciation Course.* Cambridge: Cambridge University Press.

Baker, A. 1982. *Introducing English Pronunciation: A Teacher's Guide to 'Tree or Three?' and 'Ship or Sheep?'* Cambridge: Cambridge University Press.

Benson, J. D., W. S. Greaves, and **D. J. Mendelsohn.** 1988. 'The centrality of intonation in English: an experimental validation of some aspects of M. A. K. Halliday's theory of intonation in a Canadian context' in R. Fawcett and D. Young (eds.): *New Developments in Systemic Linguistics.* London: Pinter Press.

Bowen, J.D. 1975. *Patterns of English Pronunciation.* Rowley, Mass.: Newbury House.

Brown, G. and **G. Yule.** 1983. *Teaching the Spoken Language: An Approach Based on the Analysis of Conversational English.* Cambridge: Cambridge University Press.

Catford, J. C. 1985. 'Phonetics and the teaching of pronunciation.' Paper presented at the 19th Annual TESOL Convention, New York.

Celce-Murcia, M. 1987. 'Teaching pronunciation as communication' in J. Morley (ed.) 1987.

Crystal, D. 1980. *A First Dictionary of Linguistics and Phonetics.* London: André Deutsch.

Dirven, R. and **J. Oakeshott-Taylor.** 1984. 'Listening Comprehension: Part I.' *Language Teaching* 17/4:326–43.

Dirven, R. and **J. Oakeshott-Taylor.** 1985: 'Listening comprehension: Part II.' *Language Teaching* 18/1:2–20.

Doughill, J. 1987. *Drama Activities for Language Learners.* Essential Language Teaching Series. London: Macmillan.

Esarey, G. 1977. *Pronunciation Exercises for Advanced Learners of English as a Second Language.* Pittsburgh, Pa.: University of Pittsburgh Press.

Finger, J. 1985. 'Teaching pronunciation with the vowel colour chart.' *TESL Canada Journal* 2:43–50.

Gilbert, J. B. 1984. *Clear Speech: Pronunciation and Listening Comprehension in American English.* Cambridge: Cambridge University Press.

Gimson, A. C. 1980. *An Introduction to the Pronunciation of English.* London: Edward Arnold.

Grasham, J. A. and **G. R. Gooder.** 1960. *Improving your Speech.* New York: Harcourt, Brace, and World.

Hecht, E. and **J. Ryan.** 1984. *Survival Pronunciation.* San Francisco, Calif.: Alemany Press.

Holden, S. 1981. *Drama and Language Teaching.* London: Longman.

Kenworthy, J. 1987. *Teaching English Pronunciation.* London: Longman.

Killam, C. E. and **B. Watson.** 1983. *Thirteen Language Groups: Practical Application of Contrastive Analysis for Teachers of English as a Second Language.* Vancouver: Vancouver Community College.

Klyhn, J. 1986. 'International English: Communication is the name of the game.' *TESOL Newsletter* 20/2:1–6

Knowles, P. and **R. Sasaki.** 1980. *Story Squares: Fluency in English as a Second Language.* Cambridge, Mass.: Winthrop.

Ladefoged, P. 1982. *A Course in Phonetics.* New York: Harcourt, Brace, Jovanovich.

Ling, D. 1976. *Speech and the Hearing Impaired Child: Theory and Practice.* Washington, DC: Alexander Graham Bell Institute for the Deaf.

Livingston, C. 1982. *Role Play in Language Learning.* London: Longman.

Littlewood, W. 1984. *Foreign and Second Language Learning: Language Acquisition and its Implications for the Classroom.* Cambridge: Cambridge University Press.

MacCarthy, P. 1978. *The Teaching of Pronunciation.* Cambridge: Cambridge University Press.

Maley, A. and **A. Duff.** 1982. *Drama Techniques in Language Learning.* Second edition. Cambridge: Cambridge University Press.

Morley, J. 1979. *Improving Spoken English: An Intensive Personalized Program in Perception, Pronunciation, Practice in Context.* Ann Arbor, Mich.: University of Michigan Press.

Morley, J. (ed.). 1987. *Current Perspectives on Pronunciation.* Washington DC: TESOL.

Mortimer, C. 1985. *Elements of Pronunciation: Intensive Practice for Intermediate and More Advanced Students.* Cambridge: Cambridge University Press.

Nilsen, D. L. F. and **A. P. Nilsen.** 1971. *Pronunciation Contrasts in English.* New York: Regents.

Ponsonby, M. 1982. *How Now, Brown Cow? A Course in the Pronunciation of English.* Oxford: Pergamon Press.

Prator, C. and **E. Robinett.** 1985. *Manual of American English Pronunciation.* Fourth edition. New York: Holt, Rinehart, and Winston.

Ricard, E. 1986. 'Beyond fossilization: A course in strategies and techniques in pronunciation for advanced adult learners.' *TESL Canada Journal,* Special issue 1.

Robinett, B. 1978. *Teaching English to Speakers of Other Languages.* Minneapolis, Minn.: University of Minnesota Press.

Sanderson, P. 1965. *Pronunciation of Consonant Clusters.* Oxford: Pergamon Press.

Selinker, L. and **S. Gass.** 1984. *Workbook in Second Language Acquisition.* Rowley, Mass.: Newbury House.

Skinner, E. and **T. Monich.** 1980. *Good Speech for the American Actor.* New York: Drama Book Specialists.

Smith, S. 1984. *The Theatre Arts and the Teaching of Second Languages.* New York: Addison-Wesley.

Stern, S. 1980. 'Drama in second language learning from a psycholinguistic perspective.' *Language Learning* 30: 77–100.

Swan, M. and **B. Smith.** (eds.) 1987. *Learner English: A Teacher's Guide to Interference and Other Problems.* Cambridge: Cambridge University Press.

Ur, P. 1984. *Teaching Listening Comprehension.* Cambridge: Cambridge University Press.

Ur, P. 1989. *Grammar Practice Activities.* Cambridge: Cambridge University Press.

Wong, R. 1987. *Teaching Pronunciation: Focus on English Rhythm and Intonation.* Englewood Cliffs, NJ: Prentice Hall Regents.

Woods, H. 1976a. *Sound Production: h.* Ottawa: Public Service Commission.

Woods, H. 1976b. *Sound Production: th.* Ottawa: Public Service Commission.

Woods, H. 1977. *Intonation.* Ottawa: Public Service Commission.

Woods, H. 1979a. *Rhythms and Unstress.* Ottawa: Public Service Commission.

Woods, H. 1979b. *Syllable Stress and Unstress.* Ottawa: Public Service Commission.

Woods, H. 1983. *Vowel Dimensions.* Ottawa: Public Service Commission.

CONTRIBUTORS

John Archibald is an Assistant Professor in the Department of Linguistics, University of Calgary. He is the former co-editor of the *TESL Canada Journal.* He is an experienced ESL teacher and has been involved in many teacher training programmes. His research interest is the acquisition of phonology.

Peter Avery currently teaches linguistics at the University of Toronto. He is involved in teacher training through the TESL Certificate programme at George Brown College, Toronto. His research interests include theoretical phonology and second language acquisition.

Susan Ehrlich is an Associate Professor of Linguistics in the Department of Languages, Literatures, and Linguistics at York University, Toronto. She has been involved in many ESL teacher training programmes and has taught ESL at George Brown College and the University of Toronto. Her areas of interest include second language acquisition and discourse analysis.

Nicholas Elson is an Associate Lecturer and Co-ordinator of English as a Second Language in the Faculty of Arts at York University, Toronto. He teaches credit courses in ESL and is involved in ESL teacher training. His interests include the linking of theory and practice and the impact of social and political factors on the ESL classroom.

Suzanne Firth is currently Associate Director of the International Business Education Programme, York University, Toronto. She has designed courses and developed materials related to pronunciation and has offered numerous workshops on the same topic.

Douglas Jull is Academic Co-ordinator in the Language Training Department, George Brown College, Toronto. He received an MA in Linguistics from the University of Toronto. His interests include language transfer in second language acquisition and the relationship between music and language.

Maureen McNerney is Associate Director of the York University English Language Institute, Toronto. Her field of specialization is pronunciation. Her areas of interest also include the sociology of language and teaching English as a Second Dialect.

David Mendelsohn is an Associate Professor of ESL in the Department of Languages, Literatures, and Linguistics at York University, Toronto. He has been involved in numerous teacher training courses and has published widely in the field of second language learning. His specialization is spoken English. He is the former co-editor of the *TESL Canada Journal.*

Ilsa Mendelson Burns teaches ESL at George Brown College, Toronto. She also teaches in the TESL Certificate Programme there. She has an MA in Linguistics from the University of Toronto.

Neil Naiman is an Associate Professor of ESL in the Department of English, Glendon College, York University, Toronto. He has researched and published on the characteristics of good second language learners and has developed a curriculum for a communicatively-based pronunciation course.

INDEX